ALSO BY SHEILA KITZINGER

Being Born

Birth at Home

Birth Over Thirty

The Complete Book of Pregnancy
and Childbirth

Educational Counseling
for Childbirth

The Experience of Breastfeeding

The Experience of Childbirth

Giving Birth: The Parents' Emotions
in Childbirth

Women's Experience of Sex

Women as Mothers

◆ YOUR BABY, ◆
YOUR WAY

◆Your Baby,◆ Your Way

Making Pregnancy Decisions and Birth Plans

Sheila Kitzinger

◆ PANTHEON BOOKS ◆

New York

Library of Congress Cataloging-in-Publication Data

Kitzinger, Sheila.
  Your baby, your way.

  Bibliography: p.
  Includes index.
  1. Pregnancy.   2. Childbirth.   I. Title.   [DNLM:
1. Labor—popular works.   2. Pregnancy—popular works.
WQ 150 K62y]
RG525.K53 1987   618.2   86-42983
ISBN 0-394-54573-7
ISBN 0-394-75249-X (pbk.)

Part-title photos © Nancy Durrell McKenna, except page 217,
© Suzanne Arms Wimberley

Book design by Debby Jay

Manufactured in the United States of America

9 8 7 6 5 4 3

♦ CONTENTS ♦

• AUTONOMOUS BIRTH •

• TABLES •

♦ ACKNOWLEDGMENTS ♦

Many friends and colleagues have advised me and stimulated my thinking as I considered the pros and cons of different kinds of care and obstetric intervention, and the making of birth plans. I should like to thank especially the many women who have talked to me about their birth experiences and also Dr. Michel Odent; Iain Chalmers FRCOG, Director of the National Perinatal Epidemiology Unit at Oxford; Wendy Savage FRCOG; Sally Inch SRN, SCM; Caroline Flint SRN, SCM; and Chloe Fisher SRN, SCM. Professor John Edwards enabled me to accompany women through counseling and amniocentesis at the John Radcliffe Hospital, Oxford, and I am very grateful to him for this opportunity. Dr. David Banta read through the whole book and made comments and helpful suggestions.

I should also like to thank Janet Balaskas for suggestions about active birth movements included in chapter 6, Dr. Judith Lumley for the idea on which the charts on pregnancy care were based, Penny Simkin for enriching discussions and for the concept of the charts on pregnancy discomforts and questions to ask about pain-relieving drugs, and Dr. David Chamberlain for material drawing on research in perinatal psychology, some of which I have used in chapter 14. The Open University introduced me to the practice of "learning activities" of a kind that I have woven into the text—so a woman can test what she is reading against her own experience and use the information which she has been given in order to make active choices between alternatives. The charts in this book are similar to those I developed when writing the courses, and in the text I explore some of the same subjects in a rather different way.

Margaret Pearson and Judith Schroeder have given me skilled and unflappable secretarial help, and I'm very grateful for having been able to rely on them.

I also want to thank my daughters for their constructive criticism and for a great deal of lively discussion.

◆ YOUR BABY, ◆
YOUR WAY

1

✦ CURTAIN UP ON ✦
PREGNANCY

This book does not tell you how to have a baby or what you should do in labor. It focuses instead on the range of choices open to you in the kind of care you have, both during your pregnancy and at the time of birth, and on the changes and challenges of these important nine months. There are obviously physical changes. But there are emotional changes, too, and changes in your relationships with your partner, family, friends, and people with whom you work. There is also the developing relationship with those you choose to care for you in pregnancy and labor.

Pregnancy does not happen just in the pelvis. It affects your whole self—your body, your self-image as a woman, and your sense of worth. It changes, often in subtle ways, both how you see yourself and how other people, both men and women, see you. Being pregnant may enhance and enrich your sense of self. Or you may feel that it has taken something away from you.

The information presented here is intended to help you examine the alternatives, the pros and cons of different ways of doing things, and decide what meets *your* needs. With this in mind there are suggestions throughout the book for action you can take. In each chapter there are special ideas to consider, topics to discuss with other people, issues for you to explore more deeply, or facts you need to unearth about the style of birth possible where you live and the options open to you. And all this is put into an international context, so that wherever you are, you can still make a plan of action.

Keeping a diary of your pregnancy will help; you can note down your thoughts and the results of every inquiry. You will have a detailed personal record of your pregnancy, too. So, as you go through this book, have a notebook beside you to jot down your thoughts and the facts you have discovered. The activities that I suggest—set off by diamonds in the text—are intended to help you reflect on the information given, record your feelings, and work out your own strategies. They are not tests to see if you have read the material properly or to check your understanding. If you prefer to read the book without doing these activities, simply skip them. Or you may want to come back to them later.

You will also find many quotations from women about how they felt, what they did, and how they coped with the reality of their own experiences. Some of these women may be much like you, others very different. What they say is important because a happy birth is not a matter of following a method or obeying a set of rules, like carefully following a knitting pattern or the instructions for a computer. There is no one right way to have a baby. Our personalities and lifestyles are different and no one else should—or can—dictate *your* experience.

Choices about birth are never as simple as selecting a can of beans from a supermarket shelf. They often involve powerful emotions—hope, fear, anger, guilt, to name a few. It is understandable that this should be so, because birth is not just a matter of pushing a baby out of your body, a demonstration of biomechanics, but something that concerns fundamental human *values*.

Even when we feel most free to make choices, those choices are restricted and shaped by social pressures. New choices close the doors on others. Now that we have the choice to control the number of children we bear by using contraception, women who have very large families—at least if they are poor—are labeled social deviants and problem cases. As a technology develops that gives us the choice to screen for imperfections in the fetus, and to abort a fetus that is not up to standard, increasingly women feel the pressure not to bear handicapped babies.[1] When the choice of having complete anaesthetic pain relief in childbirth is available, pressure is put on women to agree to its use and they lose the choice of laboring without drugs. When all women can choose to give birth in a hospital, it becomes more and more difficult to make the choice, and to get others to agree to it, to give birth at home.

Choice is not just an individual matter, having to do with personal and private decisions. It always takes place in a social context, and it is important to be aware of the constant pressures on us that define and limit the choices we can make.

Enormous changes have taken place in childbirth over the last half century, and women's expectations about the whole experience have altered radically. Take this account of birth written from a woman's point of view in the 1930s—and intended to reassure the expectant mother. It starts by telling her, "The thing to have firmly fixed in your mind . . . is that you are going to be a good girl," and warns her that the way to get the best out of doctors and nurses is to do what she is told. Otherwise she will be ignored and neglected. Nurses, though apparently hard-boiled, are "as sentimental as nursemaids underneath," and a woman who wants to be treated well should placate them and be a good patient. Then there is a description of what the woman can expect in labor: Indefinite time goes by and as she lies in "a merciful stupor, not knowing, not caring . . . conscious, but foggy. You are in pain but it doesn't seem real." Something jolts her out of peaceful quiescence. She is put on a stretcher and carried to another room but doesn't really know what is happening to her—because everything is completely confused, "like a nightmare," and she is aware only of pain. "Then a rubber ring is fitted over your face . . . you gulp in great breaths. Pinpricks of light and a grinding noise that goes round in a spiral zooms through your head." The woman doesn't know how long this goes on, but after a time she opens her eyes to see that there is a nurse in the room. She starts to remember that there was something about a baby—and asks, "When am I going to have the baby?" A nurse announces, "You have a fine son born three hours ago."

We are no longer prepared to hand over responsibility in quite the same way. And there are issues over and above the relief from pain that concern us: the quality of our relationships with caregivers, the side effects of drugs, the physical and emotional well-being of the baby, and our own autonomy as women.

Yet these changes have occurred at the same time as the whole of pregnancy has come to be ruled by increasingly elaborate screening

5

procedures, childbirth has been made subject to technological control, and a multiplicity of interventions of different kinds has been introduced in even the most apparently straightforward birth.

Raised consciousness has made us more alert, but has not made the experience any easier—not because of the natural processes with which we have to deal, but because of the things done to us by those in charge of childbirth that can still make the whole process a nightmare.

Many women today feel as if they have been sucked onto a conveyor belt and are being processed through pregnancy and birth like cars in a highly mechanized automobile plant. They feel guilty when they do anything that holds up the process, such as asking questions, or daring to be persistent in stating what they want. The message they receive, even though unspoken, is that they are being "bad patients," that they are naïve and selfish, and, if they reveal concern about anything other than safety, that they do not care about their babies.

This means that a woman's experience of pregnancy and birth is likely to be fraught with a sense of inadequacy and powerlessness. At the point when she is bringing new life into the world and a tremendous power is released in her body, she feels most helpless. She is trapped in a situation outside her control.

Preparing for childbirth used to be seen as a matter of doing exercises, learning what happens, and breathing and relaxing in order to cope with contractions. All that training and rigorous practice turn out to be utterly irrelevant if a woman is confronted with a medical system that takes over her labor and manages it, and with obstetricians who are convinced they know what is best for her regardless of what she prefers and what she knows about her body. Effective preparation for childbirth must include learning how to cope with the medical system and knowing how to work in partnership with your doctor or midwife rather than passively receiving care. It is your body and your baby, and though expert counsel is welcome, the decisions should be yours.

A woman who is expecting a baby is not ill. She is *pregnant*. She is performing a normal physiological function for which her body is beautifully made. But things can go wrong. Just as with other physiological functions—the intricate processes of digestion and the working of bowels and bladder, the rhythms of sleep, breathing, and heartbeats—fear and anxiety that her body may not work correctly, or that she may be subjected to treatment she does not want, affect the way a woman's uterus functions.

This is why thinking simply in terms of risk is so dangerous. It is a self-fulfilling prophecy: if doctors continually remind a woman of risk factors and all the disasters that may be just round the corner, after a while she is bound to lose confidence in her body and see it as an enemy, rather than something through which she expresses herself in giving birth. Her blood pressure climbs, or the contractions do not open her cervix, or her labor suddenly comes to a full stop, leaving her half dilated, in pain, frightened, and exhausted. She then actually *becomes* high-risk and needs the obstetric intervention and strong drugs she may have been determined to avoid.

One of your important tasks during pregnancy is to get in touch with your feelings, in order to know what is right for you. Saying how you feel is important, too, when you talk to the people who are looking after you. Sometimes a woman thinks her doctor is going to let her have what she wants because he has a pleasant manner. Later, when the doctor imposes his will during labor, she discovers that he had just been humoring her, that it was part of his method of managing patients. So it is vital to be open and honest about issues that are important to you and not to be lulled into complacency by a mixture of charm and reassurance.

Few doctors have learned in medical school how to have an equal relationship with their patients, so they feel they are treading on uncharted territory when they enter this new kind of relationship with a pregnant woman. They are usually anxious about it.

It is, on the whole, easier for midwives to treat pregnant women as equals, because they are women themselves and they too are in an unequal power relationship with doctors. It is possible for you to have most, or sometimes all, of your care from a midwife rather than an obstetrician. This is an option that will also be explored in these pages.

A price we pay for the safety of birth today compared with the nineteenth century is that we often lack resources when things go wrong—when a baby is born prematurely, for example, or is sick or handicapped. The most profound shock of all comes when a baby dies. Very few of us get any emotional preparation for that kind of experience.

As you think ahead, it is important to consider alternatives if everything is not straightforward—if you are advised to have labor induced, for instance, if labor proves unexpectedly difficult, if delivery is by forceps or cesarean section, or if your baby is in intensive care. Though women often repress these thoughts because they arouse anxiety, they tend to cluster in the back of their minds and to loom larger still in the middle of the night.

You may find that talking about these things triggers anxiety in other people, too. Friends and family, even doctors and nurses, often prefer not to discuss these possibilities. Such thoughts are branded as unhealthy, and you are urged to think positively. That does not solve the problem. And because this attitude is evasive and denies the strength of what is in your mind, it cheats you of the chance to develop skills needed to cope with an emergency and to work out what you want from other people. A woman who has never allowed herself to imagine that her baby might be stillborn, for example, has no idea of what she would want from those caring for her. Will she want to touch and hold her baby or would she prefer the baby to be whisked away unseen? Does she want time alone with the baby so she can grieve without interruption? Or would she prefer to be heavily sedated and left by herself? These are all issues that are difficult to resolve at the time if you have never thought of the remote possibility of such a thing happening.

But of course, plans are one thing, and reality is another. You can never make a blueprint for labor—or for life! Any plan has to be flexible and therein lies its strength. The branches of a tree sway in the wind; they do not meet it with rigid resistance. It is because they are flexible that they do not crack. This is why the emphasis in these pages is on learning as you go, on being willing to reassess what is happening and what you want, and on being flexible.

♦♦♦ Before you read on, note down the things that are most important to you about childbirth. Discuss them with your partner or someone else close to you, and keep them in mind as you go through the book. ♦♦♦

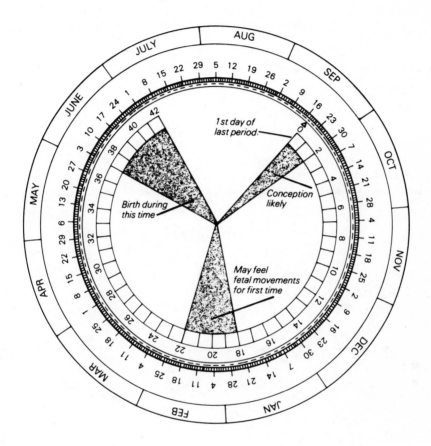

WORKING OUT WHEN YOUR BABY WILL BE BORN

Cut out the inner circle by following the dotted lines between the two sets of numbers. Rotate the inner disk until the arrow points to the first day of your last period on the outer ring. Lined up that way, the chart will show you when you can expect to feel movements and about when your baby will be born.

◆ LOOKING AFTER ◆
YOURSELF

2

⋆ THE EARLY WEEKS ⋆

Some women glow from the moment they realize they are pregnant and go right through the nine months feeling radiant. Others have times with aches and pains when they wonder why they ever got pregnant in the first place. A great many find the first three months especially difficult for two reasons: nausea, often accompanied by vomiting, and extreme tiredness.

Judi enjoyed being pregnant from the beginning and says she was "tremendously excited. I never really believed I was fertile—that I *could* have a baby. It happened as soon as we decided I should come off the Pill and we used condoms for three months so that the hormones were cleared from my system, and then I conceived—just like that! I was happy about being pregnant but it was more than that; my body felt, well, *enhanced*."

Carol did not feel like that at all. For her those first few weeks, the transition to pregnancy, were really difficult. She said, "I'm aghast at what I have taken on. There is no going back now. Sometimes I feel the baby is a kind of parasite. Then I am guilty about feeling like that. I have had the most awful nausea and vomiting, not just in the early morning but in the evening too, and I have never been so tired in my life. I have had to reassess myself. I can't go on regardless of my body—that's never happened before." And she added, "I suppose I have learned something from that, but it's frustrating."

However much you read, plan ahead, and want to achieve intellectual control over what is happening, pregnancy and birth are processes that sweep through and take over your body.

If you get morning sickness or feel exhausted in the early weeks, you may be wondering whether it is going to continue like this throughout your pregnancy and if the only thing to do is to quit work and lie in bed. Even if you are feeling fine at the beginning, you have to make decisions about whether to keep on working, and if so for how long—and if you give up, whether you can cope without the money. Or you may be thinking of cutting down on or modifying work in some way, if that is possible—maybe working part time or flex-time. Then there are all the things you normally take for granted—doing the laundry, cooking, and cleaning. You may want to have someone else to take over these tasks, or want to talk with your partner about sharing them more equally. If you already have children, you must decide if you'll need additional help with them. In making these decisions, bear in mind that the periods of greatest stress are right at the beginning of pregnancy, when your body is adjusting to its tremendous new task, and in the last six to eight weeks, when you may feel tired and heavy and find that every-day tasks—cleaning the bathtub, carrying bags of groceries, lifting a toddler, and even sitting very long in one position—cause a back-ache or wear you out.

Even at the beginning of pregnancy, for many women there come times when the pressure of trying to carry on as if nothing has changed can be overwhelming, and you may be frustrated, angry, or depressed that you cannot control your body and emotions as you used to before you were pregnant. Some women say that, apart from missing their periods, they wouldn't know they were pregnant, and they can go on just as before. But you cannot bank on this, and there is no virtue in pretending that you feel fine if you don't, and thus denying your body's needs.

A woman who is accustomed to being in charge of her life and being able to plan ahead, without having to think whether her body is going to cooperate, may be shocked by the emotional and physical changes of early pregnancy, especially if she feels extremely tired and has nausea and vomiting—which, though often described as "morn-ing sickness," can continue on and off through the day and get worse again in the evening.

You may even get a disturbing feeling that your body no longer belongs to you, and at times that you have been invaded by a hostile force. Then, like Carol, you feel guilty that you should have such negative thoughts about the baby inside you. There are often enormous fluctuations in how a pregnant woman feels. One day she wakes up sunny and full of energy, the next under a black cloud, wondering why she ever started this pregnancy.

The first surprise of those early weeks, long before anyone can see that you are having a baby, is the way your body is totally involved in producing and protecting this miniature creature, still no larger than a spool of thread. All this is happening when you have nothing to show for it, and you are probably busy working, perhaps committed to seeing through important projects in your job.

Even if other people do know you are pregnant, women have babies all the time, and your pregnancy may seem to them a secondary matter compared to coping efficiently with problems at work. There are deadlines to meet, difficulties to sort out, work schedules to keep, which don't change just because you are pregnant. To some colleagues it may seem as if you are making a fuss about nothing. Other women may be secretly envious that you are having a baby; they may feel this strongly, without even being aware of their own jealousy. Once they know you are pregnant, some men start treating you as if you were soft in the head and incapable of making decisions in your work. You may feel as if you have been written off as a responsible colleague. Whatever their attitude, if you enjoy your job and want to go on with it after the baby is born, or to take it up again when the child is older, you will probably feel you cannot afford to slack off now and need to show that you are still worth your pay.

The tiredness common in the early weeks of pregnancy is rarely acknowledged, though probably most women feel it, if only in the evening. It can be so severe that you wonder how you can ever get through a pregnancy that starts like this. It seems logical to assume that if you are exhausted at the beginning, things will get worse and worse through the later months. This, however, is not the case. Many women who are weary and lethargic in the first three months or so sparkle with energy in the later months. The final few weeks of pregnancy may prove tiring because you are carrying around such a heavy load, but even that is not like the feeling of being completely drained of energy that is often experienced as a woman's body makes its first huge adjustment to pregnancy.

Here are some things other women say they have found helpful in dealing with the most common symptoms of early pregnancy. If you are suffering from nausea and vomiting or excessive tiredness, go through the list and see what would be practical for you to do. The chances are that there is at least something you have not tried yet. Jot down any good ideas in your notebook and keep a record of the results. Allow at least four days of experiment before you assess whether a particular course of action is effective or not.

NAUSEA AND VOMITING

- Cut out foods that make you feel queasy; for some it is eggs, milk, meat.

- Take Vitamin B_6 (pyridoxine)—20 to 30 mg a day. (Since B_6 reduces the absorption of zinc, it may be a good idea to take supplementary zinc.)[1]

- Cut out greasy, fried, and spicy foods, and alcohol, tobacco, and coffee.

- Carry glucose tablets, crackers, or fruit around with you. Have frequent nibbles so that your stomach never gets empty.

- Have a snack during the night so that your blood sugar does not drop so low by early morning.

- Have a milky drink before going to bed.

- Get up in the morning very slowly. First sit up for half an hour, sipping a cup of tea and eating a slice of toast, and then get out of bed slowly.

- Eat a high-carbohydrate diet: dry toast, honey, banana, baked potato, muesli and other whole-grain breakfast cereals, steamed rice.

- Drink wheat germ dissolved in warm milk, a few teaspoons hourly.

- Drink peppermint tea.

- Drink ginger tea, made by boiling root ginger in water and then straining it. Add a little honey to sweeten. Or you may prefer capsules of powdered ginger, obtainable from health-food stores. Unlike antinausea medications, ginger works not on the central nervous system, but in the gastrointestinal tract itself. Experiment with the amount you need. Between five and fifteen capsules a day will usually keep nausea at bay. Sucking candied ginger may also be effective.

♦ If you are taking iron tablets, see what happens when you stop. They often cause nausea and vomiting in early pregnancy, when they are rarely needed anyway, but do not upset the digestion later in pregnancy.

♦ Keep away from smoky rooms and smells of cooking. If you are nauseous in the evening, rest in a darkened room after returning from work and get someone else to prepare the evening meal. Get more rest. The more tired you are, the more nauseous you are likely to feel.

♦ If you are vomiting a great deal, try a diet of one food only, one you know you can tolerate: for example, peeled grapes, small pieces of apple, banana, steamed fish, dry toast and honey or yeast extract, for one day. Then add one other food the next day. If you tolerate that well, introduce one more the following day, and continue until you are on a good mixed diet. Go back to the mono-diet if you start vomiting again. You are unlikely to need to do this for more than two or three weeks.

Nausea and vomiting do not usually last beyond the third month of pregnancy, but occasionally they are a continuing problem right up until delivery. Vomiting can be seriously dehydrating and can make you feel very sick indeed. It is known as hyperemesis, and the usual treatment involves admission to the hospital. A combination of a mixed, low-fat diet, plenty of fluids (sipped slowly), and the ginger therapy may make this unnecessary.

TIREDNESS

♦ Cut housework back to basics and put off until tomorrow anything that does not *have* to be done today.

- Make sure you are getting a nutritious diet with plenty of fresh, raw vegetables, fruit, and whole grains.

- Get your partner or a friend to go to the supermarket, do the laundry and cleaning, etc., for a while.

- Have a rest in a darkened room immediately after coming home from work.

- Spend one day a week in bed.

- If you can afford it, go to a hotel for a weekend—or explain the situation to a friend with whom you can stay—and spend most of the time in bed.

- Get regular vigorous exercise in the fresh air.

- Make some time for yourself. One way of doing this is to take up some leisure occupation that allows you to get physical rest. It may be easier to take a rest regularly if your hands and mind are occupied. Patchwork or other sewing, the traditional knitting of little booties, catching up with correspondence or other writing, taking up drawing or painting, even sorting your photo album, are possibilities.

BLEEDING

It is horrifying when you are pregnant to go to the bathroom or undress and see blood coming from your vagina, yet this happens to a great many women who go on to have normal healthy babies. As many as 20 percent experience some bleeding in early pregnancy.[2] The bleeding is often just a few drops, and after it has stopped you can forget all about it. Sometimes, however, it is heavy, like the second day of a period, or there is continuous spotting that goes on for a week or more. In either of these situations there is a 50 to 60 percent chance of miscarriage.[3] You can have an ultrasound scan to see if the baby's heart is still beating. If it is, you are very unlikely to miscarry. If it is not, there is nothing you can do about it. There is no evidence that staying in bed, or any other form of treatment, makes miscarriage less likely. On the other hand, you may feel that you want to retreat to bed, even if nobody has proved that this is any help. All in all, it is probably best to let your own feelings guide you. If you *do* lose the baby, you may need this space to come to terms with and mourn your loss. If you just keep on working as if nothing were happening, you may be denying yourself this emotional refuge and later feel cheated, depressed, and also guilty that you did not give more attention to the pregnancy.

Pregnancy gives you a chance to get to know and understand your body better. This is not only a matter of learning how it works, what happens as the uterus enlarges and the baby grows, for example; it also means accepting it in a way you may not have done previously. Perhaps this often happens because pregnancy gives you permission to concentrate on your body and its needs and on your feelings about it. With the unfolding of life inside your body, you are able to focus on what is happening and can care for and cherish *yourself*. Most of the time women serve other people's needs. You can grasp the opportunity provided by pregnancy to assess your own needs, and, by being positive and taking action, develop a strategy wherever possible to meet them.

3

◆ DRUGS AND HEALTH ◆

CIGARETTES

The evidence against smoking in pregnancy is overwhelming, and if you smoke, the moment when you realize that you are pregnant is a good time to give it up, for your own sake as well as the baby's. Tobacco manufacturers see women as a prime target for their marketing efforts and present cigarettes in terms of "the new woman" ("You've come a long way, baby"), who is slim ("Long and slender, light and mellow"), feminine (in the 1960s a cigarette was advertised as being "as feminine as the ring you wear"), assertive and liberated ("I made a decision about low tar"; "I want the best taste I can get"), and sexually satisfied and personally fulfilled ("More for that extra measure of satisfaction"). Yet a woman who smokes, whether or not she is pregnant, is gambling with her life and health. For instance, she runs the risk of developing not only chronic bronchitis and emphysema, but—especially if she is normally on the Pill—heart disease (the FDA warns: "Women who use birth control pills should not smoke"). A smoker is twice as likely as a nonsmoker to get cancer of the cervix, and the more she smokes the greater her risk. In 1980 the U.S. Surgeon General reported a steep rise in smoking-related diseases among women.[1]

If you smoked before you became pregnant, you may have given up already. Many women stop in the first few months. American research shows that almost 75 percent of women do not smoke during pregnancy.[2] A study commissioned by the Health Education Council in Britain (but unpublished) revealed that 15 percent of women give up smoking at the beginning of pregnancy. They may be concerned about the effect on the developing baby or simply find that cigarettes make them feel nauseous. But the extra stresses that come with pregnancy make some women want to smoke *more* and they long for a cigarette to relieve tension. This may be particularly the case for a woman who is under pressure from work or family, facing financial or housing problems, or who has conceived by accident and has to decide whether or not to go ahead with an unwanted pregnancy. A woman who is advised to have screening for possible handicap in the baby is also under special stress, which may make her want to smoke. This is why it sometimes seems downright cruel to tell a woman that she should not smoke during pregnancy. Criticizing a woman for smoking is all too often a matter of blaming the victim.

Yet, the facts are clear.

Smoking is a threat to your life and health and also to that of your baby. It causes 5 percent of all stillbirths and neonatal deaths.[3] A smoker runs nearly a 30 percent greater risk of having a baby who dies at or shortly after birth than a nonsmoker. Smoking results in miscarriages (a 70 percent greater risk than if a woman does not smoke) and premature births (a 36 percent greater risk). Swedish research reveals that there is also a 50 percent greater chance that the child of a mother who smokes during pregnancy will develop cancer.[4]

But the greatest risk of all is that of stunting a baby's growth in the uterus (a 98 percent greater risk), and this slow growth continues even after the child is born.[5] The children of parents who smoke are not only shorter than those of nonsmokers but are up to five months behind them in intellectual development.

The detrimental effects of smoking are compounded by those of alcohol and poor nutrition. So the woman who drinks and has an inadequate diet as well as smoking runs the greatest risk of all.

When a pregnant woman smokes, carbon dioxide forces oxygen out of her red blood cells and those of her baby, and nicotine restricts the blood vessels, including those in the placenta. Not only is there less oxygen in her blood, but the passage of blood through the placenta is restricted. Another effect of smoking is that the baby's blood gets sticky, and this further slows down the blood flow and deprives the baby of oxygen.[6]

The bad effects of cigarettes are directly related to the quantity smoked.[7] So reducing the number smoked, smoking each cigarette only halfway down, or rationing yourself to a few a day can make a great difference. If you do decide on this course of action, however, *avoid inhaling more.* The tendency is for a smoker who is trying to cut down the number smoked to increase inhalation, and poisons then remain high in the bloodstream.[8]

Passive smoking (breathing in someone else's smoke) can also affect the baby's growth and cause the breakdown products of nicotine to appear in the amniotic fluid. It is important that other people in the family do not smoke in the same room as a pregnant woman; this provides a good opportunity for a father, too, to give up smoking. If you are employed outside the home, you should not have to work in a smoke-laden atmosphere and can ask to be transferred to a nonsmoking section of an office. Even a fan on a desk can produce a little pocket of relatively fresh air.

♦ ♦ ♦ Here is how some women say they have either cut down on their smoking or stopped completely. Make a note of similar strategies you want to adopt and add any others of your own.

♦ Reward yourself by buying something you want, like a new dress, with the money saved from not buying cigarettes.

♦ If you find that small, immediate rewards work best for you, allow yourself an extra small pleasure every week you go without cigarettes—for example, meeting a friend for lunch, having a massage, enjoying a long phone call with an old friend.

♦ Get together with a small group of other people who have decided to give up smoking. Six to eight is about the right number. Or you might want to do it with just one close friend. Arrange to meet regularly to check on progress and give mutual support.

♦ If you smoke when you are bored, fill that time with something else that will take your mind off cigarettes and keep you busy: getting the baby's room ready, cooking dishes to put in the freezer for after the baby comes, going for an energetic walk, doing anything that involves your hands and makes it difficult to smoke at the same time.

♦ If you smoke when on the phone or when watching TV, keep chewing gum or a bowl of nuts and raisins by the phone or near the TV so that you can nibble them instead.

There are organizations that can help you, too. These are listed in Useful Addresses. ♦ ♦ ♦

ALCOHOL

A great many healthy babies are born to women who enjoy having some alcohol during pregnancy. They may like to drink for social reasons, for the feeling of hospitality or festivity that drinking lends to a gathering, to indicate to colleagues or others that they are now off duty, or to express a feeling of community in the family or among friends. Taking alcohol is a social signal that marks the switch from work to leisure activities, that begins the relaxation after a task has been completed or a particular stress is over, and that serves symbolically as a kind of gift, the exchange of which cements relationships. This is why when we are accustomed to drinking, the decision to give up alcohol during pregnancy can be quite difficult. It marks us off as different from many of our friends, making us feel somehow vulnerable, almost as if we were sick.

Yet, though an occasional alcoholic drink may help you relax, it is of no benefit to the baby and may actually be harmful. So there is good reason not to drink during pregnancy, or at any rate to limit yourself to an occasional mildly alcoholic drink, a glass of wine perhaps, or half club soda and half wine.

Any woman who drinks heavily during pregnancy puts her baby at risk of developing the *fetal alcohol syndrome*. Symptoms of FAS are growth retardation, neurological handicap (slow intellectual development or mental retardation), and a facial structure that gives a special look to these children: a small head, thin upper lip, and a kind of elfin or E.T. expression. The FAS baby is also more likely than other newborns to suffer from cerebral palsy.[9]

Fortunately not all babies of mothers who drink heavily—even those of alcoholic mothers—suffer in this way, though many may not realize their full potential because of the effect of ethanol on their development in the uterus.

Occasional binge drinking (more than a whole bottle of wine, or four or five stiff drinks, for example) can also be dangerous, even when the mother drinks very little at other times. Not only does she have a hangover, but the baby's development may be hindered. We do not yet know exactly when alcohol does the most or least harm, but all the evidence so far available suggests that it is during the period of organogenesis (the first twelve weeks of pregnancy when the organs of the baby's body are being formed) and also during growth spurts in the development of the brain at the very beginning and the very end of pregnancy that the risk is greatest. It may also be that at these critical periods of pregnancy babies can be affected by very low levels of alcohol. And it may be that some are more readily affected than others. One of the problems is that it cannot yet be said with any certainty that there is a minimum safe level for alcohol, below which it can be shown to have no toxic effects.

It is clear, though, that the risk of harming a baby is related to the amount of pure alcohol consumed. If you drink less than one ounce of pure alcohol (the amount in two or three glasses of wine or one or two light cocktails) a day, the risk is very small. If you have two-thirds of a bottle of wine or three or four cocktails, your chances are one in a hundred that your baby will be damaged as a result. The woman who has a bottle of wine a day or more than four cocktails has a 19 percent chance that her baby will be abnormal.[10] Smoking increases the effects of alcohol abuse. A woman who drinks and smokes runs a fourfold risk that her baby will be stunted in growth while in the uterus.[11]

There seem to be some other risks with alcohol, even in such small amounts as a couple of drinks twice a week, for example. One study revealed that a pregnant woman who drinks, even a little, is more likely to have a miscarriage.[12] Another research project, which looked at women who had one or two drinks a day, found a special risk of late miscarriages (after twelve weeks). The risk increased if a woman smoked as well.[13]

One of the risks of drinking during pregnancy is due to the presence of nitrosamines in most whisky and beer. These, as well as alcohol, can cause birth handicaps. The concentration is higher in beer than in whisky and, of course, beer is usually drunk in larger quantities. Even so, it is probably wise to avoid drinking both whisky and beer during pregnancy, not only because of their alcohol content but because of the damage that could be caused by nitrosamines.

A woman who drinks heavily in pregnancy can quickly detoxify herself if she stops drinking, or even cuts down on it, at any stage during the nine months. An encouraging report from Boston City Hospital showed that when women had counseling and help in order to reduce their drinking, their babies' growth picked up from that point on.[14]

♦ ♦ ♦   If you drink at all, now is the time to take an overview of your drinking habits. Record in your notebook how many times you drank during the last week. If you can remember, also write down the number of glasses of wine or liquor or cans of beer you had each time. Then think whether you ever drink more than this. When you have done this, you will have a rough idea of whether you fall into the category of a light, moderate, or heavy drinker. Not more than two, or at the most three, glasses of wine or cans of beer, or one stiff hard drink a day, makes you a light drinker. More than this and you come into the category of a moderate drinker. Five drinks at any one time mark you as a heavy drinker. If you smoke as well, go up one category. Then you can decide if you want to modify your drinking habits or to abstain for the rest of your pregnancy. If you want to stop all alcohol, there are now alcohol-free wines and cocktails on the market, or you may prefer fruit juices or mineral water with lime or lemon.   ♦ ♦ ♦

Reducing or eliminating alcohol at any time during pregnancy really does make a difference.

A NOTE ABOUT X-RAYS

The dangers of X-rays in pregnancy are well known. They can cause malformation and genetic damage that result in an increased cancer risk for a child, and for the children and grandchildren of an adult who was irradiated as a fetus. X-rays also increase sensitivity to dangerous chemicals. There is no safe threshold for radiation, and therefore no minimum level that is safe for the unborn baby.

If a doctor or dentist advises diagnostic X-rays in pregnancy, check whether these are really necessary, and consider getting a second opinion. X-rays of the pelvis should never be done in the first half of pregnancy. If you decide to be X-rayed, radiation should be restricted to as small a part of your body as necessary, and if the X-rays do not have to involve the pelvic area, you can ask for a protective lead shield over that part of your body.

MEDICATION IN PREGNANCY

A pregnant woman in the United States takes, on average, eleven different kinds of medication (including things like aspirin, indigestion tablets, and tranquilizers) between conception and the time when she goes into labor and has a further seven during childbirth.[15] For two-thirds of these drug ingredients consumed during pregnancy, and for a third of those used in labor, there exist no published reports showing that they are safe for the baby.[16] And of those drugs about which reports *have* been published, more than half contain one or more substances that have been shown to affect the fetus adversely, as shown in table 1.

A teratogen is any substance capable of interfering with fetal growth or producing malformation. Teratogens are likely to have the most effect during the first twelve weeks of fetal development, when major organs of the body and the skeleton are forming. But subtle effects on the central nervous system may occur at any stage of pregnancy, since a baby's central nervous system goes on developing through pregnancy, birth, and the first eighteen months of life outside the uterus.

Taking any medication in pregnancy is a matter of weighing the benefits against possible teratogenic risk. This is an equation that has to be worked out with your doctor, and there is a great deal we still do not know about the risks involved, including the risk of *not* treating an illness with drugs, as well as the risk of the drugs themselves. Some drugs are obviously useful, and some—even those known to increase the chance of impeded development—may be

TABLE 1. EFFECTS OF MEDICATION IN PREGNANCY

DRUG	*SYMPTOMS TREATED*	*POSSIBLE EFFECT ON FETUS*	*ALTERNATIVE*
Antacid	Indigestion, heartburn	None, but if drug contains baking soda increases your own fluid retention.	Milk of magnesia
Antiemetics	Nausea and vomiting	*May* cause abnormalities.	See "Nausea and Vomiting," p. 16
Antihistamines	Nausea and vomiting, hay fever	Can cause abnormalities.	See "Nausea and Vomiting," p. 16
Aspirin	Headache, toothache, flu	If taken shortly before birth, may interfere with blood clotting (though it is sometimes prescribed to get a better blood flow through to the baby).	Paracetamol, Codeine
Cascara (a laxative)	Constipation	None, but can reduce absorption of vitamins in your own intestinal tract.	Fecal softener
Ergotamine	Migraine	Miscarriage.	Discuss with your doctor
Metronidazole (Flagyl, an antibiotic)	Vaginal and urethral infections	Can interfere with cell development.	Discuss with your doctor
Tetracycline (an antibiotic)	Infections	Can slow down bone growth and stain first set of teeth yellow.	Discuss with your doctor
Barbiturates (some kinds of sleeping pills)	Insomnia	Can cause severe breathing difficulties in the baby at birth.	See Table 3, pp. 32–35
Iodides (some cough medicines contain potassium iodide)	Thyroid conditions	Can cause goiter.	Discuss with your doctor
Monoamine oxidase inhibitors (usually called MOIs)	Depression	Can affect central nervous system (but you must come off MOIs gradually): can cause poor musculature, delayed breathing, spells of not breathing (apnea), and feeding difficulties.	Discuss with your doctor

DRUG	SYMPTOMS TREATED	POSSIBLE EFFECT ON FETUS	ALTERNATIVE
Diazepam (Valium)*	Anxiety	Baby may be slow to breathe at birth, have poor muscle tone, spells of not breathing, and feeding difficulties.	Discuss with your doctor
Lithium*	Manic depression	Can interfere with balance of chemicals in body and cause goiter.	Discuss with your doctor
Chlordiazepoxide (Librium)*	Anxiety, depression with agitation, alcoholism	Probably little effect but baby *may* have some breathing difficulties at birth and may be slow to suck.	Discuss with your doctor
Anticoagulants	Thromobsis	Interferes with clotting of baby's blood.	One kind of anticoagulant, Heparin, does not cross placenta
Live vaccines	Guard against rubella (German measles), measles, polio, and yellow fever	May infect baby.	Avoid contact with anyone likely to have any of these diseases

* If you want to come off any of the mood-changing drugs during pregnancy, do it gradually, or you may have withdrawal symptoms, including vomiting, stomach cramps, sweating, anxiety, depression, and inability to sleep. Ask your doctor for help.

vitally necessary for chronic conditions such as diabetes, heart disease, epilepsy, and asthma.

There may also be over-the-counter drugs you have never thought of as harmful—a drug you occasionally take or have around your home for emergencies, for example—that could be hazardous in pregnancy. You often cannot tell whether a drug is dangerous simply by looking at the information with the package. More than two-thirds of the over-the-counter pharmaceutical products taken by pregnant women contain no reference to their use during pregnancy.[17]

♦ ♦ ♦   Make a list of the medications you take. The package insert will sometimes give you enough information to judge whether the drug is suitable for pregnancy. Ask your doctor about any for which you do not have this information. Before you take any medication, whether prescribed or over-the-counter, ask the following questions:

♦ What does it treat, and how?

♦ Are there other options?

♦ What are the possible side effects?

♦ Could it affect the baby? If so, is it known how?

♦ If I *don't* have it, how could this affect me?

♦ If I *don't* take it, could this be bad for the baby, and if so how?

If you decide that you do not want to take a particular drug during pregnancy, and you continue to suffer the condition it is designed to treat, talk about this with your doctor, since there may well be an alternative for use in pregnancy.   ♦ ♦ ♦

HERBS

Maybe the answer is herbs? Some women prefer to treat themselves with herbal remedies during pregnancy and believe that this is a more natural way of healing.

Curative herbs have been used from time immemorial. In the fifth century B.C., Hippocrates described 400 such herbs, and a Sumerian document recording a wide variety of medicinal plants survives from 2200 B.C. Many herbs are pharmacologically potent and modern drugs have been derived from them, though sometimes to treat conditions other than those for which they have been used traditionally. Approximately 50 percent of all drugs used in prescriptions are based on herbal remedies. Foxglove leaves, for example, contain the powerful drug digitalis. The leaves of aloe vera are a strong laxative. Aspirin is derived from the willow.

It is sometimes taken for granted that drugs in the form of herbs have more healing properties because they are more natural and that they must be safer than drugs in the form of pills and capsules. In fact, many people do not think of them as drugs at all. If you decide to take herbs in their natural form in preference to prescribed drugs, you should bear in mind that they are sometimes less effective than pharmaceutical preparations because the quantity and strength of the active principle in them cannot be controlled as they can be in the manufactured product. The maturity of the plant, state of the weather, time of day when it was picked—even the soil in which it was grown—may all affect the concentration of the active principle present. It has been estimated for example, that when comfrey, the active principle of which is allantoin, is used to fight infection, you may need anything from eight ounces to eight pounds of dried leaves in a quart of a water to make a mixture which is pharmacologically active.[18]

There are other—more serious—problems with herbs, too. When plants are gathered in the wild, not only may one plant be mistaken for another, resulting in poisoning, but there may be contaminants present which themselves have a toxic effect. And even the most efficacious herb, when used unwisely or in an excessive dose, can result in poisoning. Ginseng, for example, which is often advocated for female complaints, and in oriental medicine to help adaptation to stress, when used long-term is associated with hypertension, difficulty in sleeping, skin rashes, and morning diarrhea. This has been called the "ginseng abuse syndrome."[19]

Table 2 shows some herbs and other substances women have told me they have found helpful in pregnancy. Most can be bought as herbal teas in health food stores. Unless I have specified otherwise, about one teaspoonful of the herb is used with half a pint of water. Either pour boiling water on to the herb and let it steep for about fifteen minutes, or bring the water to a boil with the herb in it, remove the mixture from the heat as soon as it boils, and then allow it to steep for about ten minutes. When roots are used, the steeping has to be much longer—up to an hour.

Some herbs, though, are known to have dangerous side effects and should be avoided in pregnancy. Lobelia may bring on vomiting, sweating, pain, paralysis, low temperature, rapid and feeble pulse, collapse, and coma. Aloe vera has been associated with cramps, nausea, vomiting, diarrhea, miscarriage, and teratogenic effects. It's obviously best to avoid them.

TABLE 2. HERBS FOR COMMON DISCOMFORTS IN PREGNANCY

SYMPTOMS TREATED	HERB
Nausea	Chamomile
	Spearmint
	Ginger
	Wormwood
	Raspberry leaves
Heartburn and indigestion	Lemon verbena
	Chamomile
	Cinnamon
	Cloves
	Ginger
	Nutmeg
	Peppermint
	Caraway
Constipation	Rhubarb
	Senna pods
	Dandelion leaves
	Brewers' yeast
	Garlic
High blood pressure	Rosemary
	Hawthorn flowers and fruit
	Garlic
	Nettles
	Spinach
	Meadowsweet
	Rue
Increased uterine muscle tone for effective contractions in labor	Raspberry leaves: one cup every day from seventh month of pregnancy
	Lady's mantle
	Blue cohash
Hemorrhoids	Witch hazel in ice pack for local application
Thrush	Lady's mantle
Difficulty in sleeping	Hawthorn flower and fruit

PREGNANCY DISCOMFORTS AND WHAT TO DO ABOUT THEM

For many women, the physical changes of pregnancy result in stresses and strains on the body. These are often called "the minor discomforts of pregnancy" and are brushed aside as of no importance. When you have a nagging backache, throbbing varicose veins, painful hemorrhoids, or feel like the baby is dropping out between your legs as you waddle about like a duckbill platypus, this casual dismissal of what you are enduring can make you feel much worse. But there is usually something you can do to ease these aches and pains, as shown in table 3.

♦ ♦ ♦ Make a note of the decisions you have made about drugs in pregnancy and any plans you have for alternative forms of treatment, either with safer drugs or by nonpharmaceutical methods. ♦ ♦ ♦

TABLE 3. TREATMENTS FOR COMMON DISCOMFORTS IN PREGNANCY

DISCOMFORT	CAUSE	WHAT YOU CAN DO
Need to empty your bladder very often, especially at night	Due to pressure of the uterus on the bladder when the uterus is still low in your pelvis; again when the baby's head has engaged in the pelvis.	Avoid drinking just before you go to bed. Lie down for a while before you go to sleep—can reduce pressure and give you a chance to empty your bladder. Cut out coffee, tea, and alcohol, which stimulate urine production. Empty your bladder before you go out.
Indigestion/heartburn (a hot feeling in your chest and throat as a result of bringing up acid from the stomach)	Sometimes due to high levels of progesterone and other hormones which soften the valve at the top of the stomach. Can also be due to the uterus pressing on the digestive organs late in pregnancy. Affected by what and how you eat.	Eat little and often. Eat slowly, chewing everything well. Sip ice-cold milk after food. Do not eat late in the evening. Sleep propped up on lots of pillows or a cushion. Reduce or stop taking iron tablets. Avoid greasy foods and fried foods. Do not jump up from the table to serve. Ask others to clear the dishes.

DISCOMFORT	CAUSE	WHAT YOU CAN DO
Cramp low in the abdomen or in the groin, on one or both sides	Caused by sudden stretching of the ligaments that link the front of the uterus to either side of the groin and hold up the uterus. It happens especially if you sneeze, cough, laugh, or stand up quickly.	Move slowly. Avoid jerky movements and changes of position. If you're about to sneeze or cough, bend forward at the hip before you do.
Aching or steady throbbing between your legs when standing	Due to pressure of the weight of the uterus on the pelvic floor muscles and the softening effect of pregnancy hormones.	Practice pelvic floor exercises (see chapter 5) regularly throughout the day. Sit with legs raised to hip level on a couch or stool whenever you can.
Cramp in legs	Metabolic changes resulting in imbalance between calcium and phosphorus.	Before bed, sit on floor and stretch one leg out. Hold toes and press heel down till you feel stretch in calf muscles. Repeat with other leg. Try more milk in diet or take calcium tablets.
Backache	Primarily due to your posture in response to the growing weight of the uterus. The baby may press against your sacrum, the big bone where your pelvis joins the spine.	Sleep on a firm bed; avoid a sagging mattress. (Put a board under the mattress or put the mattress on the floor.) Stand straight, tucking in your bottom, and avoid hollowing your back. Sit on a straight high chair; tuck a cushion in the small of your back. On long car journeys stop and get out for some exercise every hour. When shifting or lifting heavy objects, bend your knees and use the muscles in your legs, not those in your back. *Avoid:* high-heeled shoes, standing or sitting still for a long time—keep on the move.
Difficulty sleeping	Because the baby kicks so much; because you need to empty your bladder, or you have physical discomfort; because of vivid or bad dreams, or anxiety.	Do some vigorous exercise every day. Take a hot bath before bed, use relaxation techniques, read a boring book, do crossword puzzles, play music. See if lying on your side with a pillow under your upper knee is more comfortable. If you are anxious about the birth, the baby, or life afterward, talk to someone about your worries: your partner, a friend who understands, your doctor or midwife, your childbirth teacher.

DISCOMFORT	CAUSE	WHAT YOU CAN DO
Dizziness when lying on your back (supine hypotension)	Because the weight of the uterus is pressing the main blood vessels in the lower part of the body. This slows down the rate at which the blood returns to the heart and thus makes your blood pressure too low.	Avoid lying on your back. Have extra pillows at night.
Varicose veins (and aching legs)	Pressure of the uterus on the blood vessels.	Keep moving whenever possible. Rest with your feet up. Wear support pantyhose or stockings. When you get the opportunity, draw circles or the letters of the alphabet with your toes while sitting down. *Avoid:* sitting with knees crossed, or on a chair whose edge presses against your legs.
Hemorrhoids (piles) and varicose veins of the vulva	Pressure of the uterus on the blood vessels. Made worse by constipation.	Change your diet to include plenty of fiber; avoid constipation. Drink plenty of fluids. Never strain to pass a bowel movement. Ask your doctor for a prescription to soothe them. Try a small peeled clove of garlic eased inside the anus.
Skin changes Particularly dry or greasy skin	Pregnancy hormones.	Use oil in your bath, and rich moisturizer for dry skin; skin cleanser and toner for greasy skin.
Brown patches around eyes, nose, or on neck		Avoid sunbathing or use a complete sun block. The patches will disappear after birth.
Stretch marks on thighs, buttocks, breasts, abdomen	Pressure from enlarging uterus and breasts and all-round storage of fat.	Special creams are sold. They can help keep your skin supple but the strain is beneath the skin. Will fade to silver streaks after the birth.
Red raised patches (vascular spiders)		Nothing. Will disappear after birth.
Brown line from navel to pubic hair	Shows where the rectus muscle down the center of the abdomen has begun to peel open inside so there is more space for the uterus.	Nothing. Will disappear after birth.

DISCOMFORT	CAUSE	WHAT YOU CAN DO
Constipation	Sometimes due to hormone changes slowing down intestinal action to allow increased absorption of nutrients and water. Uterus may also press against large intestine. Iron tablets can cause or exacerbate constipation (may also cause diarrhea). Diet is a crucial factor.	Drink plenty of fluids: 6–8 glasses a day. Eat fiber-rich foods—whole-grain bread, bran, legumes, raw fruits and vegetables, especially figs, prunes. Licorice may help. Get some exercise every day. *Avoid:* sugar and refined foods, aspirin and iron pills (or take iron only with food).
Infections: It is normal for your vagina to be moist and juicy during pregnancy, but if you have an irritating discharge or one that is yellow or green, this is a sign of infection:		
Thrush (Candida albicans)	Being run down and under stress; antibiotics; diabetes of pregnancy.	Use suppositories or cream prescribed by doctor. Omit sugar from diet. Avoid wearing tight trousers or pants. Wear cotton pants, not synthetic fabric. Wash daily, but avoid long hot baths. Soak in tepid water with half a cup of vinegar in it. Suck natural yogurt into a bendable straw and then press yogurt through straw into vagina.
Trichomonas	Can be acquired from partner by sexual intercourse.	Use suppositories or cream prescribed by doctor. You and your partner should take a course of antibiotics prescribed by a doctor. Get your partner to wear a condom.
Bacteria (chlamydia, gardnarella, gonorrhea)	Can be acquired from partner by sexual intercourse.	Suppositories or cream for you and antibiotics prescribed by doctor for both partners. Get your partner to wear a condom.
Local irritation or allergy	Synthetic fabrics, vaginal deodorants, contact with rubber condom.	Avoid vaginal contact with deodorants, talcum powder, strong-smelling soap, bath, foam, rubber. Wear cotton underclothes.

4

◆ CHOOSING THE ◆
RIGHT FOOD

The aim of this chapter is not to prescribe a diet for pregnancy, but to get you to look at your nutrition and decide if it can be improved. There are various ways in which you might do this, and the choice is up to you.

There are nine months—or actually thirty-five weeks from the time when you first realize that you may be pregnant—in which to nourish the baby inside your body and to build a strong and healthy human being able to cope with all the challenges life presents. I believe that there are several things wrong with the way in which a good deal of counseling about diet in pregnancy is offered: it is often very dogmatic—implying that you must drink two pints of milk a day and have liver three times a week or you are starving your baby. It is also often presented as exclusively of benefit to the unborn baby, not the mother. She is supposed to ignore her own preferences and put the right raw materials in so that she will turn out a quality-controlled product at the end of the nine months. It is as if she were a machine to make a baby. If for any reason she does not stick to the rules, she feels guilty. If her baby happens to be premature or handi-capped she may even believe that this is all her fault, and that it is a kind of punishment. This approach to nutrition in pregnancy is dangerous and misleading. It blames the victim and ignores the many genetic and social causes for prematurity and handicaps.

The right kind of food is as important for the mother's own health as it is for fetal growth and development. She is not merely a passive container for a fetus. Pregnancy makes demands on her whole metabolism and without good food she can get very weary and exhausted.

The countries with the lowest perinatal morality rate (deaths of babies between the twenty-eighth week of pregnancy and the first week after birth) and the fewest babies born with handicaps are those where there is no poverty and wealth is shared with greatest equality—Sweden, Finland, Denmark, and the Netherlands. A preterm baby or a low-birthweight baby may be as much the result of socioeconomic conditions as of anything an individual woman has the power to control. Many of the things that could make childbirth safer and improve the health of babies entail social and political changes. The gap between the rich and poor needs to be reduced.

In any impoverished society, women are the poorest of the poor—and the most badly fed. Custom may add to this malnutrition. In some Asian cultures, women are undernourished because they eat only scraps after the men have finished. In the privileged countries of the West, and increasingly in the Third World, the power that food manufacturers and the multinational companies exert over eating habits leads to malnutrition because the nutrients have been removed from processed foods. So prenatal nutrition is not just a personal matter. It is a political issue—for all women everywhere.

LIKES AND DISLIKES

There is no single right diet for pregnancy. Innuit women eat whale meat and fish, few vegetables and no fruit—and have healthy babies. Many African mothers eat large amounts of grain and vegetable and fruit proteins, but little animal protein—and have healthy babies. In New Guinea, insects form an important protein addition to a diet that otherwise is very high in starch—and mothers there have healthy babies, too.

So there is no reason why you should force yourself to eat anything you cannot enjoy. In Western society there are always alternatives that can provide the same food value, though sometimes, if your diet contains no animal products at all, you need to do a bit of juggling to make sure nutrition is balanced.

You will obviously need to bear in mind what you can afford. If you are on a limited budget, some kinds of high-protein food and, depending where you live, fresh fruits and vegetables that are out of season may prove expensive. Think in terms of priorities that fit your own lifestyle so that you can add to, modify, or vary your diet to suit your needs in pregnancy.

Pregnancy changes your metabolism so that, even when resting, you are using up more energy. As outlined on table 4, your whole physical organism adapts to meet the new demands that put stress on your cardiovascular system and affect your breathing and digestion, as well as renal (kidney), adrenal, thyroid, and pituitary functions (the glands regulating the way your body uses energy). The pituitary gland, for example, gets bigger and produces special pregnancy hormones that change the entire hormonal balance in your body. Your heart enlarges and works harder. The total volume of respiratory gases inhaled and exhaled increases throughout pregnancy. At the end of pregnancy, you are using about 15 percent more oxygen than you were before you conceived.

With all these changes taking place, it is not surprising that many pregnant women—sometimes even as early as the fourth month—feel dizzy or faint if they go a long time without food, and that those who were happy not to eat breakfast or often skipped lunch before they were pregnant, discover that they need some protein to start the morning or have to stop and sit down and eat a high-energy snack at midday.

♦ ♦ ♦ To work out your nutritional needs, start by looking at what you actually eat now and at your personal preferences and dislikes. In your notebook, jot down everything you ate and drank in the last twenty-four hours. As you read through this chapter, check whether you are getting the nutrients you need. You can then add some foods and perhaps cut down on others. ♦ ♦ ♦

You do not need to go on a special diet in pregnancy—with one special exception: if as a baby you had phenylketonuria (PKU, the metabolic disorder for which a blood check is done on every baby after birth), there is an increased chance of having a baby with an abnormality of the central nervous system or heart if you do not go on a low phen-

TABLE 4. NOURISHING YOUR UNBORN BABY

SPERM AND OVUM MEET	*FIRST 3 MONTHS*	*MIDDLE 3 MONTHS*	*LAST 3 MONTHS*
The baby	Cells differentiate. Heart starts to pump. Organs form and develop.	Cartilage begins to harden into bone. Fetus grows.	Brain cells develop. Nerve fibers become covered in fat (myelination). Bones harden. Fat builds up under skin. Iron is stored. Carbohydrates are stored in baby's liver and muscles in form of glycogen. Liver functions. Fetus grows.
The placenta	Lining of uterus nourishes developing cell cluster. At 8 weeks placenta starts to function and is fully working by 12 weeks.	Placenta grows, stores nutrients, excretes waste products, keeps pregnancy hormone levels high.	
The mother	Breasts enlarge. Uterus starts to grow. May have nausea. May feel very tired and need extra sleep.	Surge in appetite.	Uterus enlarges further. Deep fat is stored for breast-feeding. Calories are stored as energy for labor and after the birth.

Source: Based on Phyllis S. Williams, "Time Line for Good Perinatal Nutrition," *Sharing* 3:1 (January 1981).

ylalanine diet in pregnancy. If you know that you were a PKU baby, talk to your doctor about this and seek guidance from a dietician.

It used to be assumed that educated middle-class women automatically ate well. But many women restrict their calorie intake in the last three months of pregnancy in order to hold their weight down. They may cut out or reduce salt because they are told it is bad for them, and some are still prescribed diuretics (pills to increase the flow of urine) to reduce milk edema (swelling and puffiness caused by water retention in the tissues). Occasionally they even try to lose weight.[1] *Do not go on a strict weight-loss diet at any time in pregnancy.* Instead, cut out sugar and reduce fats.

Good nutrition enables your immune system to function effectively so that you can resist infection and cope with some poisons— such as those in air and water—that you may not be able to avoid. Absorption of lead, for example, is affected by nutrition. Lead is particularly dangerous if you do not have enough calcium (good sources are milk—whole, skim, or buttermilk—and cheese) and iron (green vegetables are an excellent source—spinach, broccoli, cabbage, Swiss chard, kale, mustard and collard greens, alfalfa, sprouts, lettuce). When nutrition is poor, any poisons from the environment also *stay* in the body longer. If you are well nourished, you have a defense system able to resist the effects of any poison you accidentally absorb.

The simplest way to get good nutrition is to base your diet on whole foods: grains that retain their inner germ and outer husk, fruit including their skins (well washed) when these are edible, and vegetables eaten raw, or steamed or boiled in very little water with their skin when possible. Priority number one is to have plenty of fresh food and avoid highly processed foods. This is not only a matter of choosing raw fruit and vegetables when you can, but also of eating them—whenever possible—within a short time of being gathered. Though this may seem impossible in a city, it is easy to grow parsley and other herbs on a windowsill, and perhaps you can drive out to a farm to buy fresh-picked fruit and vegetables at regular intervals. The foods to avoid or cut down on are refined foods like polished rice and white flour from which much of the goodness has been artificially removed. When you eat bread, pancakes, pasta, and cereals, select them in their wheat-germ form whenever possible. You can also sprinkle wheat germ and brewers' yeast over other foods. Wheat germ can be added when baking, and brewers' yeast does not taste too bad in orange juice. Combinations of nuts, grains and beans, peas and lentils make complete proteins.

The basic building blocks of a good diet are protein, carbohydrate, and fat. Proteins are essential for your own health, for the baby's growth, and for the development of the placenta and maintenance of the amniotic fluid. Protein is stored in the body so that all the systems involved in labor can function effectively, and after the baby is born you have an ample supply of breast milk. Protein foods include milk, yogurt, cheese, meat, fish, eggs, beans, lentils, peas, nuts, and tofu (soybean curd).

Carbohydrates, together with fats, give energy and assist the storage of protein. Some carbohydrate foods are bread, cereals, pasta, rice, potatoes, and bananas. Fats—for example, butter and oil— offer a transport system for the fat-soluble vitamins A, D, E and K, as well as providing concentrated calories.

Vitamins and minerals—shown in tables 5 and 6—are vital constructional materials, sometimes compared to the cement that holds the bricks together.

Folic acid, one of the B vitamins, is the only vitamin, and calcium the only mineral, for which the need as much as doubles during pregnancy.[2]

♦ ♦ ♦ Check through the following list of foods rich in folic acid and make sure you have at least one food from it every day.

♦ Brewers' yeast and yeast extract (richest of all)

♦ Kidney, liver, brains, and sweetbreads

♦ Bran and bran products

♦ Peas and fresh, preferably raw, green leaf vegetables—for example, endive, broccoli, spinach

♦ Nuts

♦ Whole grains—for example, whole-grain bread and oatmeal

TABLE 5. VITAMINS

VITAMIN	WHAT IT DOES FOR YOU AND YOUR BABY	CONTAINED IN
A	Important for baby's cell, tooth, and bone growth. Helps keep your own skin and mucus membranes healthy.	Dandelion greens, sorrel, carrots, parsley, green leafy vegetables, dairy foods, liver.
B complex	Involved in protein synthesis (which makes energy available from food) for the baby and you. B_{12} helps development of the baby's brain.	Yeast and yeast extract, whole-grain cereals, meat (especially brains, liver, kidneys), eggs, bran, dairy foods, fish, nuts, some green vegetables, dried fruit. If you do not eat any animal products, it is wise to take a supplement of vitamin B_{12}.
C	Protects body cells, maintains connective tissue, and helps you both absorb iron.	Red peppers, black currants, parsley, sorrel, green peppers, citrus fruit, tomatoes, potatoes in their skins, watercress.
D	Helps absorption of calcium and phosphorus and enables the baby to develop strong bones and teeth.	Fortified milk, fortified margarine, dairy foods, spinach, parsley, dried figs, almonds, watercress, soy flour, liver, herrings, sardines. Sunlight on the body also forms vitamin D in oils in the skin.
E	Helps growth and maintenance of red blood cells in the baby and you, and the healing of wounds.	Vegetable oils, cereals, meat, eggs, milk, wheat germ, nuts.

Then look back at the table of minerals and make a similar checklist for daily calcium. ♦ ♦ ♦

When a woman does not have enough folic acid in her diet she may run the risk of having a baby with a neural-tube defect (anencephaly or spina bifida). A doctor in an area where this handicap was common prescribed B vitamins and folic acid for a group of women who had already had a baby with a neural-tube defect. They started taking the supplements at least one month before they began the next pregnancy. Another group of women who had previously had an anencephalic or spina bifida baby did not get these extra vitamins. In the group given the B vitamins only three babies suffered from a neural-tube defect. In the unsupplemented group, twenty-four ba-

TABLE 6. MINERALS

MINERAL	WHAT IT DOES FOR YOU AND YOUR BABY	CONTAINED IN
Calcium	Works with vitamin D to build healthy bones and teeth and helps growth and protection of nerves.	Cheese, milk, spinach, parsley, dried figs, nuts, watercress, soy flour, yogurt, egg yolk.
Iron	Helps form red blood cells which carry oxygen around the body. Needs vitamin C to work efficiently.	Blackstrap molasses, liver, lean meat, bran, wheat germ, parsley, soy flour, dried fruit, millet, egg yolk, prunes, dried peas, beans and lentils.
Sodium and Potassium	Together regulate body fluids. Sodium is a constituent of amniotic fluid and is needed for the increased blood volume in pregnancy. Oversalting of foods, however, prevents absorption of potassium and can cause high blood pressure.	Blackstrap molasses, yeast extract, dried fruit, soy flour, bran, parsley, wheat germ.
Magnesium	Assists the function of B vitamins and retains potassium in body cells.	Bran, nuts, wheat germ, soy flour, millet, whole-grain flour, oatmeal.
Phosphorus	Necessary for health of bones and teeth and development of the baby.	Available in a wide range of food. Deficiency is extremely unlikely.
Zinc	May play an important part in the functioning of the reproductive organs. Helps growth of baby. Needed for normal concentrations of vitamin A.	Oysters, red meat, liver, kidneys, whole grains, bran, fiber-rich foods, nuts, cheese.
Iodine	Minute quantities only are necessary for correct functioning of thyroid gland and baby's mental development.	Fish, vegetables grown in iodine-rich soil, agar and carrageen (vegetable gelatine), sea vegetables, iodized salt.

bies had neural-tube defects.[3] Even without vitamin supplements, improving maternal nutrition reduces the chance of neural-tube defects.[4]

Iron Tablets

Many doctors prescribe extra iron routinely in pregnancy. This is because the baby takes iron from you to form its own red blood cells. Iron tablets can cause indigestion and constipation and make nausea and vomiting much worse. There is no need to take extra iron in the first three months anyway, because extra demands are not yet being made and you are saving iron by not menstruating. After that time, one tablet a day is usually enough. If you find that supplementary iron is causing indigestion or making you constipated, go back to your doctor. Iron in another form may suit you better. Your hemoglobin (red blood cell) level should not fall below eleven (written on your notes as 11g/dl), but the hemoglobin normally falls by 7 to 12 percent by about the thirtieth week of pregnancy, as the volume of blood increases.[5]

HOW MUCH PROTEIN,
HOW MUCH SALT?

Poor nutrition is associated with the rise in blood pressure, albumen (protein) in the urine, and excessive edema (retention of fluid in body tissues) that characterize the condition known as preeclamptic toxemia (PET for short). A preeclamptic woman often feels well, but the placenta may function less efficiently and fetal growth slow down, so that the baby is of low birth weight. Preeclampsia and fetal growth retardation are most likely to happen in the last few months of pregnancy. The doctor usually orders bed rest. Induction of labor may be recommended.

Some kinds of preeclampsia can be dangerous for the mother as well as the baby. In serious cases she becomes eclamptic. The signs of impending eclampsia are severe and persistent headaches, flashes or spots in front of the eyes, nausea and vomiting, and extreme agitation. Her blood pressure shoots up and she starts to have convulsions. Medical help should be sought immediately if any of these symptoms are experienced.

One well-known study claims that PET is always the result of malnutrition.[6] Whether or not this is so, even in an affluent nation like the United States, poverty, hunger, and eating junk food cause reproductive problems, including prematurity and stillbirth. Some of this malnutrition is actually iatrogenic (produced by doctors)— the result of medical advice given some pregnant patients to eat less.

Weight-reducing or weight-holding diets, sometimes with diuretics (water pills) to get rid of excess fluids, are still advocated by some doctors in order to prevent or treat PET. But they don't succeed in bringing down blood pressure or preventing protein in the urine. An overview of nine randomized trials of diuretics reveals that in almost half the cases reported they did not reduce preeclampsia or the number of stillbirths. Fortunately, neither was there evidence of any severe side effects of diuretic treatment.[7] There are many questions about PET that remain unanswered and need to be explored.

Since protein deficiency is thought to affect birthweight, a number of studies have investigated the effects of giving mothers protein supplements in pregnancy. One of these studies, carried out in Guatemala, where there is great poverty and hunger, showed that protein supplements produced bigger and healthier babies. Another research project, in Harlem, New York, found, however, that protein supplements had very little effect.[8] One problem with giving out vitamin pills or protein supplements is that researchers often do not find out what the women they are studying usually eat. This happened with another research project that entailed giving Asian women in an English Midlands city extra protein and other supplements during pregnancy. Though extra protein made the women put on more weight, it had no effect on their babies' birthweights. The researchers commented that if they had provided supplements only for those women who were underfed they might have learned more from the project.[9] So they did another study, providing supplements only for those women who were obviously not well nourished. This time they found that extra protein did produce bigger babies.[10] Protein deficiency stunts the baby's growth. But having *more* than you need is of no benefit to the baby. Two helpings daily selected from among the following foods will meet this protein need: milk and dairy products, eggs, meat, fish, whole-grain cereals, legumes (peas, lentils, beans), and protein-rich vegetables (potatoes, cabbage, broccoli).

Nearly all processed foods are highly salted, and adding salt at the table increases the amount even more. Excess salt overloads the renal system and causes high blood pressure. There is a strong case to be made for reducing salt consumption, whether or not you are pregnant. Salt occurs naturally in many foods, so with a good mixed diet you are very unlikely to go short of it.

When you are pregnant, you may find you like salty, spicy, strongly flavored foods, especially in the first months. This may be because there is an increased need for salt at that time to form the amniotic fluid. Provided that you have not developed a taste for oversalted food before pregnancy, your personal preferences are the best guide. If you concentrate on natural whole foods, rather than processed products, you are unlikely to have too much salt. Onions, garlic, lemon juice, herbs and spices, and roasted seeds and nuts all enhance flavor, as well as provide trace minerals and other valuable nutrients.

WHAT DO YOU EAT?

A few pages back I suggested that you make some notes about what you ate yesterday. Look at these now and check whether your diet contains the nutrients your pregnant body needs. Can you improve your nutrition? Here is what some women discovered.

Clare, in England, is in public relations and has been trying to lose weight.

♦ Morning: Coffee

♦ Lunch: Cottage cheese and crackers, lettuce and tomato salad; coffee

♦ Afternoon: Chocolate bar "because I was so hungry"

♦ Supper: Chinese takeout spare ribs and spring rolls; diet cola

♦ Evening: Peanut butter and enriched white bread; 2 glasses of skim milk: "I couldn't sleep. I was hungry."

Clare's diet is short of B vitamins and protein, though her appetite led her to have some unplanned food after she had gone to bed which partly made up for this since peanut butter contains both protein and B vitamins and enriched bread has B vitamins, too. But she needs whole-grain bread and other whole-grain cereals such as brown rice, and should add dark green vegetables to her diet for extra iron, magnesium, vitamin A, and the B vitamins, especially folic acid. She could get more protein from fresh fish, which would provide her with zinc and iodine as well. In spite of the salad at lunch, she is short on vitamin C. If she had some potatoes and added citrus fruits, berries, and more green vegetables to her diet, not only would her nutrition be much better balanced but she wouldn't feel so hungry.

Sherry, in the United States, has a child aged fourteen months, is alone with the baby most of the day, and has an evening meal with her husband.

♦ Morning: Prune juice and muffin

♦ Lunch: Rest of baby's cereal and mashed beets; hamburger; scoop of ice cream; tea

♦ Supper: Chicken, broccoli, squash, mashed potatoes; fruit pie; milk

Though Sherry has vegetables in the evening and finishes up the baby's beets midday, she is short on vitamin C and would do better with some raw fruit and vegetables at each meal. A fresh fruit salad would be better than the fruit pie. Some citrus juice, an orange or grapefruit, strawberries, or melon would be a good idea at both breakfast and lunch, and she could add tomatoes, watercress, or celery to the midday meal. Since she needs a lot of energy to cope with her fourteen-month-old, starting the day with more protein at breakfast would help—perhaps two boiled or scrambled eggs and a helping of yogurt, or a Dutch-style breakfast with cheese. A good high-protein, high-energy snack to keep her going in the late afternoon, when she says she gets very tired, would be a handful of nuts and raisins.

Kerstin, in Scandinavia, is a vegetarian.

♦ Morning: Fresh orange juice; whole-grain cereal with dried fruits

♦ Lunch: Lentil soup; yogurt; brewers' yeast

♦ Supper: vegetable curry with onions, turnips, spinach, and brown rice; salad; soy milk whisked with banana and molasses

Kerstin's diet is high in most vitamins and minerals because of the variety of fresh and cooked vegetables, but unless she is getting sunlight on her skin she is short of vitamin D, and it would help if she had fortified margarine or milk, or took a vitamin A and D supplement. If she chooses the supplement, the dosage ought to be carefully controlled because these vitamins are toxic to the fetus in excessive quantities.

♦ ♦ ♦ It is all very well working out a balanced diet when you shop and cook for yourself. It's another matter when you have to eat at your place of work, in a cafeteria, or in a restaurant. Here is a self-service cafeteria. Starting at the left-hand side with your tray, work your way along, putting a circle around the dishes you would choose.

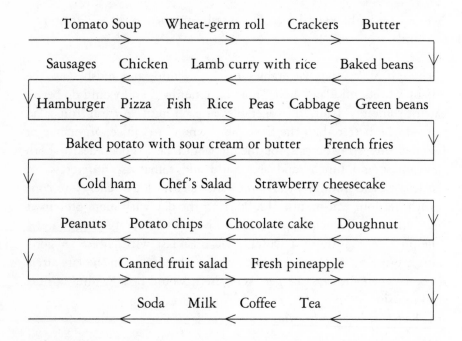

When you have done this, write down in your notebook the things you have on your tray. Then check whether you have enough protein and vitamins B and C. You have protein if you chose a meat, fish or egg dish, cheese, baked beans, or milk. Vitamin B is in the whole-grain roll, milk, meat, beans and peas, leafy green vegetables (in the salad), and peanuts. In most cafeterias the food is kept hanging around so long that it loses vitamin C. Even so, you will get some vitamin C if you chose the salad, baked potato, or fresh fruit. The cooked vegetables may have been overcooked and exposed to the air, so you can't rely on them for vitamin C.

The cheesecake, canned fruit, and doughnut are all high in sugar. There is often hidden sugar in commercial soups and other canned and processed foods. Sugar occurs naturally in fruits and some vegetables, but when you consume extra sugar in soft drinks or added to tea and coffee, and in the form of desserts and baked goods, this often overloads the system and feeds you only empty calories. Since concentrated sugar actually draws on stores of vitamins and minerals, especially the B vitamins, the overall effect is even worse. If you discover that your meal was lacking in important nutrients or that you were filling up with empty calories, think of some snack foods you could take to work with you to supplement your diet. ♦ ♦ ♦

AT THE SUPERMARKET

Most convenience and instant products are deficient in vitamins B and C and in minerals. Some B vitamins are eliminated entirely from sausages, processed meats, and milk products like processed cheese, ice cream, and commercial yogurt, for example. Even if you have a large proportion of protein foods in your diet, you are not necessarily eating the right *kinds* of protein, for the more protein you have, the more B vitamins you require. If you rely on sausages and processed cheese as your main sources of protein, you may not be getting enough. Moreover, highly processed foods such as packaged desserts, cakes, cookies, sausages, and other convenience foods "steal" nutrients from other foods. Whole foods contain vitamins and minerals that enable you to make use of all the nutrients in them. But junk food leaches vitamins and minerals from your body's stores. Highly processed and refined foods are also very low in fiber and high in calories, so there is a temptation to eat too much of them.

In addition to extra sugar and fat, processed and packaged foods on supermarket shelves often contain special additives to preserve and color them and give a pleasing texture. Red dye No. 2, though banned in the United States (as well as France and eastern Europe) because it is associated with birth defects and cancer, may still show up in some imported jams, jellies, sausages, canned foods, and soft drinks. Check the labels; by law, food packages have to list their ingredients in order of weight—there is most of the first ingredient and least of the last. But even a speck of a poisonous substance may be harmful, so you cannot go by weight alone.

It is worth reading the labels on all packaged and processed foods. Artificial colorings and sodium nitrite are ingredients to avoid, together with excessive amounts of sugar and fat. Coca-Cola contains caffeine, caramel coloring, sugar, phosphoric acid, flavoring, and carbonated water. Many breakfast cereals are mostly sugar and are artificially colored. Sodium nitrite makes processed meat keep its pink color. It is added to bacon, ham, Spam, hot dogs, salami, bologna, and liverwurst.

NUTRITION IN PRACTICE

It is all very well talking about what we *should* eat, but convenience, the need for speed, the cost of many high-quality foods, and the food preferences of a partner or of other members of the family all play a part in dictating what we actually eat. Children often have very strong likes and dislikes. If you already have a family, you may plan to have salads, only to discover that they want french fries with everything. Then it becomes important to think about how you are going to introduce those foods, or more of them, that you know are healthy for you in pregnancy in such a way that the rest of the family can enjoy them, too. But sometimes, as a last resort, a pregnant woman needs to have her own nutrition plan and eat foods different from her partner's or those of the rest of the family.

The cost of some foods may be a problem. Out-of-season fruits and vegetables are expensive, and because carbohydrate foods are cheaper than high-protein foods, you may feel guilty and self-indulgent if you spend money on the more expensive protein foods. On the other hand, there is no need to choose expensive cuts of meat, and there are many sources of protein in vegetables, legumes, and grains that together with cheese, eggs, milk, fish, or a little meat make appetizing dishes. A good vegetarian cook book will help you plan meals that are nutritious and can give ideas on how to make use of other sources of protein.

The appearance of food on a plate, or different foods to be eaten together, can be a help—and color is especially useful. Have something white or brown, something green, and something yellow, orange, or red at every meal. It will look much more appetizing than, for example, chicken, rice, and mashed potatoes, and will be a better balanced meal.

♦ ♦ ♦ Bearing in mind your own eating habits and what you have noted down about the food you ate yesterday, decide what, if any, changes you want to make in your diet in order to have really good nutrition in pregnancy. You are more likely to make changes if you limit them, at first anyway, to just two or three decisions that you can build into a realistic plan. Write down your main decisions about how you want to improve your nutrition in the remaining months of your pregnancy. ♦ ♦ ♦

5

✦ EXERCISE ✦

You may be wondering what exercises you should be doing in pregnancy and whether there are any that are best avoided altogether. If you are accustomed to a daily jog or run, for example, or enjoy a friendly game of tennis, you may be uncertain whether you should stop as soon as you learn you are pregnant, whether you can continue right through pregnancy, or if there is a special time when it is wise to avoid this activity. Even if exercise in general is not harmful, you may question whether certain movements can be risky.

There is, in fact, no systematic medical information to guide you about this. It is a matter of common sense and, above all, your own feelings. *You are the expert about your body, in pregnancy as at other times, and only you can really judge what makes you feel good and what is a strain.* That is the litmus test. Exercise that brings a glow of well-being is bound to be good for both you and your baby—and this applies throughout your pregnancy.

The major benefits of energetic physical activity in pregnancy are that it tones up your muscles, improves circulation, helps balance and physical coordination as you change shape, and makes you feel good and look good. Movements specially adapted to pregnancy which you can learn at childbirth classes help avert aches and pains as you get heavier and enable your body to work efficiently so that you avoid some of the things that can make pregnancy a misery—like constipation and hemorrhoids, accidentally wetting your pants, indigestion, and difficulty in getting off to sleep or staying asleep. Exercise throughout pregnancy also means that you are more likely to feel fit and energetic after the birth and to recover your figure quickly.

Physical activity has other advantages, too. Exercise done for pleasure stimulates the production of hormones called endorphins that are natural opiates (pain-killers) related to morphine. As you jog, for example, the endorphin level in your blood may rise by as much as 60 percent. At the same time, there is an increase in prolactin of about 40 percent. This is the hormone that stimulates the breasts to make milk. In animals it is a powerful trigger for nurturing behavior.

To get a release of endorphins and prolactin you need to stretch yourself. A stroll around the shopping mall will not achieve it. Endorphins are liberated as a result of *stress*. Endorphins are produced in labor, too. They contribute to the sense of deep satisfaction that many women experience with the hard work of childbirth.

So regular exercise that you really enjoy during pregnancy tones your muscles, encourages good posture, body mechanics, and complete breathing, stimulates an efficient blood flow to the baby, and produces the prolactin you will need for breast-feeding. It also gets you in good condition to get your figure back after the baby is born. And if you start labor with your endorphin level already high from energetic activity, you may experience less pain. When you have enjoyed coordinated physical movements throughout pregnancy, you are more likely to be well prepared to work *with* your body and with the power of your uterus as contractions follow one another like great waves in a strong sea.

Here are some simple and straightforward guidelines about exercise in pregnancy:

You should enjoy it! There is no need to push yourself into doing exercise you do not like. If a particular kind of exercise proves wearisome and becomes a chore, your body is probably trying to tell you to stop.

It should be rhythmic. During pregnancy hormones are liberated in your bloodstream that soften tissues and make the connecting ligaments between bones more flexible. The research on this was originally done on guinea pigs, who apparently became very supple when pregnant. For some time it was not known whether a similar process occurred in human beings. But now research shows that it does. This softening process prepares your body for birth so that the bony pelvis has extra give and the cervix and vagina open easily. This means, however, that it is possible to overstretch ligaments that are already very flexible, especially those of the pelvis, and in particular in the small of your back. A bad backache after any exercise that involves vigorous movement—anything which entails hollowing your lower back, for example—could mean that you are stretching these ligaments too much. If you keep to smoother, rhythmic, dancelike movements, this is much less likely to happen.

It should be noncompetitive. Being paced by someone else or trying to surpass their performance could be harmful because you are likely to lose touch with the messages your body is giving you. A woman who is highly motivated to keep herself in shape during pregnancy and remain active and energetic may be particularly at risk of overdoing exercise in this way. Though it is good to know what you want and prepare yourself actively to be in the best condition during pregnancy and ready to meet the challenge of labor, if you know that you have an obsessional personality and tend to tackle things with tremendous energy, you will be aware that your very determination may itself prove a handicap if it drives you to demand too much of yourself. It is important to listen to your body in both pregnancy and labor. You are not taking an exam that has to be passed and you do not need to prove yourself as a woman.

Start any new form of exercise gradually. Tone your muscles step by step and learn how to perform movements smoothly without straining. When you begin a new movement or position, do it for a short time only and then gradually lengthen the time or increase the number of repetitions.

Energetic activity should be interspersed with a regular break for relaxation. Muscular relaxation and release from tension are as vital as exercise. Exercise works best for you and for the baby inside you when it is partnered with refreshing rest periods, even if they last only a few minutes each.

As your uterus enlarges, you may notice that you tend to breathe more quickly. You also take in and breathe out a larger quantity of air and this enables more oxygen to reach the baby. Your heart beats faster even when you are resting, going up from about seventy to about eighty-five beats a minute. Heart and blood-flow changes mean that you get a reduced blood flow to your uterus and placenta *during* exercise but increased blood flow afterwards. So short bouts of energetic exercise are much better than prolonged ones. Every time you take a rest, the flow of oxygenated blood to the baby is increased.[1]

Exercise should not leave you feeling exhausted. Your own feelings about any activity are the best guide. If you feel worn out, maybe you are going at it too strenuously. Maybe those particular movements are wrong for you at this stage of your pregnancy. Trust your body. After each exercise session, take a little time to tune in to how you feel. For this reason, brief, regular sessions are much better than a weekly workout. If you are in pain after any activity, stop it and, if you can, lie down for at least twenty minutes. Then choose an activity that involves different muscles from those you have been using before. There is a lot of exercise in housework. If you have been cleaning windows or hanging wash on a clothesline, for example, both of which entail stretching, get down on your hands and knees and wash the kitchen floor, so that you take the weight of the baby off your spine and flex your arms and legs.

Some women notice that they get contractions when overtired or under stress. Occasionally, exercising because you think you *ought to,* rather than because it feels good, steps up these Braxton-Hicks contractions until they become quite painful. Even walking, if done strenuously, does this sometimes in pregnancy. It is a sign that you need to have a rest or change your activity.

Swimming is marvelous in late pregnancy because the water supports the weight of your body, and even if you feel rather like a stranded whale on dry land, in water you can move almost effortlessly and feel light and graceful.

Do not hold your breath when exercising. The baby depends on you for oxygen. Any movement that makes you stop breathing is too stressful and should be abandoned or modified so that it is easier. One advantage of vigorous exercise is that it helps you to breathe fully, using all of your lungs instead of merely the top part. But if an exercise results in breathholding, it defeats the purpose. When the breath is held, the diaphragm is fixed. If at the same time you are exerting effort, the return of oxygen to your heart may be impeded and you may feel sick and dizzy. This is why energetic aerobics or workouts on exercise machines are not a good idea.

The balance of gases in your blood could also be affected by scuba diving, so it is probably unwise to dive in pregnancy.[2] If you want to go on diving, restrict your dives to thirty feet.[3] One study has shown that more babies with abnormalities are born to mothers who continue, especially with deep dives.[4] Many women get a stuffy nose and congested sinuses in pregnancy because there is an increased blood supply to mucous membranes throughout the body. For this reason, deep dives can sometimes also cause burst eardrums in the mother.

Exercise should take place in air that is as clean as possible. Avoid exercising in smog, smoke, fumes, or chemically polluted air. Jogging by the highway forces polluted air into your lungs, and though the placenta can filter out some of the toxic elements, it is unable to detoxify your bloodstream completely. When you can, exercise in the countryside, or in a park, or by the ocean.

Special Exercises for Pregnancy

Exercise should tone the muscles that work to carry the extra weight of the enlarged uterus and the baby—those in your legs, lower back, abdomen, and feet, for example. Sometimes an exercise does nothing to help the efficiency of these muscles. Bending straight-legged to touch your toes is one such exercise. Some movements, such as lying on the floor and raising straight legs off the ground, put a strain on muscles already under stress, and pain or discomfort can guide you to know when this happens. The muscles most affected by pregnancy are those of the abdominal wall, the pelvic floor (which supports all your pelvic organs), and your back, especially your lower back. Supported squatting and doing gentle pelvic movements on all fours help to strengthen lower back muscles and ease backache. But an exercise often taught in birth classes, involving a pelvic rock on hands and knees, humping the lower back and then swinging it down so that it is hollowed, strains the muscles and can make back pain worse. This exercise is fine if you remember always to keep your lower back *flat* as you swing down from the humped position. A good exercise for firming the abdominal muscles is to sit (either on a chair or on the floor) with your hands on your abdomen. Breathe in slowly, letting your abdomen bulge out, and then exhale fully, pulling in your abdominal muscles more and more as you do so. Sit-ups and lying on your back lifting a leg straight up in the air, though intended to strengthen the abdominal muscles, often have the opposite effect. In pregnancy the rectus muscle down the middle of your abdomen, which you may see as a dark line from your navel to your pubis, is under stress. Anything that puts excessive strain on this muscle can make it literally fall apart. The longitudinal bands of muscle fiber can separate like a zipper. It can be difficult to regain tone in this muscle after childbirth, and then this must be done very gradually, starting with the breathing movement I have just described and progressing to more difficult exercises.

It is important to exercise invisible muscles, not only those you can see. The pelvic floor muscles—which surround your vagina and anus and form thick layers of muscle fibers further up, supporting your uterus and bladder—open up as the baby is squeezed down between them to be born. They need to be well toned to cope with the extra weight of pregnancy and to open completely during the birth itself. Knowing how to contract and relax these muscles at will enables you to have good internal posture during and after pregnancy and also helps you open up to give birth.

The *elevator exercise* can be done any time during the day, and it is best to link it with often repeated activities like sitting in the car waiting for the light to change, going up or down in an elevator, or walking up and down the stairs. Imagine that the circle of muscles around your vagina and your urethra is like an elevator inside you that can go up five stories. Tighten the muscles first as if the elevator is going up one floor. Hold the contraction firmly. Then tighten further as you ascend to the next floor. Hold. Go further up, and up. Then gradually release the contraction and go down gently and deliberately. Do not let the elevator shoot to the bottom. When you reach the ground floor, go further down to the basement by bulging the muscles downward. (This is what you do when you push your baby out.) Then go *up again* one floor so that you finish the exercise with the muscles well toned. Repeat two or three times. If either during pregnancy or after the birth you find yourself wetting your pants when you laugh or sneeze—a common experience—this exercise, performed with the upward movement of the elevator only, will help tone your muscles.

CHOOSING THE EXERCISE
THAT SUITS YOU

Now think about the physical activities you already enjoy and list them in your notebook. Are there any others you would like to take up that might meet your body's needs in pregnancy? Add these to the list as well.

Ros is three months pregnant and her list was

- ◆ Swimming

- ◆ Walking

- ◆ Exercise Class

- ◆ Horseback riding

- ◆ Cycling

She decided to find out if her exercise instructor taught special classes for pregnant women or, if she didn't, whether she would be able to adapt the standard movements suitably. The exercises were usually done to rather fast music, and as Ros found keeping up with the brisk tempo tiring, she decided to discuss this with her instructor, too. Walking would be very good, and there were special classes for pregnant women at a nearby swimming pool. She would continue cycling, though a friend who cycled throughout her pregnancy advised her that as she got bigger a regular bicycle with upright handlebars would be much more comfortable than one with racing handlebars. She couldn't arrive at a definite decision about riding, though she decided not to jump in case she was thrown. She was going to see how she felt, and make sure that she always had a well-schooled horse.

Shirley made out her list as

- ◆ Yoga

- ◆ Dancing

- ◆ Aerobics

- ◆ Running

She thought the dancing might not be a good idea since they usually danced in smoky rooms where everyone was drinking pretty heavily, too. She found an aerobics class for pregnant women, and after searching around also discovered a special yoga class. She had been running every morning before breakfast for a year or more, and while she was still feeling so fit she would keep this up, perhaps slowing down the pace. She would be guided by how her body felt as pregnancy went on.

♦ ♦ ♦ In your notebook jot down your plan of action for the exercise you have chosen, how to contact people who can help or join you, and any information you need to get. ♦ ♦ ♦

Many women are now choosing to attend special pregnancy exercise classes. This is in addition to classes for childbirth, though there is often an overlap between the two. Sometimes they involve *dance*. In ancient Greece danced formed a central theme in the worship of Cybele, goddess of birth and of the moon, and later on, of Artemis, goddess of birth and of all perilous passages. The pelvic rocking and circling movements a laboring woman and the other women attending her made in childbirth were not only of practical help; they had deep religious significance and expressed through each human birth the power of the great mother goddess. These same pelvic movements, forming what we know today as belly dancing, have also been used in childbirth and in preparation for it among women in Egypt and other parts of North Africa, and are often still used today.

Yoga forms the basis of other pregnancy exercise classes and includes exercises in deep breathing. In yoga, breathing and posture, breathing and movement, are united. It is a way of learning not only how to discipline your body, but also to trust it. It demands serenity, flexibility, and balance, rather than muscle power.[5] It is a good idea to use a chair to help you adopt any vertical head-down positions so that you can unfold gradually, or alternatively slowly walk up a wall with your feet. It is vital to have a good teacher who understands the special needs of pregnancy.

Aerobics must be specially adapted to pregnancy and the teacher should understand the physiology of pregnancy. Each exercise session should start with a warm-up, go on to vigorous movement, and finish with a cool-down. You can check that your heart is not being made to work too hard by taking your pulse regularly.[6]

In an active birth a woman is free to move around spontaneously as and when she wishes, and is not restrained in any way.[7] In classes beforehand she learns movements and positions that encourage the maximum opening of her pelvis. If you can find birth classes in your area that incorporate stretching exercises and movements for active birth, you have the advantage of combining pregnancy exercises with rehearsal for a labor in which you are upright as much as possible, change position often, and give birth squatting, kneeling, or on all fours (or in modifications of these positions) rather than reclining or lying down in the "stranded beetle" position.

Although in the twentieth century the labor bed and delivery table have been treated as essential items of equipment in every hospital, all over the world from time immemorial women have chosen to labor moving around, getting into positions in which they feel most comfortable, and to push the baby out with their feet planted firmly on the ground and in upright or semiupright positions. Medieval midwives delivered women on low, horseshoe-shaped birth stools, and until the introduction of hospital births it was normal practice for women to walk around during labor and to carry on working in the house, often until the onset of the second stage. The postures our great-grandmothers chose were modifications of the squatting, kneeling, and crouching postures still used in Third World countries today.[8] In these positions the uterus is not pressing on the largest blood vessel in the lower part of the body, the inferior vena cava, thus reducing fetal oxygen supply, and gravity helps the delivery of both the baby and the placenta.[9]

A woman in labor tends to be more comfortable upright and walking around, though she may enjoy lying down for short intervals. In a British study women who were encouraged to move around needed fewer pain-relieving drugs and were sometimes reluctant to get on the bed when they were told they could do so. Their contractions were more effective in opening up the cervix, so the first stage was shorter, and at birth the babies were in better condition than those whose mothers lay in bed.[10]

An upright posture produces greater pressure within the pelvis and lets the uterus form a globular shape during contractions. If you are leaning forward, as a woman usually does spontaneously, the baby's head is tipped forward away from her sacrum, the bone that forms the back of the pelvis. This reduces backache and encourages the rotation of the baby's head into the correct position for delivery.

It is all very well deciding in advance that you would like to be out of bed and walking around during labor, but when it comes to doing it there often seems to be nowhere to go and you find yourself wandering around the bed or aimlessly up and down a corridor. It is a good idea to think ahead to some different kinds of movements and positions you might find comfortable and can help you handle pain. These movements should be started as early as possible. In the Third World women crouch or squat as a matter of course instead of sitting for all kinds of daily activities. Because in the West we usually sit on chairs, it can be uncomfortable to squat or crouch for more than a minute or two; ligaments and muscles in the pelvis and back tend to be stiff and our knees and ankle joints tight. Careful, gentle practice done regularly throughout pregnancy will help you to loosen up progressively for childbirth. Aim for smooth, full, flowing movements and avoid jerky, erratic ones. When a muscle is contracted suddenly or very hard, spasm may result and instead of being flexible and stretched, it springs back and becomes shorter.

EXERCISES FOR ACTIVE BIRTH

Many childbirth classes now include both exercises for physical well-being in pregnancy and positions for active birth. The concept of active birth is based on the belief that the woman in labor is an active birthgiver, not a passive patient. So instead of lying down for doctors and nurses to do things to you, you get into positions you find comfortable and move around as and when you wish. This means that you are not restricted to a labor bed or even a birth chair but are free to move around on the floor, in a shower, leaning against the wall, the furniture, or your birth companion. Changing position as often as you want, you work with the process of birth.

Exploring Different Positions

Squatting is most comfortable when you hold on to something firm or someone in front of you, or when you are supported by two helpers, one at each side. When you first start practicing squatting, do so for a short time only, and either wear shoes with low heels or slip a pillow under your heels to avoid putting strain on the Achilles tendons. As the muscles stretch, you will be able to hold the position for longer and gradually lower your heels to the ground.

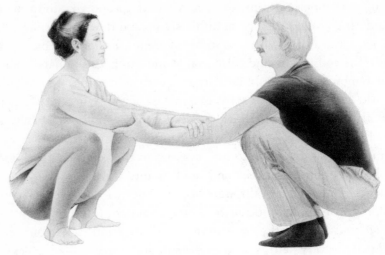

SQUATTING

Experiment, too, with *half-squatting, half-kneeling,* with one knee bent down on the floor, the other bent up with your foot on the floor, as this can be even more comfortable in labor than a full squat. Many women spontaneously seek positions in which the pelvis is asymmetric like this, and the tilting of the pelvis, especially if it is combined with pelvic movement, may help the baby's head to rotate into the correct position for delivery.

There are a variety of good *kneeling* positions, too, in which you do not necessarily need to hold on to anything or be supported. Try changing between a position in which you are sitting up on your heels, leaning forward onto a pillow placed on a chair, and then further forward still, legs wide apart, with your forearms on the floor. A special chair designed for people with back problems that enables you to kneel with your bottom slightly raised and supported is now widely available. This could be one of the things you have with you in case you want to use it in labor. Or you may want to

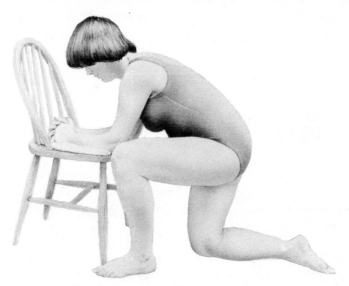

HALF-SQUATTING, HALF-KNEELING

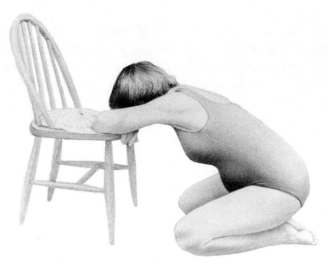

KNEELING

kneel with your partner kneeling behind you so that you have the support of his or her thighs. These positions can feel good if you have a backache labor, and they are all ones in which it is easy to give lower-back massage.

ALL FOURS

Another variation is to get onto *all fours,* knees and arms well apart, thus tilting the baby away from the small of your back and forward on to your abdominal wall. This position is excellent if you have a backache, which often happens if the baby's spine lies parallel with yours, with its face and limbs forward (occipito-posterior position). It can also be comfortable during labor if the baby is in the breech position.

Standing is another good position to practice. Explore different ways in which you can use a wall or a piece of heavy furniture, or lean against your labor companion. Try leaning over a table or onto a windowsill.

With all these positions you do not have to be static. You can change from one to another and then back again. Ask someone to help you—preferably the person who is going to be your birth companion—to experiment with different kinds of movement in each position. See how it feels when you move your pelvis rhythmically. Try rocking or swaying and slow circling. Find ways in which your companion can help you best. Do you want your helper to be still or to move *with* you? Would you like firm holding, massage, or light stroking? How can your partner give physical support and also be in a position where you can make eye contact if this is what you want?

STANDING

Experiment with positions and movements that might be good in the bath or shower. Water can feel wonderfully refreshing in labor.

If you are having your baby in a hospital, the journey there can be uncomfortable unless you work out in advance some comfortable positions in the car. The back seat is often best. See how pillows can help support your back, allow you to be on all fours, or recline on your side.

Imagine, too, how you might want to lie if you are feeling extremely tired. Lying on your side is better than on your back—if the heavy uterus is pressing on the vessels that deliver the blood back to your heart, you may feel dizzy and faint.

Imagine needing to vomit, pass urine, or empty your bowels and work out easy positions for these natural functions.

♦ ♦ ♦ Make a note of the positions and movements you prefer, so that when the time comes there is little chance of getting stuck lying on your back, or in a position that you dare not change either because your whole body feels too heavy or because you are afraid that the pain will get worse if you do. As pregnancy advances, your center of gravity changes and the positions and movements you prefer may also change. ♦ ♦ ♦

EXERCISE PLANS FOR AFTER THE BIRTH

This is time to make inquiries about exercise or yoga classes for after the baby is born. Many classes have babysitting facilities, so you can work out knowing that your baby is cared for while you take time to concentrate on your own health. Some classes are designed for mothers and babies together, so if yours is not sleeping peacefully or enjoying watching, you can include the baby in the movements. A baby a few months old loves energetic activity and doing exercises together can be great fun.

Even if you cannot get to classes regularly, this is something you can do at home, especially if you have learned how. One advantage of classes, however, is that you meet other women there, and this social contact is a great help as you cope with what can be the daunting experience of learning how to be a mother. If you have left your job and are taking time off to get to know your baby, it is important not to become housebound and socially isolated. For far too many new mothers the high point of the day is a trip to the supermarket. It is hardly surprising that women cut off from all their usual social contacts, who don't see another adult for hours on end, often get depressed. This kind of depression has nothing to do with hormones. It comes from being terribly lonely and not having the emotional and social support you need.

In postnatal exercise classes, you and your baby can benefit from the stimulus that comes not only from vigorous activity, but also from having regular outings together and meeting and talking with other women who are going through the same experience.

♦ ♦ ♦   In your notebook jot down your plans for exercise after the baby comes, along with addresses and phone numbers that will be useful then.   ♦ ♦ ♦

6

◆ PREGNANCY AND YOUR ◆
ENVIRONMENT

Whether you are working outside or in the home, or—as with most women—in both places, pregnancy is a time to look at your environment, find out whether it needs improving, and change it if possible.

Are there chemical dangers in the places where you work? Do you breathe clean air? Is the temperature right? (When pregnant, you feel hotter.) Can you sit comfortably? Do you have to stand for long periods? Are you in positions in which you get a backache, neckache, shoulder tension, or pain in your legs or feet? Is the lighting good? Are noise levels acceptable?

It is not only the physical environment you must consider. Look also at the stresses and strains under which you work. Are you under pressure to meet unrealistic deadlines? Are you without any control over your own timetable or unable to plan ahead? Do you work with machines that dictate your pace and allow you too few breathing spaces? Are there enough breaks when you can use the bathroom? (In early and late pregnancy you need to empty your bladder more often than at other times.) Do you feel that you are never able to finish any task properly, that your work has to be skimped because you are pulled in every direction? Are you at too many people's beck and call? Are the hours you work long and exhausting? Are you exposed to sexual harassment at work, having to run the gauntlet of comments about your body or crude jokes, or put up with being pawed? If you work outside the home, there is the journey to and from work, too. Is that stressful?

Living in any big city exposes us all to the stress of constant impersonal and meaningless human contact—the pressure of crowds and of people competing for living space, the tedium of waiting at the check-out counter or for the bus, of driving in heavy traffic, delayed when we have an urgent appointment—all these things irritate, frustrate, and exasperate, and they trigger the release of stress hormones that push blood pressure up, increase breathing rates, contract muscles, and result in general body tension and mental stress. Stress is often talked about as if it should not exist. Yet a certain amount of stress is normal—and we can even enjoy it. It is also inevitable. After all, we shall only be completely stress-free when we are dead.

Because stress produces challenge, it can push us out of a rut, make us rethink things we took for granted, and stimulate problem solving and creativity. Stress is there to be *used*.

The ability to enjoy a certain amount of stress depends, however, on several important factors in our personal lives and our relationships with other people. Physical health is important. When we are physically run down, stress can easily tip over into distress. We are also unlikely to manage stress effectively if we are deprived of any sense of autonomy and personal space because we are constantly at the service of other people, satisfying *their* needs, obeying *their* orders. Stress then results in our feeling put upon and exploited. This is the kind of stress, concerning work both outside the home and inside it, that is worth acknowledging. We may then negotiate changes with those who are making these demands on us, and, if we possibly can, organize life so that stress is reduced.

I realize that, put like this, the list of potential hazards may seem almost endless, your work place full of threat. This is because most of us have to work under pressure and suffer the effects of living in crowds and in a polluted environment. It is probably impossible to escape this altogether. Sometimes it seems that we are surrounded by dangers that we can do very little about and every time we open a newspaper or watch a TV documentary new hazards are reported. Life in the twentieth century is a dangerous process! And when you are having a baby you become even more alerted to all these risks.

Alarming as they are, it does not follow that there is nothing we can do about them. Even if there are many things we cannot change, there are certainly others that, with determination, effort, and by joining with other people who feel the same way, we *can* improve.

This is not just a question of achieving a safe working environment during pregnancy. When poor working conditions affect a pregnant woman's health, or harm an unborn baby, they need improving for the benefit of all of us. Certain pollutants damage sperm too, and a man can become impotent. *All* workers may suffer a deterioration in health or, at the very least, not be functioning at full capacity. This is an urgent social issue.

VIDEO DISPLAY TERMINALS

If you are working with computers, word processors, or video equipment, you may be worrying about their possible harmful effects on the development of the baby. There has been a good deal of publicity recently about the risks of video display terminals (VDTs) for developing babies, especially in the first eight weeks of pregnancy.[1]

The first hazard is that X-rays emitted may be teratogenic (harmful to fetal development). In fact, the energy from these X-rays is low and cannot be detected beyond the glass screen of the tube. A study of mothers of babies with birth defects found no evidence that a higher number than usual had worked with VDTs in early pregnancy.[2] But even if VDTs do not cause birth defects, are women who work with them more likely to have miscarriages? This is the other worry.

In Britain, the Trades Union Congress has recommended that pregnant women be given the option to switch to other work because "worry as a result of uncertainty about VDT work might, itself, prove a significant threat to the success of the pregnancy."[3]

VDTs certainly adversely affect health in other ways. The furniture and lighting in offices are usually designed for reading and writing at desks, so working at VDTs there can be hard on the eyes (though this does not make eyesight deteriorate) and cause a bad working posture. Spots and rashes sometimes appear on the jaw area—a result of electrostatic fields and a dry atmosphere, coupled with electrostatic charges in synthetic office carpeting, poor ventilation, and contaminants in the air. All in all, worry about the possible dangers of VDTs ought to make us reexamine our working conditions generally and improve the environment for everyone.

PESTICIDES

There has been a lot of publicity about pesticides and their effects on the organs and central nervous system of the developing fetus. If you live and work in the countryside, or just do some gardening—even if only with plants on a patio—you may wonder about the chemicals you are using.

The U.S. Environmental Protection Agency states that approximately a third of the active ingredients of registered pesticides are poisonous and a quarter are highly carcinogenic and mutagenic— they cause cancer and damage genes.[4]

Chlorinated dioxin is known to cause miscarriage, stillbirth, and birth defects (cleft palate and kidney abnormalities especially). Dioxin—the active chemical of Agent Orange, used in Vietnam— was sprayed over thousands of people in an explosion at a factory in Seveso, Italy. In Oregon it was used to spray forests, and a study by the EPA shows that women had a high rate of miscarriage in that area, most of the babies being lost in June and July, after the peak spraying period in March and April.

When cattle feed on dioxin-sprayed grass, the chemical is concentrated in their fat. Dioxin is also present in the wood preservative pentachlorophenol and in some plant sprays. On the label it may be indicated as 2,4–D, or 2,4,5–T or TCDD (the TC stands for tetrachlorine and the DD for dioxin).

In the United States, the Food and Drug Administration restricts the use of organochlorine compounds, including DDT, so organophosphates (Malathion, parathion, Mipofax) have largely replaced them now. But we do not know if their long-term use is safe. Though they do not cause damage to organs, they may have more subtle effects on the central nervous system and on learning behavior.

+ Before buying or using any pesticide, read the label.

+ Check through cupboards where you keep insect sprays and plant pesticides and throw out any that contain toxaphrene or other chlorines.

+ If you use organophosphates, wear a mask.

+ Pyrethrum is probably the safest insecticide for domestic use.

♦ If any food plants are likely to have been sprayed with a pesticide, wash carefully before cooking or eating raw.

♦ Always wash your hands after using any pesticide.

OTHER CHEMICALS AND MINERALS

Carbon monoxide in the blood of an unborn baby exceeds that in the mother's blood by up to 15 percent.[5] It deprives the baby of oxygen and growth may be retarded. Some Americans living and working in cities have carbon monoxide blood levels of 4 percent, the equivalent of smoking a pack of cigarettes a day.

If you live in a city and can cut down on the time you are exposed to air polluted by carbon monoxide, it will benefit you and your baby. You may be at greatest risk on the journey to and from work if traffic is heavy at that time. Here are some things you can do.

♦ Stagger your working hours so that you can travel to and from work when there is less traffic.

♦ Whenever possible, avoid waiting behind a car with its engine running—for example, in a gas line.

♦ Avoid jogging where there is heavy traffic; choose a park instead.

♦ If the air you have to breathe is contaminated with carbon monoxide, do not run the extra risk of smoking as well, and whenever possible avoid other people's smoke.

Another dangerous chemical, ethylene oxide, used by nurses to sterilize instruments, can cause miscarriage. Other people who may come into contact with ethylene oxide are workers in the pharmaceutical industry who sterilize drugs, and those employed in factories where certain kinds of food are chemically sterilized. Glutaraldehyde and formaldehyde are safer chemical agents than ethylene oxide.[6]

Hexachlorophene, a cleansing agent much used in hospitals, aniline, benzene, and turpentine may also cause birth defects. Occasional contact with these substances is unlikely to be dangerous, but if a pregnant woman works with them daily she and her baby are exposed to special risk.

Three heavy metals, mercury, lead, and cadmium, are known to be hazardous. Mercury concentration in the brain of the unborn baby is twice that in the mother's brain. In the 1950s and 1960s, mercury poisoning from fish and shellfish affected villages around Minamata Bay in southern Japan and babies were born brain-damaged. The source was traced to a plastics factory that discharged its effluent into the bay. Yet even after this was known, a further outbreak occurred in another part of Japan resulting from similar industrial discharge. Mercury is also used as a fungicide. There was a disaster in Iraq caused by grain bought from Mexico that had been treated with methyl mercury. Though there was a warning on the sack that it should not be used for making bread, this warning was in Spanish.

Lead poisoning results in damage to sperm, miscarriage, and possible fetal handicaps. Evidence linking it to birth defects is conflicting. But when young women workers at a chemical factory in Willow Island, West Virginia, wanted to keep jobs that required exposure to lead dust they had to agree to be sterilized. Five women were sterilized and some later regretted it.[7]

Yet a woman is not just a container for a fetus or a set of ova. Her own health is important, and if that is damaged by exposure to lead she should not have to work with it. And since lead poisoning not only harms sperm but can adversely affect men's health too, men should not be forced to suffer exposure to lead in their work either. As a speaker at a British women's TUC conference said: "While women are being discriminated against, men are being conned."

The women workers in Willow Island sued the company, Cyanamid. As a result of this political action and the publicity it generated, maximum lead levels have been fixed by law for all U.S. workers.

Cadmium is used in electroplating factories (which discharge it into the sewage system), is a constituent of tobacco smoke, and is produced as rubber tires wear out. In high concentrations it can cause birth defects and growth retardation.

Other minerals that may be dangerous are nickel and selenium, though the evidence is not conclusive.

But there is no question about the dangers of asbestos. Inhaled asbestos can cause an otherwise rare form of cancer. Research has focused on the diseases caused by working with asbestos (in shipyards or car factories, for example) rather than on the possible effects on the unborn baby, but animal studies show that asbestos dust can pass through the placenta. So avoid contact with flaking asbestos—on an old ironing board, for example, or a deteriorating insulation panel behind an electric heater—for both your own and the baby's sake.

When jobs are few, women may be fired on the grounds that they are unsuitable because they may get pregnant and the work could cause miscarriage, premature birth, stillbirth, or birth handicaps. They lose their jobs and the place is still not cleaned up. The fetus is protected at the expense of the woman, and since chemical pollution, for example, can harm male fertility at levels as low as those set for women, at the expense of male workers, too. The woman is treated merely as a potential container for a baby. The man is ignored, considered too tough to be affected, and forced to go on being exposed to these toxins.

Yet women are often exposed indirectly to dangers their partners encounter in *their* workplaces. If your partner, or anyone else in the family, does work that involves contamination with chemical or metal dust, work clothes should either be laundered at the place of work or be put in a plastic bag before they are brought home and put straight into the washing machine. Dust can also be carried in hair, even when protective clothing is worn. Workers should shower and wash their hair to avoid bringing this dust into the home.

Pollution at work is not a matter for women only. It is a challenge for everyone.

BUILDINGS

Foam insulation is used in many modern office blocks, public buildings, hospitals, schools, and homes. Formaldehyde is sprayed into the wall cavities and produces a toxic gas as it dries. This usually disperses into the air outside, but if it leaks into the building it can cause headaches, breathlessness, runny nose, eye irritation, coughs and colds, skin rashes, sore throats, drowsiness, and lapses of memory. Sometimes this gas is still present in the air long after the building has been insulated, and its presence can be detected by a strong chemical smell.

Old buildings sometimes have lead water pipes. You are more

likely to find them in your home than in a modern office building or factory. They contaminate drinking water, especially if it is naturally soft or if a softener is used, since soft water dissolves lead. The placenta is unable to filter out lead, which passes through and becomes concentrated on the side of the placenta nearest the baby. It can cause genetic damage.

You can tell if pipes are made of lead because they are dark and rather soft—a knife cuts through them rather than just leaving a scratch. They should be replaced with copper. If you cannot avoid drinking water from lead pipes, let it run for thirty seconds to clear any deposits. First thing in the morning, allow the water to run for a couple of minutes to flush out any lead deposits that have built up overnight.

♦ ♦ ♦ Either on your own, or better still with a small group of women colleagues at work, or with other women who also work at home, critically examine your workplace to see if it provides a healthy environment and how it could be improved. Make your own checklist for this. If it is difficult to find out whether, for example, the air is polluted in any way, devise a plan of action to get information about this. You may need to ask the advice of your local environmental control agency or community health office concerned with preventive medicine. Sometimes a union can help. Make a note of all the things that concern you.

Food habits are also likely to be affected by your work. Whether you eat in the company cafeteria, grab a snack wherever and whenever you can because of the pressure of work, or entertain in restaurants as part of your job, look at chapter 4 for suggestions on how to improve your nutrition.

If there aren't any no-smoking areas in your place of work and you have to breathe other people's tobacco smoke, this is another issue you may want to consider, bearing in mind the material on smoking and pregnancy in chapter 3.

If the air is polluted, use a fan or air filter, or improve ventilation by opening a window when possible. Use a mask or other protective clothing if necessary. Seek a single standard to control each hazard at work to ensure maximum protection for all workers, male and female. ♦ ♦ ♦

STRESS

If you decide that stress is a major problem at work, consider what action you could take to reduce it. It is not a trivial matter. Constant excessive stress can make people physically and mentally ill. Many medical conditions—asthma, migraine and other headaches, eczema, indigestion, constipation, high blood pressure, and heart problems —are stress-related. Here are some of the questions you may want to ask yourself and discuss with other women who do similar work:

♦ Do you need to be more assertive?

♦ Can you organize regular breaks from work, especially if it is monotonous or especially demanding?

♦ Can your work be rearranged so that particularly stressful tasks do not follow immediately one after the other and you have a breather in between them?

♦ Do you need more time on your own, or, alternatively, working alongside other people?

♦ Can the job be done in a different sequence or methods employed which would make it less stressful?

♦ Can noise be reduced and lighting be improved?

♦ Can you cut down the number of interruptions that make it difficult to concentrate?

Other things that can also help are:

♦ Taking time for relaxation and learning how to relax physically and mentally.

♦ Getting more exercise.

♦ Being out of doors sometimes rather than in a building all day.

♦ Sharing the work or getting someone else to take over part of it.

♦ And, perhaps, also reducing the demands you make on yourself.

These can all help you to manage stress more effectively.

IF YOU ARE WORRIED

What if you have already been exposed to chemicals or enormous stress that you feel might have harmed you or the baby? Since the greatest effect is in the first eight weeks of pregnancy, even before you knew you were pregnant, what should you be doing? What *can* you do?

Take comfort—the chances are high that your baby will be perfect. Our concern about teratogens in the environment has come about as a result of large-scale statistical studies involving enormous numbers of births. Even with powerful chemicals, the chances of your baby being harmed are very low indeed.

If you are healthy, well nourished, and do not smoke, any effect of poisons on your unborn child is much reduced. If damage had been done in those first eight weeks, the chances are that you would have had a miscarriage. A great many miscarriages occur because there is something wrong with the developing embryo.

One consequence of our raised consciousness about pregnancy and our rights as women is that we develop an often frightening sense of responsibility and have to learn how to handle the anxiety that stems from this. Anxiety can be used constructively if it leads to joining with others to improve the conditions under which we work.

7

◆ EMOTIONAL CHANGES ◆

In one sense, of course, a woman has no choice about the emotions she feels during pregnancy. They just come and have to be lived with, the good and the bad. In another sense, you *do* have choice. You can acknowledge your feelings or try to escape from them by denying them. You can seek to understand them, dismiss them as too disturbing or dangerous, or avoid them because you think it is wrong or silly to have such feelings. You can decide to be open about how you feel with someone close to you—your partner or a friend— or you can put on an act of being placid and unruffled throughout pregnancy.

All this doesn't apply just to emotions like fear and anxiety about whether the baby will be normal. It is sometimes a temptation to suppress or try to hide from others feelings or tremendous elation, even ecstasy, because they seem silly too, and "no one would understand."

In this chapter, I want to look at some of the dominant emotional states of pregnancy so that you can explore how you feel, understand what you share with other women, and decide if there is any action you can take in response to these emotional challenges.

Pregnancy is for some women a time of deep emotional satisfaction and an oasis of content. There is a feeling of being in tune with life. Senses are heightened. For one woman the first crisp, cold air of winter produces a tingle of excitement. When storms toss the trees and she is heavy with child she sometimes feels as if she too is like a great tree, its roots deep in the earth. For another, pregnant in the spring, flower shoots pushing through the earth and fronds of green unfurling on the branches echo the physical sense of life moving inside her body. As a woman lies in the sun, her abdomen like a great curved melon soaking up its heat, she may feel a tremendous inner energy—the power of her uterus, which now cradles her baby and will later knead and squeeze the child out of her body. Watching the ocean, she senses the movement of waves and the rush and swirl of water as it too flows in the inner world of her uterus. There is a symmetry with nature, a unity with the elements, which brings a feeling of rightness about her body.

We do not often talk about these feelings because they are so distinctly womanly that it can be difficult to find the words to describe them. They are not part of the language we normally use. So we tend to be embarrassed talking about them, or even never grasp the experience for ourselves—because there are no words with which to understand and encapsulate it.

Even a woman for whom pregnancy was an accident, or who conceived before she was quite ready for it, may go through it with delight. And though weary with the heavy load she carries, there are still likely to be precious times when she feels her whole body glowing and radiant with life.

Yet an inescapable fact about pregnancy is that—emotionally—each woman is as if on the rim of the void. More than any explorer in frozen wastes of ice, more than any sailor in an expanse of uncharted ocean, she is alone in the face of a momentous event, the drama of birth, which is going to open her body and bring from its depths a new human being. She has only to think about that to feel awe at the magnitude of what must happen, to know eager anticipation and wonder—and sometimes also fear.

The paramount and overwhelming theme of every pregnancy is change. Nothing stays as it was. Everything is in a state of flux. The woman's appearance changes from one month to the next. Emotions change, even perhaps from day to day. Pregnancy is growth. It is also metamorphosis—for the child from embryo to fetus and from fetus to newborn baby. For the woman it brings a gradual and inexorable swelling and ripening until her body is ready for birth. In terms of emotions and relationships, it transforms a woman into a different kind of social being, with often incredibly passionate bonds of love and responsibility to one small human creature, as she becomes a mother.

This nine months' journey may be marked by some of the most profound and powerful emotions a human being can ever feel. It is often claimed that pregnant women are placid and, indeed, many women are concerned that they may get cowlike, their brains so softened by maternity that they are incapable of logical thought. The recurrent advertising stereotype of pregnancy is that of an expectant mother knitting contentedly in the lamplight or dreamily picking daisies in a meadow, far removed from and untouched by the turmoil of everyday life. An expectant mother, these advertisements seem to be saying, is fulfilled as she dreams of the coming baby. A vessel for the new life, her mind is tranquil, and no needs of her own intrude on this harmony.

The reality is different. Pregnancy is often a time of deeply disturbing emotional conflicts and many woman are exposed to stresses from outside—in the environment and in their relationships—that make of it an arduous passage. Far from being insulated from the external world and its stresses, it may all have a greater and more painful impact, as the woman faces the life crisis of pregnancy and birth.

The first emotional conflicts may come when she realizes that she has conceived. However much a baby is wanted, however careful the planning, the reality of discovering that you are pregnant can be almost unbelievable, thrilling and strangely disquieting. For now you have to face up to it. You have started something that cannot be stopped except by a deliberate act of termination or an accident of nature. There is an inevitability about the whole process that can be both awe-inspiring and alarming.

The first movements are felt between eighteen and twenty weeks and from that moment you are constantly reminded that there is someone else inside you. This creature is not just part of your body, but has its own life and, though still growing from and dependent on yours, is nevertheless distinct and different. Sometimes it feels wonderful to have this other life developing inside you. At others it may feel like an intrusion and you think of the fetus merely as a kind of parasite—and then, perhaps, feel a wave of guilt at having such thoughts. This sense of two people in one body can be threatening.

Even a woman who welcomes her pregnancy is likely to have times when she asks herself, "Is this what I really want?" There is nothing abnormal about these feelings. There are times in almost any pregnancy when a woman feels that her body is completely taken over and that she has been swallowed up and has disappeared inside it. She may wonder whether she will ever be able to find herself again.

Sally felt like that through much of her pregnancy. She had been an athlete and an avid horsewoman, but after she had some bleeding in early pregnancy, even though there was no evidence that her riding had caused it, her doctor advised her not to ride again until after the baby was born. She said:

> I hated being pregnant. I hated looking pregnant. I had always been slim and taken pride in my body. I thought my swollen body was revolting. And mentally I felt that I was losing my grip. The doctor treated me like an irresponsible child.

For some women pregnancy entails a loss of identity, a death of self. They resist what is happening to their bodies and try to carry on exactly as before. It can be a very frightening experience. Becoming a patient, and being forced to surrender one's identity as an adult capable of making rational judgments, increases this sense of loss of self. One way of counteracting it is to get together with other pregnant women to start exploring childbirth choices and weighing up the alternatives, and thus start functioning as an adult again. A woman who feels that she is trapped inside her pregnant body may feel quite different once she starts exercise classes and learns how to breathe and relax and prepare for an active birth, since the movements learned in groups like these help her get in greater harmony with her body.

Any link between such emotions and how a woman feels about her baby once it is born is extremely tenuous. It is astonishing how often a woman who hated pregnancy falls head-over-heels in love with her baby at birth or in the days following. For some women there is a vast difference between the feeling of having a baby inside the uterus and a baby in their arms and they can welcome one, but not the other. And there are women, too, who like being pregnant but feel emotionally numb for a time once the baby puts in an appearance.

Many pregnant women say they respond with strong emotions to suffering, whether of human beings or animals. Tears come quickly; television programs that extol violence or vividly depict the consequences of war and newspaper photographs of starving children with their swollen bellies and sticklike limbs prove unbearably distressing. It is as if approaching motherhood sensitizes you to the needs not only of your own child, but of all the world's children. This increased awareness of suffering, the overwhelming compassion, and the urge to help those hungry and in need, are part of the spontaneous emotional changes that precede birth. They prepare us to nurture a child. The world is in short supply of these qualities of nurturing. We often repress such emotions because the exposed nerve causes too much pain. Yet this nurturing concern that spills over from pregnancy and the experience of motherhood should not be dismissed lightly. It is important in politics (in the peace movement, for example), in bringing aid to famine-stricken people, and in the struggle for social and economic justice. It can be a power for good in the world, and, difficult as it can be to do so, perhaps this new emotional vulnerability should be welcomed.

A major doubt in a woman's mind may be whether she is ready to be a mother. If you have never had much to do with babies, or thought of yourself as a mother, you may wonder whether you have any "maternal instincts." In human beings mothering is learned behavior. Though there is an instinctual element, no one could rely on instincts alone to see her through the highly complex series of tasks involved in being a mother in today's society. We learn from books, the media, and parenting classes. But we probably learn most by simply watching other women with their babies—seeing how they handle and respond to them, what they do, how they talk to, hold, rock and soothe them, and thus pick up information often when we are least aware of it. It is very different from academic learning.

Many women who have never had a chance to care for a small child and who do not have younger brothers and sisters lack confidence in their mothering skills. But you will find that your baby soon teaches you what to do and will leave you in no doubt about what she likes, when she needs to be fed, played with and talked to, and exactly what makes her feel comfortable and contented. You do not have to rely on maternal instincts for that.

Pregnancy may be marred by the dread of going into the hospital and what "they" will do to you. This is another realistic anxiety about the loss of autonomy.

Robin, for example, spent six months trying to find an obstetrician who was willing to help her have a natural birth. The first "treated me like a schoolgirl, in a very condescending way," and it was not until twenty-six weeks that she was able to switch to a doctor who was newly arrived in the area and interested in natural birth. He worked with her to build a personal birth plan. Only after this was she able to relax and start to enjoy her pregnancy.

Anxiety that stems from being powerless and having other people make all the decisions about you and your baby can be dispelled only by constructive action. It entails either improving communication and understanding with your caregivers and changing the balance of power, or changing your caregivers and the environment in which you give birth. There is no easy solution by means of facile reassurance, breathing deeply, or meditation. You should not have to try and change yourself to fit the system. Somehow you have to change the system to suit your needs.

One element in worry about what happens *after* the baby comes is concern about the sheer practicalities of looking after a baby. If you are going back to your job immediately, or after an interval, getting good child care may be looming large in your mind: its cost, whether it is going to be reliable, and what you can do if it does not work out. It pays not only to plan ahead but to make all your contacts, with alternative arrangements if your first choice does not work out, as early in pregnancy as you possibly can. Otherwise you may spend the whole nine months worrying about it.

You may not have decided yet about going back to your job. It is best to keep your options open if you can, since no matter how sure you may feel now, you may feel quite differently once the baby is born. A woman who plans to go back to work immediately often feels she cannot leave her baby, and one who plans on being a full-time mother finds that it is driving her up the wall! So all plans should be flexible.

Whether or not she is working outside the home, every woman with children needs a good informal support network of people who can help out, or substitute for her, when the going gets tough. In the days of large extended families this existed automatically, but many modern women are alone and isolated. You might think any woman ought to be able to cope with one child at least, but a first-time mother with a new baby especially needs people to help her feel that what she is doing is right and that, even though she is a complete novice, she is a good enough mother. It is not so much advice she needs as someone to listen and, when she cannot cope, to take over tasks like shopping, cooking, and cleaning.

Many women having their first child are far from their own families and friends with whom they grew up. They are preoccupied with their jobs, and social contacts have been mostly with work colleagues, many of whom may not have children. They may never have met the people living in the same block. If they move before the baby is born, or soon afterward, as many do, they know no one at all in the area. At the stage when a woman is completely preoccupied with the baby and finds that the day-to-day tasks of baby care take up all her time, it can be very difficult to make new friends.

So it is important to make plans well before the baby is born and develop survival strategies for afterward. Anxiety now can provide the spur for planning ahead like this. You can build up a support network both by having a list of emergency contacts whom you can pay to take over essential tasks (your phone book may be able to help here) and also by setting out to meet people, through clubs and voluntary associations—childbirth, church, and women's groups, for instance—with whom you can create a mutual support network.

Besides a peer support group of women roughly the same age and all coping with the same kinds of challenges in their lives, it is helpful to have older women friends who are not trying to cope at present with the same day-to-day problems. Though they may not do things quite your way, they can still be a valuable resource, and their experience and confidence stands you in good stead when you are feeling overwhelmed. It is fashionable nowadays to deride and criticize the help that such older women can give. It is a way in which some professionals try to isolate new mothers from the support they can get from other women, preferring that they should rely on *their* advice alone. But it is not really advice that you will need. It is someone to listen, someone who can give you the warmth of friendship and the occasional break from the baby that allows you to rediscover a little personal space.

When Maureen and Jim had their baby, they got to know a woman in her sixties who lived a few doors up and whose husband had died recently. She was obviously lonely and her own grandchildren were half a continent away. Mrs. Smith was worried about insurance and other money matters with which she had to deal—something she had never done before. Maureen and Jim were able to help with these, and Mrs. Smith, in her turn, was delighted to babysit and soon became an adopted grandmother.

Many support networks grow spontaneously, but when you are pregnant it is risky to leave your postbaby network to chance, and to do so causes unnecessary anxiety. So reach out and make friends now!

Some pregnant women are tortured with the fear that the baby may be abnormal, and even those who dismiss such thoughts from their minds during the day often feel anxious at night. Mental handicap is the thing they most fear. One woman said:

> I lie there thinking that I could face almost any physical handicap but I just don't have the courage to deal with a mentally handicapped child. Last night was awful. Yesterday I saw a woman leading a Down's syndrome girl by the hand. Her tongue was hanging out. She must have been in her twenties. I thought, "What if my baby grows up like that?" I couldn't face it! It would wreck our lives!

It is not difficult for any pregnant woman to think back to something that occurred in the first weeks of pregnancy that might have harmed her baby: drugs, alcohol, cigarette smoke, or something else that could have interrupted fetal development. Few of us live in such an unpolluted environment that we can't point to some toxic chemical that might have caused damage. As one woman said:

> I worry about a lot of things because, however careful I am, I can't be sure that the baby isn't being exposed to poisonous chemicals. Over the weekend we went hiking. It was great to get out of the city. But farmers were spraying the crops—I don't know what with. The air was quite still at first, but after we had been walking for about an hour a wind got up and I got really scared. We turned back. It spoiled the day and last night I had a terrible nightmare about a deformed baby.

Occasionally a woman who suffers from anxiety is given medication, which adds further to her fear that the baby will be abnormal. Heather, for example, had been taking tranquilizers over a period of nine years. "Though I reduced my dosage by half before becoming pregnant, I took tranquilizers through my pregnancy," she said. "I was very, very scared about the effect of the drugs on the baby. I couldn't believe the irresponsibility of what I had done and felt my baby and I would be blighted for life." She needed to talk this through with her doctor. But unfortunately she felt so guilty about taking the tranquilizers that she never dared raise the subject with her. If you take medication for any chronic condition, it is wise to have a discussion about this with your doctor well *before* you get pregnant. You can then decide whether to reduce or cut out medication or to switch to another kind, or whether, if the effects of the illness would be worse than any side effects of the drugs, it would be more sensible to go on taking them.

Stress in a job may also cause anxiety during pregnancy. Catherine, for example, was a psychiatric nurse working with patients who were physically as well as mentally sick.

> Most could do very little for themselves. There was a lot of lifting and bathing, as well as the occasional aggressive and violent outburst. I was terribly afraid that the baby would be hurt in some way.

She had to keep on working because they needed the money. But it might have been possible for her to be moved to less demanding work in the hospital. Her anxiety was obviously rooted in reality, and it certainly could not be dismissed as merely a figment of a pregnant woman's imagination due to her special emotional vulnerability.

It is well know that German measles (rubella) in the first eight weeks of pregnancy can damage the fetal heart, brain, sight, and hearing. Diana had not been immunized against rubella and contracted the disease shortly after she became pregnant.

> I went for a blood test. It came back positive. My husband and I were absolutely devastated. We desperately wanted a baby. We told the doctor that we would continue the pregnancy. We were told that there was a 20 percent chance of the baby being

born with a handicap of the eyes or ears. From that day on till the end of my pregnancy we went through hell. Some days we could discuss it. Other days we refused to accept that anything could be wrong. I was under terrible strain. Not many days went by without crying either in the bathroom, at work, or at night in bed. I will never know how my husband and I survived those everlasting forty weeks. [Her baby was perfect.]

A woman who has lost a baby previously, from a late miscarriage or stillbirth, is often waiting for the same thing to happen with this pregnancy. She may be on her guard until the time has passed when she miscarried before, or right until the baby is safely delivered. An experience like that casts its shadow forward, and even though you feel you have come through the grief and are now starting out with fresh hope, it is there in the background and may haunt the present pregnancy. There may be special dates in your pregnancy when you think, "At this stage last time I felt very much as I do now. Perhaps this means that something is wrong," or something else happens that is like an echo of the previous pregnancy and so gives rise to anxiety.

Janice had a stillborn baby two years ago. She called me after a visit to her doctor.

He said, "You leave the worrying to me. That's what I'm here for." He obviously forgot, but he said that before when I told him I couldn't feel much kicking in my last pregnancy.

When a woman becomes pregnant soon after the death of another child, without enough time to grieve over the loss, she may also feel guilty about replacing the dead baby. A woman who had lost a baby to crib death was advised by her doctor to get pregnant again as soon as possible, and she conceived a few months after the baby's death. She told me:

We bought a lot of things when I was pregnant with Roseann [the baby who died]. I can't help feeling it's all wrong to use them for this baby. It's like closing the door on her—as if I don't care anymore.

Another woman, who had a stillbirth, said:

I keep thinking, "The baby would have been a year old now," and wondering if this baby will look like her. Sometimes it is

almost as if she has come back and I'm still pregnant with *her*.
It's as if I want to make amends to her, give her the chance of
life she lost.

Grieving takes many months. Some women need a year or more. A
pregnancy that begins before the mourning process is completed may
result in very mixed and disturbing feelings.

Often when things have gone wrong and a baby has died, parents
have found it very difficult to get full and accurate information about
why it happened. Sometimes doctors themselves don't know. But
many parents feel that the true facts are being withheld from them
by doctors in case of litigation. This may be true.

With the next pregnancy a woman usually feels an urgent need to
know and be quite sure that nothing is being hidden from her. She
may decide that she wants to make this absolutely clear to her doctor.
Anne's last pregnancy ended in the stillbirth of a baby with multiple
handicaps. When she was pregnant again, she asked her obstetrician
to give her full and frank information.

He encouraged me to listen to the fetal heart, and when I had
an ultrasound scan, took time to show both of us our baby's
limbs, the heart beating, and all the internal organs. We could
see the fully formed spine and even watched the bladder emptying. And he described exactly how he was going to measure
the baby's growth and development and reassured me that all
was well.

A previous abortion, which a woman thinks she has put behind
her, even one a long time back, can cause feelings of inexplicable
depression and anxiety in the next pregnancy.

Beth was talking to me about her overwhelming fear that her baby
would be malformed. She did not go through a day without brooding
on this. It was only when we talked about the termination she had
three years ago, and her feelings then, that she said: "I feel that this
baby is going to be abnormal as a punishment for getting rid of that
baby."

However rational we want to be, many of us have a similar dread
of retribution during a pregnancy following a previous abortion. It

isn't just a matter of having lost a baby before, but of abortion. Women who have had a previous miscarriage are not especially likely to feel like this.[1]

It can take a long time to get over a distressing labor and look forward with joy to the next one. People sometimes advise you to try and forget, but that is impossible. A better way is to find out all you can about exactly what went wrong last time, and why, so that you can make sense of what happened and prepare for the coming birth with fresh knowledge and understanding.

Elaine's previous labor was a ghastly experience. She had gone into it relying on the obstetrician to do everything for the best, because he was the expert. It turned out to be a high-tech labor culminating in a forceps delivery. She said that one of the worst things about it was that a crowd of medical students piled into the room to watch the delivery and the obstetrician talked to them rather than to her: "I was merely exhibit A. It was," she added, "like a gang rape." With this pregnancy she changed her obstetrician and made sure such a thing could never happen again.

I wrote a list of questions before I went to see my obstetrician and had a long talk with my husband, so that he understood exactly what I wanted. He agreed to come with me to talk with the doctor and was as concerned as I was to make sure that I could have this baby the way *I* wanted. I stressed that, even if intervention was necessary, I would like an intimate atmosphere.

Fear of birth itself is very complex. It is often a mixture of anxiety about being deprived of autonomy—trapped in a situation completely outside your control and exposed as inadequate and worthless —and anxiety that you will not be able to handle the pain. Fear that the baby will be malformed or that it will die—or that it will be dreadfully malformed and will *not* die—and fear of injury to yourself, even fear that *you* might die, are all part of this pervading anxiety that many women experience, often in the dead of night.

It is important to be able to talk about birth fears openly with someone who understands and does not dismiss them. Your childbirth teacher might be the right person, or a sympathetic doctor or midwife. In childbirth classes where there is full and free discussion, women are often surprised to discover that others share the same fears and many find this sharing very helpful.

For most women anxiety in pregnancy is concentrated on the birth, which is perceived as a time of testing, and even, by some, as one of judgment and punishment. The dread of pain is only one aspect of this, which is why a doctor's reassurance that pain-relieving medication is readily available and that there is no need for any woman to suffer in labor is largely irrelevant.

One way of dealing with fear of birth is to take constructive action so that you feel well prepared to cope with whatever challenges it presents. That means understanding exactly what happens and what labor feels like in its different phases, and knowing what you can do to help yourself. Those looming fears can be replaced with the confidence to work *with* your body instead of against it and, regardless of whether it turns out that you can do it all by yourself or require help to get the baby born, to approach birth as an active and creative experience.

In any major transitional phase of life there is bound to be anxiety, even if we do not always acknowledge it. It has an important function in stimulating us to seek information, make changes, and adapt to new tasks. Anxiety can be used and worked with.

♦ ♦ ♦ Spend a little time thinking about your own anxieties. Cast your mind back to the beginning of pregnancy and make a note of anything that worried you when you first realized you were pregnant. The worries you started out with may have disappeared. If so, think how this happened and make a note of what occurred. You may, for example, have made personal contact with a caregiver who was previously just a shadowy and rather ominous figure. You may have gotten the important information you needed. You may have someone who can give you emotional support and understanding, or be in a group of pregnant women or couples who are helping each other.

Now look at any anxieties that are still on your mind and see what you can do to use them constructively, thus reducing their power. The first step is often to talk about them with someone who can accept what you feel. ♦ ♦ ♦

It isn't always realized that fathers can be very anxious, but because they are not pregnant themselves, they feel that they should not express their worries. Whoever is going to be your support person in labor, whether or not it is your partner, may be apprehensive about what is going to happen, too. Talking together about this provides an opportunity for your relationship to grow and for each of you to show what you need from the other.

SEX

In the first few months of pregnancy you may find that you go off sex, or that you prefer gentle stroking and affectionate cuddling to sexual intercourse. Many women feel tenderness and subtlety is lacking in their relationship with a sexual partner, whether or not they are pregnant, and in pregnancy this feeling that sex should be slower, gentler, and more caring often crystallizes with still more clarity. You may want to take the opportunity to discuss this with your partner so that pregnancy can draw you closer together, rather than driving you apart, as it does some couples.

There is nothing like nausea and vomiting to turn your thoughts from sex and make you feel drained of energy and very negative about your body. Fear of miscarriage also puts a damper on sex, and both partners may be very frightened of somehow dislodging the developing embryo. For many women, too, the medicalizing of pregnancy results in a feeling that their bodies are no longer their own and that they are primarily patients.

Nausea and vomiting, and the tiredness so common at the beginning of pregnancy, do not usually last longer than three months, and then you may suddenly feel completely different. As one woman told me: "After the morning sickness was over I felt like a queen!" Feeling good about yourself like that, rather than the stimulation of the genital organs, is the basis for enjoying sex.

In the middle months you may feel more quickly aroused than usual and enjoy sex a lot. This is partly because of the excitement of knowing that the baby is growing inside you, partly because you and your partner share happiness in the pregnancy and often feel really clever—as if this were the first baby ever to be conceived—and partly because the pressure of the enlarged blood vessels in your pelvis and against your pelvic floor muscles and vagina has a physically arousing effect. As the pregnancy becomes obvious, women often say they like their bodies more, feel more mature, womanly, feminine, fulfilled, proud, special, and wonderful. "I loved to be big," Lindsey said. "I felt very attractive. Lovemaking was better than before and I had more powerful orgasms."

In her fifth month of pregnancy, Angela was in a state of almost continuous arousal.

> My body is now at its most attractive. My hair is soft and sleek, my skin taut and smooth, my cheeks softly glowing. I'm very aware and proud of my firm, rounded breasts and belly. My nipples are erect and big with dark areolas. I masturbate to orgasm at least twice a day. I am enjoying sex to the full in the knowledge that I may only have another four or five weeks of such fun before our sex life becomes curtailed because I feel too cumbersome.

For some women this sexual exhilaration continues right through pregnancy. Sara told me that she enjoyed sex so much she began to worry that she was abnormal and asked the doctor if there was something wrong with her.

> He said I was one of the lucky ones. I enjoyed it up until the night I had the baby. We made love at twelve-thirty and my waters broke at three while I was asleep. I kept thinking they would know in hospital, but no one said or asked anything.

She felt rather bewildered because her increased sexual drive did not fit with her image of maternity. Our culture creates an antithesis between sexuality on the one hand and motherhood on the other, as if pregnancy and birth were at the polar extreme to the passion that originally created them. Women are now rediscovering the sexuality of pregnancy and birth.

Even so, as the baby grows and she gets larger a woman is unlikely to enjoy intercourse if her partner is rough, insensitive to her needs, or too quick, and many women say they enjoy masturbation in pregnancy—sometimes for the first time. "I was surprised by my increased drive to masturbate," one woman said. "It didn't fit the maternal image at all but I masturbated regularly to orgasm, though I couldn't have orgasms with my husband." It may be that her husband could have learned something from her about where and how to caress her. Pregnancy can sometimes throw up difficulties like this in a sexual relationship, but it can also provide an opportunity to explore sexual feelings more deeply.

Many women find the last weeks difficult because they are too tired to enjoy sex and feel heavy and distended. Some have a very negative picture of their bodies. "I felt like a whale," one woman told me. And another said: "My stretch marks look like a map of the world. I feel very ugly. I have not wanted to make love as I have a lot of heartburn and am extremely uncomfortable, and I can't wait to get some sort of figure back!" If this is how you feel, a loving partner can give reassurance by reaffirming delight in your body and helping you feel good about it.

Some men are anxious about sex in pregnancy and very frightened of hurting the woman or the baby, and as a result they withdraw from the physical contact a woman may be desperately longing for. Even though it may seem to you unfeminine and demanding to ask for it outright, it is important to bring this out into the open and say what you want. Otherwise you each retreat into a private shell.

It often happens, too, that just as a woman is feeling sexually exuberant in mid-pregnancy, she discovers that her partner seems to have switched off. This can occur because of fear of harming the pregnancy or, sometimes, dislike of the pregnant body and its curves and fullness. Men do not often care to admit that they are afraid, and try to maintain a casual nonchalance which women may interpret as withdrawal of love. "I thought my husband found me repulsive," one woman told me, "as he abstained totally from sex during my pregnancy. However, after much talking and agonizing he told me it was not revulsion at my body, but his fear of hurting the unborn child." It is sad that it was not until after the baby was born that this couple got down to talking about it.

A man may also treat a pregnant woman as "not sexy, but sacred," in another woman's words and deliberately repress all erotic feeling because he believes it is inappropriate or wrong. Some women feel like this, too: "My body felt sacred and special. Lovemaking ceased as soon as the pregnancy was confirmed."

Right at the end of pregnancy, a man who was fairly carefree about sex earlier on may be almost overwhelmed by a sense of responsibility for this new life and fear that he may hurt the woman.

In the last three months my husband became increasingly reluctant to have intercourse. He still wanted to be touched, kissed, and caressed and wanted me to stimulate him to orgasm, but he wouldn't touch me. At the time I thought he didn't fancy me. Now that we've talked about it I realize that he was just scared of hurting me.

Not all men are like this, of course. Sometimes a woman who does not feel erotic in any way has a partner who is really turned on by pregnancy. Jo did not enjoy her pregnant body at all, and could not understand how her partner could. "But he said I was daft. He couldn't have wanted me more and he thought I was beautiful when pregnant."

Is sex harmful in pregnancy? An American study investigated whether intercourse in late pregnancy causes premature rupture of the membranes and resulting infection. The researchers discovered that infection was the *cause* of premature membrane rupture, not the consequence, and that there was no relation between premature rupture and the number of times a couple said they had intercourse. However, if an amniotic fluid infection is present, sexual intercourse is likely to make it more severe.[2] This suggests that if a pregnancy is going well and you are feeling healthy, you can trust your own feelings to do what is right for you and make love as often as you want. But it also suggests that if there is premature leaking of amniotic fluid, even though slight, or you are feeling run-down and ill yourself, it would be sensible not to have intercourse and to find other ways of showing your love for each other instead.

Semen is rich in prostaglandins which ripen and soften the cervix at the end of pregnancy. When you explore an unripe cervix with your finger, it feels like the hard tip of your nose. A ripe cervix feels like a soft, relaxed mouth. One way of inducing labor is to introduce prostaglandin gel into the cervix to prepare it for labor, and if the baby is ready to be born this will actually start contractions, often within hours.

If you notice any bleeding after intercourse and are not yet within three weeks of your due date, it is wise to avoid intercourse and enjoy pleasuring, stroking, and cuddling instead. If you are near term or past the date when your baby is due, intercourse is not only harmless but may help labor start, especially if combined with nipple stimulation. Lie still for half an hour after intercourse, while your partner continues to suck and stroke your breasts. It is one of the pleasantest ways there is to start labor, and even if you do not go straight into labor, you will know that this has probably softened and ripened your cervix further.

♦ ♦ ♦ Think about the choices you would like to make about sex during your pregnancy, considering not only the things you *don't* want, but also those you do. The basis of a mutually satisfying relationship between lovers is good communication. How do you want to indicate your wishes to your partner, in words, gesture, and touch? Are there any aspects of each other's sexual feelings and behavior it would be helpful to discuss together now—any fears, doubts, hopes, or longings? You can find out a good deal more about sex in pregnancy, as well as the sexuality of birth and sex after the baby comes, in my book *Women's Experience of Sex.* ♦ ♦ ♦

The variety of feelings and personal experiences in pregnancy is so great that it is impossible to claim that any behavior is normal or abnormal. You can be sure, however you feel, that there are other women whose experience is very similar to yours. You are certainly not alone.

For many couples pregnancy is a time of wonder and delight, a vital part of which is the newness and sense of discovery as the woman's body changes, burgeons, ripens. It brings fresh tenderness and passion into their relationship and this excitement and joy prepare them to welcome a new life into the circle of their love.

It is just as well that babies do not emerge a few weeks after they are conceived. A great deal is happening emotionally during pregnancy that needs time to unfold and develop. There are alternatives that need to be explored, about the kind of care that is right for you and your baby and the degree of responsibility you want to take. Sometimes other people assume that you do not *have* any choices, so you have the additional task of making it clear that they do not make decisions *for* you. It is a time when you need to be able to communicate effectively and sometimes stand up to opposition, to learn more about yourself, and to discover how to work with and express yourself through your body in the most satisfying and harmonious way.

Pregnancy may be uncomfortable—not only physically, but emotionally, too. Occasionally you may wish you had never started a baby. Yet this stress can be challenging. It can stimulate fresh thinking and a new understanding of yourself and your relationships. The insights you gain during this time can help you cope with stresses and changes throughout your life.

Pregnancy is a learning time. It is a process—often stormy and sometimes tumultuous—that encourages a kind of emotional ripening and maturation that gives the strength and the sensitive awareness to take on responsibility for a new life.

8

◆ WHAT KIND OF ◆ PRENATAL CARE?

Though it is often taken for granted that seeing a doctor regularly during pregnancy must be a good thing, and that the more medical care a woman has in pregnancy the better, there is very little evidence to support that assumption. It is true that women who have the most prenatal visits have fewer premature babies—but that is because, by definition, premature birth makes pregnancy shorter, so fewer visits are possible.

Seeing a doctor regularly throughout pregnancy cannot be of any benefit unless the care given is appropriate to a woman's needs. Moreover, in the vast majority of pregnancies, the care a woman gives herself, and that which is provided by a partner and other family members, has more significance for her and her baby's well-being than any provided by doctors. It is easy to lose sight of this fact. Basically, prenatal care is not something conferred on a pregnant woman by the medical system. Obstetric services can provide a safety net, but cannot ensure that a woman has good care throughout her pregnancy.

If you do not want to be merely at the receiving end of medical care, but want to look after yourself in the best possible way and get the most effective service from those caring for you, you need to be able to assess what you are offered. In order to do this, it is important to think through what you want, if necessary shop around to find it, and also work out how much *personal* responsibility you wish to take for yourself and your baby.

A woman's idea of what she wants from prenatal care may be very different from how an obstetrician sees it. She expects time to talk about worries and fears and wants a good deal of information about the day-to-day experience of pregnancy, how to care for herself, and how to prepare for labor. He—for in most cases it is a "he"—is usually primarily concerned with screening for a wide range of deviations from the normal, and, according to how she measures up, placing the woman in categories that determine treatment. For many obstetricians, especially those working in large, overcrowded hospitals, it is rather like checking for flaws on a factory production line.

This kind of prenatal care is of relatively recent origin. In the past, in different cultures all over the world, women have most commonly had babies in a system of community-based care in which other women were the caregivers. Historically, the modern professional organization of care in a medical system staffed by doctors and nurses is the exception rather than the rule. In concentrating exclusively on physical safety, we have lost the emotional support that other women can provide.

THE BACKGROUND TO CARE

Midwives have counseled women about nutrition and health, massaged them, and given advice on how to prepare for birth from the time of the earliest historical records.[1] There are references to midwives in Genesis. Pregnancy and birth, female "mysteries" that men knew nothing about, were under the protection of the great mother goddesses, called by many different names—the Earth Mother, the Many-Breasted One, the Queen of Light, the Moon Goddess, the Huntress, and later, Mary, the mother of Jesus.

Women supported each other in birth, shared knowledge that had been handed down from their mothers, and drew on the experience of those who had already borne children. In this way a network of beliefs and practices was created which, in their disintegrated form, we now know only as old wives' tales.[2]

In the Third World today, two systems of prenatal care coexist. The official one, run by doctors and trained nurses and midwives, is accessible to only a small section of the population. The indigenous system draws on practical skills women have learned, handed down, and adjusted to that particular environment, and is closely linked with the religion and belief system of the culture. Inevitably, the two conflict. The first employs techniques of measurement and clinical assessment that aim to be objective and identical for every patient. It provides a standard system of care that often treats each woman as if she were merely an ambulant pelvis. On the other hand, there is no doubt that it saves the lives of many babies—and mothers—when pregnancy is abnormal. The second system draws on the power of spiritual forces, and sees the woman in the context of a unique set of social relationships, past and present, with both the living and those who have died, which are thought to affect her and her baby. And it puts special emphasis on the psychological conditions it is important for her and her family to create if she is to have a healthy child and an easy labor.

In Mexico, for instance, it is believed that a pregnant woman must be protected from emotional upset and from people who cause her stress. In the past she used to wear a red cord around her waist with which she herself assessed the progress of pregnancy by measuring the expansion of the uterus. (In modern clinics, professionals do the measuring, not the woman herself.) She took personal responsibility for looking after herself, keeping clean, and having daily baths lest the baby get sick, and was familiar with a range of herbal teas to treat minor conditions. Today in Mexico, urinary infections common in pregnancy are still treated with ancient Aztec herbal remedies—tea brewed with corn tassels or sarsaparilla.

Throughout the Caribbean the pregnant woman regulates her diet carefully so that her blood is neither too "hot" nor too "cold." She believes that she should have regular exercise in order to be strong for labor, and in late pregnancy the local "nana" (the folk midwife) visits regularly to talk encouragingly to her and to "shape" the baby by massage and to "make it grow right."[3]

In South Africa the Zulu woman goes to the door of her hut every morning, where she breathes slowly and deeply for a few mintues as the sun rises, and prays that her baby will grow healthy. Through large parts of Africa it is believed that if labor is to be straightforward, a woman must not quarrel with anybody in the preceding weeks, and that she and her husband must seek forgiveness for any anger they have for each other. An easy, straightforward labor is thought to depend on the right ordering of relationships.

MODERN PRENATAL CARE

The kind of care we know in the West was started by doctors, not midwives. It was first proposed by Dr. Ballantyne of Edinburgh in 1901, though no special clinic was opened until 1915 and a network of clinics was set up later still, at the end of the First World War. The aims of these pioneers were noble: to remove anxiety and discomfort, ensure the early treatment of complications, increase the proportion of normal labors, and lower the maternal death and stillbirth rates.

Today the principles of prenatal care have been described by one woman obstetrician as follows: to identify any abnormality and try to correct or minimize it; attempt to prevent conditions developing that are hazardous for the mother or her baby; if complications occur, select the best time and style of delivery; and help the woman and her partner and family understand and enjoy the birth experience.[4] These objectives have not changed much, but others have been added: the detection of congenital abnormalities and preparation for childbirth and parenthood. Most recently, concern has focused on what happens even before conception and on the effects of social deprivation and poverty: poor mothers and babies face greater danger than those who are well off.

Doctors are learning that social factors have a greater influence on pregnancy and its outcome than anything they can do.[5] In Britain, for example, 16 babies in every 1,000 whose fathers are in semi-skilled or unskilled occupations die at or around the time of birth compared with 11 of those whose fathers are in the professional classes.[6]

In all Western countries the highest rates of death and sickness occur in the babies of working-class mothers and of recent immigrants from Third World countries. And a woman born in Pakistan but having a baby in the West is more than twice as likely as a British-born woman to lose her baby at or around birth.[7]

Such factors as lack of education, poor housing, inadequate nutrition, unemployment, and working in a toxic environment can all adversely affect the well-being of the mother and her baby. The kind of care provided today does little or nothing to reduce the impact of social pressures like these which put many women under physical and emotional stress during pregnancy, and are a threat to them and their unborn babies. Poverty is the major cause of baby deaths—and no amount of microchip technology can make up for that.

But it is not just a question of babies dying—neonatal *mortality*. Many babies are born prematurely, with low birthweight, sick, or in some other way handicapped—neonatal and infant *morbidity*. In the words of a sociologist, Ann Oakley: "Reducing social disadvantage —whether in the form of poor housing, inadequate disposable income, deficient diet, or whatever—is not a different issue from the issue of improving the perinatal mortality and morbidity, but the same issue."[8]

PROBLEMS IN HIGH-TECH CARE

At the beginning of this chapter, I pointed out that everyone more or less assumes that there ought to be more prenatal care. It is put forward as an example of the best kind of preventive medicine.

Yet when we try to measure its success and cost-effectiveness, little data is available. In fact, prenatal care has grown piecemeal from the last century, bits being added to it over the years without proper assessment, and without anybody finding out at what phase of pregnancy specific kinds of care are appropriate or to which women different elements should be offered.[9] It is taken for granted that it must be a good thing, however complicated it becomes, whatever the cost, and whatever the effects on the pregnant woman and her family. Caregivers, often with the best will in the world, use their authority to indoctrinate the pregnant woman with the idea that she should passively undergo any and every investigation—however stressful to her—for the sake of her baby. She is, after all, the container for the fetus, and society demands of her that she submit to whatever screening procedures can enable obstetricians to know more about exactly what is happening inside the uterus—that tantalizingly locked cupboard which, by a seemingly inexorable process of advancement in science, is becoming more and more like those transparent plastic snap-shut cases in the models of the female body used to demonstrate our reproductive anatomy.

Technology has enabled doctors to introduce a whole range of new screening tests into prenatal care. But these have produced new problems. One is that of the *false positive* diagnosis, and the unnecessary intervention that often takes place because of it. A false positive occurs when, as a result of a test that gives incorrect information or is misinterpreted, a diagnosis is made that attaches to a woman a disease or high-risk label. That label sticks even if other tests show later that nothing is wrong after all. The anxiety it produces often remains with the woman and those caring for her, and this may affect their actions later and lead to unnecessary intervention when she goes into labor, too.

One common false positive is the diagnosis, following an ultrasound scan at sixteen weeks, of a low-lying placenta, which may mean a cesarean section. But a low-lying placenta is very common in the first half of pregnancy, and as the uterus enlarges later in pregnancy the placenta is often found to be in a good position. Or, again following a scan, a woman may be warned that the baby is not growing in the uterus, but in spite of this later gives birth to an eight-pounder. One study revealed that 5 false positive diagnoses of intrauterine growth retardation (IGR) were made for every 2 correctly diagnosed. [10]

Doctors, on the whole, do not worry so much about false positives as about false negatives. They prefer to err on the side of overdiagnosis of problems than to miss signs of malfunction or disease, and the idea of failing to note evidence that a physiological process is going wrong triggers a great deal of anxiety and, especially in North America, worry about possible litigation. Yet the consequences of a false positive diagnosis can be catastrophic for the woman—unnecessary hospitalization, induced labor, cesarean section—as well as for the baby exposed to the dangers of prematurity.

False negatives are obviously dangerous, since they suggest that everything is all right when, in fact, something is wrong. They have the effect of switching off the warning light that clinical judgment and human experience turned on. Although assessment of fetal growth results in more false positives than false negatives, a good many instances of intrauterine growth retardation are not revealed by standard prenatal care. In one study doctors suspected it in only 44 percent of women who later had low birthweight babies. [11] Obviously diagnoses of intrauterine growth retardation are very much a hit-and-miss affair!

When tests are performed the woman is rarely asked what she knows, and what she says is usually ignored. Another kind of false negative can result when the baby's heartbeat is recorded in pregnancy and no abnormality is indicated, though the woman herself realizes that she is no longer noticing any movements, and after some days the baby dies. It is a rare occurrence, but one that shatters confidence in high-technology care. The mother felt that something was wrong—but nobody asked her what *she* knew about her baby and the doctors relied on technology instead.

Prenatal care, even when given conscientiously—and it isn't always—and even when professionals are up to date with knowledge —and they aren't always—can be ineffective, and sometimes dangerous.

Some people think the lesson to be learned from this is to have still more routine investigations and more sophisticated technology. Others believe there is a great deal to be learned from women themselves, and that what a woman knows about her body and the way in which she can be in touch with her baby inside should form a major theme of care through pregnancy.

Yet medical care usually makes a woman distrust her own first-hand experience and her awareness of her baby. Her medical records present the sole validated reality. The only things we are supposed to know about our health and the progress of pregnancy are those that can be recorded and measured by observers and entered in charts and case notes. Everything else is considered irrelevant. An elaborate system of procedures has been developed, one effect of which is to deny women knowledge they can have about themselves.

Many of these routines have become heavily ritualized—part of a symbolic process by which a woman is turned into a patient. One example of a ceremony of this kind is the regular weighing at each visit—as if she were not capable of keeping track of her weight at home. These rituals are employed routinely on all women, though they can be shown to be useful only in certain specific high-risk cases. Ultrasound is also used in a ritual manner, though the benefits of routine ultrasound investigations have never been scientifically demonstrated. It has become an insurance against disaster.

You do not *have* to agree to any interventions. If your doctor cannot provide you with evidence that a screening procedure or a treatment is going to do you any good, you are free to refuse it.

The authors of a midwifery textbook suggest that the label "high risk" ought to be replaced by a different concept—that of "levels of care." [12] Some women need more concentrated care than others or care of a different kind. As pointed out earlier, risk-oriented prenatal screening often leads to care inappropriate to a woman's needs and harmful intervention.

Though doctors treat pregnancy as a medical condition, it really is not. Eighty percent of women have completely normal pregnancies and labors. Twenty percent are at some special risk. But only half of these are discovered to be at risk during pregnancy. The others' problems are recognized only during labor. So at present the whole system of prenatal care works efficiently for only 10 percent of women.

Even when prenatal care is accurate, the way a woman *feels* about the care she gets and how she is treated by doctors is of paramount importance. For pregnancy and birth are biosocial processes. They do not simply operate like a process in mechanical engineering, though obstetric textbooks often give this impression. A frequent effect of prenatal care is to drain away a woman's self-confidence and, through medicalization of the whole experience of pregnancy and birth, to deprive her of autonomy and make her feel inadequate, helpless, and often guilty, because she feels that if she really cares for her baby she should not mind being treated like this.

When a woman becomes a patient, she also tends to be isolated from the help and emotional support of other women. In the past, the announcement of a pregnancy was an occasion for reinforcing solidarity among women in the family and neighborhood. In medieval times a woman starting labor called together her "God sibs" (a word that later became corrupted to "gossips") to care for and comfort her during childbirth, bring food and strong drink, and have what amounted to a celebratory birth feast. The men might grumble about it, but they were expected to leave the house and fend for themselves. Birth was women's business! Similarly, in colonial America, pregnancy and birth were primarily social processes based on reciprocity—women caring for each other and giving practical help and emotional support.

In contrast, today a woman is taught to put her faith in medical advisers and distrust all that other women can teach her, which is dismissed, in one obstetrician's words, as a "cartload of rubbish." [13] He warns expectant mothers not to listen to "wicked women with their malicious, lying tongues." The ideal pregnant patient should, according to this view, be the doctor's obedient pupil, with ears only for his instructions and a willingness to follow them unquestioningly.

Prenatal clinics are so poorly organized in many countries of the West that some probably do more harm than good. Those women who do not have a private obstetrician or an individual midwife who cares for them throughout, and who attend large hospital clinics, are exposed to the risks that come from lack of continuity in care and the muddle and confusion that results. They say things like: "There was a conveyor belt feeling. I saw a different doctor each time." "Treatment was impersonal. Confusion over dates was never resolved. Twice they told me I ought to be induced." (The baby would have arrived five weeks early!). "The clinic was extremely bureaucratic. We were constantly being herded from one line to another. I came away from each visit in tears, feeling that motherhood was being degraded."

In a hospital clinic a woman may feel she is the passive object of management. Fed into the system, her progress through it from point to point is controlled as if she had no wishes of her own. Large hospitals are often located far from where those they are intended to serve live or work, so that women must travel a long way to attend. Then they have to wait, for an hour, two hours, three—sometimes even more—in surroundings that are often extremely uncomfortable and depressing. In almost any large clinic, a visitor can see rows of women sitting waiting for the doctor. The assumption is that though the obstetrician should never have to wait for a woman, it is acceptable for a woman to wait to see an obstetrician. The doctor's time is always more valuable than the patient's.

Few hospitals provide anything for women to do *except* wait. Facilities for childcare are usually absent and toddlers become fractious and weary. The clinics are also often overcrowded and the atmosphere is that of a badly managed cattle market. Women tend to get conflicting information and advice.

Any discussion with the obstetrician is restricted to a few minutes. Many women see this as the whole point of the visit and their planning and waiting is directed toward this moment. They are desperately disappointed when they are in and out of the examination room in a matter of minutes and have no opportunity to ask questions or voice their anxieties. Instead, they find themselves lying flat on their backs, pants off and exposed from the waist down, being prodded and poked while all they can see is the hair in the doctor's nostrils. This done, the doctor often disappears to see the next patient and the women is told that she can get up and dress now.

When that kind of thing happens to you, and you get upset, it is easy to feel that there must be something wrong with *you*. *Other* women do not seem near tears. You blame yourself for being oversensitive or expecting special treatment. When talking with pregnant women, I am often struck by the way in which they feel trapped in a situation they are powerless to influence and in which they are completely isolated. Yet this experience is so general that you are not really alone with it. It is worth talking with other women about how you feel and seeing if there is anything you can do to change the situation.

Many caregivers are concerned about what is happening, too. Women sociologists have stressed the negative experience that women have of prenatal care and have shown how anxious it makes them, and some doctors and midwives are well aware that things need changing and may welcome any help you can give them in order to effect change.[14]

In many hospital clinics, the doctors, nurses, and midwives are also under stress. When a great many women converge on an overcrowded clinic in a short period of time, there is bound to be anxiety among the staff as well as the mothers, since they are under pressure to keep the flow moving and often feel frustrated and guilty because it is impossible to give adequate care. Their work is fragmented, and as it is task-oriented rather than person-oriented, they, as well as the women, feel as if they were on an assembly line.

Yet private obstetrics, though it offers more continuity of care and more comfortable—sometimes even luxurious—conditions, still does not ensure that you get the kind of care you want. All too often a woman is coaxed along by an obstetrician who is trying to reassure her, but who does not really intend to allow her any choice, except in trivial matters. Women wanting natural childbirth often encounter filibustering and insincerity, and sometimes outright deceit, from obstetricians who want "the little woman" to take them on trust. "You can have your baby hanging from the chandelier as far as I'm concerned," (another version is "standing on your head") "but if you are in too much pain I'll have to intervene." "Of *course* you can have a natural birth. *All* birth is natural." The same authoritarianism, the same paternalism, that control women in the large hospital clinics may be hidden behind the face of the salesmanship inherent in private obstetrics.

MIDWIVES AND OBSTETRICIANS

You do not have to have an obstetrician. In many countries you can choose to have some, most, or all of your care from a midwife. She may work independently, as in the Netherlands, or as part of a team of midwives, or with a family practitioner who does obstetrics, as community midwives do in Britain. Trained midwives are able to take full responsibility for care in pregnancy, at the birth, and afterward. They can call in other help when they think it is needed. In practice, though, in many European countries this professional responsibility is being removed from midwives, so that increasingly they work as members of hospital-based teams headed by obstetricians. This means that more and more they take their instructions from obstetricians and in some countries—Italy and Germany, for example—midwives are becoming like North American obstetric nurses, assistants to the obstetricians. In Britain more than 75 percent of those midwives who work in teaching hospitals are supposed to refer to doctors about the conduct of normal deliveries—though in practice this often does not happen. Over 90 percent of the midwives who work in hospital clinics are not required to use their skills and judgment to the extent to which they are qualified.[15] They are used as receptionists and chaperones, or to test urine and weigh patients. It is not surprising that in Britain only one of every five midwives who qualifies actually practices, and of these most leave midwifery within five years. Even so, around 80 percent of babies are delivered by midwives, and within the National Health Service doctors usually do only the complicated deliveries.

Because things have become so bad, midwives are now organizing themselves to redefine the role of the midwife and make a clear distinction between midwifery and obstetrics. There is a strong and growing movement of "radical" midwifery—a term that means literally "going back to the roots."

In North America, where the medical profession forced it into virtual extinction in the early years of this century, there is now a rebirth of midwifery. Many women prefer to be cared for by a midwife. Yet many states (and many provinces in Canada) refuse to recognize midwifery or to register women as midwives. As a result, many lay midwives are practicing illegally, though there are some places where they can be registered. Sometimes they are called "empirical" or "practical" midwives. In those areas where midwifery is illegal, both lay midwives and nurse-midwives (who go through training as a nurse before they start their midwife training) live continually under the threat of possible prosecution and imprisonment for practicing medicine without a license. Some lay midwives are excellent. Others have suffered because there is no systematic training. Similarly, some nurse-midwives who are working closely with obstetricians are more like doctors than other midwives. Others are skilled in supporting the natural process of labor. In America midwifery is almost synonymous with home birth, since in most states midwives are not allowed to deliver babies in the hospital. If they do catch babies, it is because the obstetrician did not arrive in time, or occasionally because they have been given another name, such as "extended role nurses," as part of a research program to compare the safety of midwife-attended birth with doctor-attended birth. Many midwives also work in out-of-hospital birth centers where birth is treated as a normal life process and there is little or no intervention.

It may not be easy for you to get one-to-one care from a midwife. And if you want care different from that usually offered, you may have to seek far and be extraordinarily persistent.

In considering the type of care you want during pregnancy, you will obviously have to think ahead to the birth, too, because this usually involves the same people, and your choice of caregivers for the birth will almost certainly limit those available to look after you during pregnancy. You need to bear both in mind at the same time.

Though there are vast differences between practices in different countries, and in the United States, for example, between the West Coast and the Midwest, and between rural and urban areas, in general the differences between midwives and obstetricians are those shown in table 7. This list is obviously oversimplified, and it is important for you to find out the situation in your area if you want to make choices between alternative kinds of care.

TABLE 7. MIDWIVES AND OBSTETRICIANS

A MIDWIFE	*AN OBSTETRICIAN*
Is almost invariably a woman. (Midwifery is open to men, but very few choose it as a career.)	Is usually a man. (But more and more women are going into obstetrics these days.)
May be a specialist in natural birth.	Is a specialist in dealing with things that go wrong.
May work independently or as part of a small group.	Is likely to work as part of a team with other specialists—neonatologist, anesthesiologist, physical therapist, etc.
May not have easy access to specialized equipment if she does not work in a fully equipped hospital.	Has access to specialized equipment —electronic fetal monitors, ultrasound, X-ray, certain lab tests.

◆ ◆ ◆ Look at the list again, and when you have found out about conditions in your area, alter it as necessary to apply more accurately to the situation there. Then add information about particular midwives and doctors whom you are considering. Allow a column for each midwife and doctor about whom you have information.

If you live somewhere where a midwife may not have hospital privileges or work with a doctor who does, include this information in your list. If you can discover rates of intervention—for instance, what percentage of women have a perineal shave, suppositories or an enema, an intravenous drip set up, labor augmented with synthetic oxytocin, artificial rupture of the membranes, episiotomy, or a cesarean—include these facts in your list, too. (These subjects are discussed in chapter 11.) You will then be in a better position to decide on an appropriate caregiver or, if you have one already, to consider the advantages and disadvantages of this person compared with others and decide whether you want to change. ◆ ◆ ◆

THE PRELIMINARY VISIT

Your first visit to an obstetrician or midwife may be a preliminary one to see if you get along and if you share the same view of childbirth. You may not want to make a firm decision before you have had such a meeting. In some care systems, it is difficult to arrange any personal contact like this and you are expected to go on trust and simply hand yourself over to the professionals, relying on them to do what is best for you. If this is how you are expected to act, be especially careful to shop around first, talking to other women who have had babies recently. Ask local childbirth organizations and birth educators for their advice. You may need to do some quite complicated detective work. This is an important decision. You would make careful inquiries about a hairdresser before letting him give you a new hairstyle, or an architect before asking her to design a house for you. You have the right to be at least as careful about the person you choose to look after you in pregnancy and birth.

Though you will obviously want to assess whether your caregiver understands your approach to childbirth and is sympathetic toward it, avoid going with a list of demands. Statements put in terms of do's and don'ts are invariably oversimplified and do not take into account new information that may cause you to modify your views. The important thing is whether you can communicate and work together well. On the other hand, you need to explain exactly where your priorities lie. Otherwise there may be serious misunderstandings. Do not be put off by soothing noises and reassurance. Get everything right out in the open.

It is useful to have some written notes you can refer to so that you remember to discuss the aspects of care that are most important to you. Chapter 10 may help you say what you want and negotiate effectively, and chapter 11 can give you some idea of the different styles of birth to consider.

So far as the place of birth is concerned, bear in mind that a doctor may not always be the best person to advise you about where to have the baby—and is certainly not the only one. You need to talk with other women about this and find out what they liked or disliked about the places where they gave birth. Childbirth education organizations and women's health centers can help you, too.

THE FIRST CONSULTATION

Once you have decided on your caregiver, the first consultation is important because you are likely to have more opportunity to talk than at subsequent visits. A doctor or midwife takes your history on this occasion. This includes details about your own health—and any previous pregnancies and births—and, if the information is available, that of the baby's father and both your families. You are given a complete physical examination. Your height is measured and you are weighed. Several tests are made, as shown in table 8. A sample of blood is taken to measure the ratio of blood cells (which gives your hemoglobin level), check your blood group, find out whether you are Rh positive or negative, and test for syphilis. If you are in a vulnerable group, you may also be tested to see if you are a carrier of sickle-cell anemia, or Tay-Sachs disease. You are also asked to give a midstream specimen of urine so that it can be checked for bacteria and for sugar, which might indicate diabetes.

A vaginal examination is usually done to assess the size of your uterus and check it against the date of your last menstrual period. A cervical smear may also be taken to test for precancerous cells in the cervix. If you have any vaginal discharge, the doctor can take a swab and test it for thrush (candida) and sexually transmitted disease. You should be offered a chest X-ray if you come from an area where TB is common.

Another test that is often performed at this or the next visit involves measuring the level of alpha-fetoprotein (AFP) in your blood. If it is high, there is an increased risk of the baby having a neural-tube defect (a central nervous system handicap such as spina bifida, in which a part of the spinal cord protrudes from the back). This test cannot be done before sixteen weeks (from the first day of your last period). Women over thirty-five are usually also offered amniocentesis, which tests the water in which the baby floats to discover whether or not the fetus is suffering from a range of conditions, including chromosomal disorders, such as Down's syndrome,

TABLE 8. TESTS DONE AT THE FIRST VISIT

TEST	*WHY IT IS DONE*
Weight	Have base from which to assess weight gain during pregnancy.
Blood	Ascertain blood group.
	Reveal possible rhesus (Rh) incompatability.
	Measure hemoglobin.
	Check for sexually transmitted disease so that it can be treated.
Urine	Check for presence of bacteria, so bladder infection can be treated.
	Check for sugar, possible symptom of gestational diabetes.
If it is your first baby, nipple examination	See if there are likely to be breast-feeding difficulties because of inverted nipples. (This is pointless, because once you can get a baby well fixed, the baby shapes the nipples beautifully.)
Palpation of abdomen	Feel size of uterus and level of top of uterus.
Possible vaginal examination	Confirm pregnancy. Take swab in case of discharge so that infection can be treated.
	Do cervical smear to check for precancerous condition of cervix.
Blood pressure	Find base level against which any later rise can be measured.

and neural-tube defects. Again, this test cannot be done until sixteen to eighteen weeks. There is no cure for these conditions, but you can choose to have the pregnancy terminated. Although it may be too early to have these tests done at your first prenatal visit, it is a good idea to discuss them then and to let your doctor know how you feel about them.

Many obstetricians perform routine ultrasound examinations at sixteen weeks—some earlier than this—in order to check your dates. Some make regular ultrasound checks to record the baby's growth throughout pregnancy. Since there is no evidence that routine use of ultrasound is of any benefit, you may have your own ideas about this, too. If so, you should discuss them with your doctor.

During this first visit, you should also discuss where you are going to have your baby—at home, in the hospital, or in some kind of alternative birth center. If you decide on the hospital, you may want to consider a birthing room in the hospital, if it is available. The range of options varies in different countries. But if you are to choose between alternatives, you must know exactly what is available and the pros and cons of each. If you find you cannot come to an agreement about this, it is not too late to change your caregiver.

Visits usually take place every four weeks until twenty-eight weeks, then every two weeks until thirty-six weeks, and each week from then on—largely to administer the routine tests shown in table 9. For most women—those who start pregnancy in good health and continue to feel well—this number of visits to an obstetrician before thirty-six weeks is pointless. A pregnant woman is perfectly capable of charting her own weight gain and, using a dipstick, of checking her urine for the presence of protein (one symptom of pre-eclamptic toxemia, a metabolic disorder of pregnancy) and of sugar.

What many women feel they need most, however, is the chance to talk to knowledgeable and understanding women who have first-hand experiences of pregnancy and birth.

RAISED BLOOD PRESSURE AND PREECLAMPTIC TOXEMIA (PET)

You will notice that many routine pregnancy tests are concerned with the detection of preeclampsia. This is important because you may feel perfectly well and not realize that anything is wrong. Pre-eclampsia leads to a reduction in blood supply to the placenta, the baby's life-support system. The symptoms are raised blood pressure, albumen in the urine, marked edema (retention of fluids under the skin), and sudden weight gain. Raised blood pressure (hypertension) can exist by itself or as one element in PET. Mild preeclampsia in

TABLE 9. TESTS DONE EVERY TWO WEEKS

TEST	WHY IT IS DONE	HOW TO DO IT YOURSELF
Weight	Assess growth of baby and reveal any sudden weight gain, a possible symptom of preeclampsia.	Weigh yourself at about the same time of day, wearing similar clothing. After the first 3 months some women put on weight in swoops and starts. Most weeks there is a steady gain of 7–14 oz. (200–400 g), with a total weight gain of up to 26 lbs. (12 kg). The baby can still be a good weight if you gain less or more than this.
Urine	Check for presence of bacteria, so bladder infection can be treated.	Cannot be done yourself. Specimen must be sent to a lab.
	Check for sugar, possible symptom of gestational diabetes. Check for presence of albumen (protein), one symptom of preeclampsia.	Use dipsticks, which change color to indicate presence of albumen or sugar. You can buy them from a women's health center or pharmacy.
Blood pressure	Check whether there is any rise —a sharp rise is one symptom of preeclampsia.	Get a friend to help you, using a sphygmomanometer (blood-pressure gauge).
Palpation of abdomen	Feel size of uterus and level of top of uterus. Feel position and size of baby.	See chapter 12. Ask your midwife or doctor to show you how to do this.
Fetal heart monitoring	Check baby's heart rate— normally 120–160 beats per minute.	Use a long stethoscope or get a friend to listen using the cardboard cylinder from a toilet tissue roll. Listen for 15 seconds and then multiply by four.
In late pregnancy also:		
Possible vaginal examination	Reveal position of baby's head and whether cervix is ripe for labor.	Best done by a doctor or midwife.

the last few weeks occurs in approximately 25 percent of all pregnancies.[16] It is so frequent as to be normal. But preeclampsia that starts earlier in pregnancy (before thirty-six weeks), or which is severe— when blood pressure is higher than 160/100—even with late onset, is serious. This severe kind occurs in only one-fifth of all cases of preeclampsia. If the diastolic pressure—the lowest level to which blood pressure falls between heartbeats—goes up to 110 or more, or there is albumen in the urine *and* the diastolic pressure is 90 or more, of if the woman actually develops eclampsia and has fits, there is a risk that the baby may die.[17]

Blood pressure readings are recorded with the systolic pressure (the highest pressure reached during a heartbeat) as the upper figure and the diastolic pressure underneath it. The upper figure changes at different times of the day and when you are feeling angry or anxious. If you have to rush to get to your appointment, or drive through heavy traffic, it will probably go up. The lower figure is the important one.

For a blood pressure reading to be accurate you should be relaxed. It is often difficult to feel at ease when you visit your doctor, especially if you are worried that your pressure may be up. The expression "white-coat hypertension" has been coined to describe what happens when blood pressure shoots up in the presence of a doctor.[18] Your blood pressure is likely to be lower at home than in the hospital.[19] It will vary at different times of the day and is usually lowest first thing in the morning. Single blood pressure readings are unreliable.[20] Some heart specialists suggest that the most accurate records result when patients take their own serial blood pressure measurements at home, or when a friend or someone in the family helps them do so. In Britain, where community midwives sometimes still come to the home for prenatal visits, pregnant women often notice that their blood pressure is higher when taken by the general practitioner, higher still when done in the hospital, and lowest when measured by the community midwife at home. So if your blood pressure is slightly up at the end of pregnancy, as it is for many women, and there is concern that it may be rising, you may want to borrow or buy a blood pressure gauge and learn how to take blood pressure readings at home.

Women nearing the end of pregnancy who have preeclampsia are usually advised to have labor induced. Those with marginally raised blood pressure are often told that they are developing preeclampsia and thus ought to have labor induced. It is best not to agree to induction of labor unless your blood pressure is dangerously high.

There are all sorts of ideas about what causes preeclampsia: not only poor nutrition, as we have seen in chapter 4, but also being tense and under pressure, poverty—and our whole Western way of living. It certainly seems to be a physiological stress disease. A woman is more likely to develop it if her body has to adapt to cope with a twin pregnancy, for example, or if she is especially young or old. First-time mothers (primigravidae) are also more likely to get it than those having subsequent babies (multigravidae).

If symptoms of preeclampsia are diagnosed, a doctor will want to admit you to the hospital for bed-rest and may advise drug treatment. Diuretics, drugs that promote the flow of urine, are often used since they lower blood pressure. However, there have been eleven randomized trials of diuretics in pregnancy that showed there is no reliable evidence of the value of this treatment.[21]

The other drugs used are beta blockers, which block the action of adrenalin on the heart. There have been few controlled trials of these, though one systematic study with follow-up when the babies were a year old revealed no major disadvantages.[22] But it has to be remembered that there is rapid development of a child's central nervous system throughout the first three years of life and some problems may not crop up till much later. In view of this, some researchers believe that "follow-up until the age of seven years is mandatory before a drug given to the mother during pregnancy can be considered even relatively safe."[23] Doctors are under great pressure from drug companies to employ these drugs, but their use at present is, on the whole, more or less unevaluated and uncontrolled.[24]

If preeclampsia becomes severe and rest in bed does nothing to reduce it, there may be no effective treatment other than induction of labor. There comes a point when the baby is better out than in.

♦ ♦ ♦ Since one pregnant woman in four is classified by doctors as having some form of preeclampsia, even though mild, it is sensible to think ahead about what you would want if you developed any symptoms. Talk about this with your partner or with someone else who could take over your responsibilities and make a plan of action together. Jot down a rough outline of this in your notebook. It will help to look at your lifestyle and see how you can simplify it and cut out stress. If you are planning to have a break from work outside the home, for example, the time to do so is when you get the earliest symptoms of preeclampsia, rather than waiting till it is severe and then having to go into the hospital. Your partner, or someone else, will need to take over the household chores so that you can rest as much as you can. The relaxation exercises you learn in childbirth classes, breathing slowly and fully and relaxing a little more with each breath *out,* can help lower your blood pressure. Since raised blood pressure tends to occur at a stage of pregnancy when sleep is most likely to be disturbed, you may want to try a natural sleep-inducer consisting of amino acids—tryptophan. This is available from health food stores. If you do not have to wake several times in the night to empty your bladder, a milk drink before you sleep can help. At the end of pregnancy you may sleep better in a separate rather than a double bed.

Outline a plan of action in case your blood pressure should go up after thirty-six weeks or there are other symptoms of possible pre-eclampsia. To be forewarned is to be forearmed.

Note any questions you might want to ask.

Make a list of people you could call on for help and the arrangements you would need to make. ♦ ♦ ♦

The anxiety many women feel in pregnancy cannot be explained away by saying that they are in an emotionally vulnerable state and that it is all a matter of hormones. When a baby is coming, social and economic problems that did not seem daunting before can become overwhelming because you are taking on responsibility for a new life. It may be important to discuss stresses in relationships, worries about financial matters or living conditions, or fears about the birth or how you are going to manage afterward, with someone who understands and can help you reduce these stresses. If they cannot be removed, you at least have the opporutnity of working out ways of coping with them better.

9

◆ DECIDING ABOUT ◆
SPECIAL TESTS

The borderline between the tests done routinely in pregnancy and the special screenings done if there is reason to suspect abnormality is a fuzzy one. In many countries an increasing number of tests designed to detect slight and unimportant deviations from the normal, on the one hand, and rare conditions which can have serious consequences, on the other, are being introduced into routine care. Knowing about them, what they are, and why they are done can help you decide whether or not you want to have them. The choice is yours. Even if it has been proved conclusively that a test is valuable, you still have a right to refuse it. No one can compel you to agree to any medical intervention whatsoever.

Some of these screening procedures entail further analyses of the blood which is taken as a matter of course at the first visit or soon after that. Others involve an extra blood test or other kind of investigation. It is very important that a woman with diabetes, for example, has regular monitoring of blood glucose concentrations during pregnancy. Previous obstetric practice has often been to deliver the baby early by inducing labor at about thirty-seven weeks, but it is now being shown that with careful control of blood sugar it can be safe for women to wait to go into spontaneous labor. Women can monitor their own blood glucose concentrations effectively at home. When they do, there are fewer hospital admissions, a reduced cesarean section rate, and the babies are in better condition.[1] This is one situation where scrupulous monitoring throughout pregnancy is extremely important and where women themselves, instead of being merely at the receiving end of prenatal care, can take personal responsibility and an active role in looking after themselves.

AFP BLOOD TEST

The level of alpha-fetoprotein (a substance produced by the baby's liver and gastrointestinal tract) in the mother's blood can be measured to find out if the baby is likely to have a neural-tube defect— a handicap resulting from failure of the spinal cord to form correctly or to close. Screening is done between sixteen and eighteen weeks. A higher than usual level of AFP suggests that the baby may have a congenital handicap involving the spinal cord. In some places this screening is done routinely on all mothers. In others it is done only if, because of family history or because a woman has already had a baby with a congenital handicap, there is cause for concern. There are many arguments for and against routine screening. Some people say that if a woman is not told that her blood is to be used for this purpose it should not be done. Others say that to introduce the possibility of congenital handicap, with no evidence that it exists, is to sow seeds of anxiety in the pregnant woman's mind. Some doctors point to the low incidence of abnormality revealed by AFP testing and therefore consider it an unnecessary and costly procedure. Only 10 percent of women who have a raised AFP level in their blood and go on to have amniocentesis actually have babies suffering from central nervous system abnormalities, so there is a very wide margin of error.

One reason for this is that a woman may have her dates wrong. The level of AFP roughly doubles every five weeks in the second three months of pregnancy, and the gap between a normal and a very high level is greatest between the sixteenth and eighteenth weeks. If you are further along in your pregnancy than you think, the AFP level will be higher than expected. A twin pregnancy will also push up the AFP level. If you have viral hepatitis, it will also be raised.

In America, the rate of neural-tube defects is 1 in 1,000 pregnancies, whereas in Britain it is a good deal higher—4.5 for every 1,000 pregnancies. This is one reason why AFP screening is more usual in Britain than in the United States.

AFP testing cannot completely rule out the possibility that a baby may have a neural-tube defect. In 2 percent of cases where there is no raised level of AFP, the baby has spina bifida or anencephaly.[2]

If you ask for an AFP test, or if your obstetrician advises it, bear in mind that if the level is up this will cause a lot of anxiety until you have the results of your amniocentesis. Think about how you would want to cope with this and the support you might need. Many women find that an understanding woman friend who has been through it all herself is a great help. Many talk it through with their partners and face it together. Whatever happens, do not try to push it to the back of your mind and pretend that it has not happened. It is better to bring the anxiety out into the open and acknowledge it, while at the same time keeping busy with other things and living life as fully as possible.

AMNIOCENTESIS

Amniocentesis is a test of the amniotic fluid in which the baby floats. It cannot be done until sixteen to eighteen weeks because until then there is insufficient fluid. A needle is introduced through the mother's abdominal wall into the uterus to draw off a sample of fluid so that it can be examined to show the level of alpha-fetoprotein (AFP), and so that fetal cells cultured from the fluid can reveal a range of chromosomal abnormalities, including Down's syndrome, and spina bifida and anencephaly.

If amniocentesis reveals that the baby is suffering from a congenital handicap, the mother can decide whether or not to have an abortion, something which most women have thought about in advance of having the test—and, indeed, some say there is no point in having it because they would not agree to an abortion.

To be able to predict which babies will be handicapped or may die from a congenital abnormality is a major scientific advance. For women at special risk of bearing handicapped babies because certain kinds of abnormality run in their families, or who are in an at-risk age-group (the risks increase with the mother's age; see tables 10 and 11), it may be an enormous relief to know whether or not the fetus is affected, and be able to choose to terminate the pregnancy. The equation is different for every woman, and her personal feelings, which are often very mixed, must be an important part of any deci-

TABLE 10. RATES OF DOWN'S SYNDROME IN LIVE BIRTHS BY MATERNAL AGE

MOTHER'S AGE	INCIDENCE
35	1 in 365
36	1 in 290
37	1 in 225
38	1 in 180
39	1 in 140
40	1 in 109
41	1 in 85
42	1 in 70
43	1 in 50
44	1 in 40
45	1 in 32
46	1 in 25
47	1 in 20
48	1 in 15
49	1 in 12

Source: J. Simpson, "Antenatal diagnosis of cytogenetic abnormalities," *Seminars in Perinatology*, 4, 3 (1980): 168.

sion she makes. It is not something that can be worked out with a slide rule.

The U.S. National Genetic Foundation advises that the following women should have amniocentesis:

♦ All women over thirty-five.

♦ Any woman who knows, as the result of a genetic test, that she and the father of her baby carry the same gene for congenital disease.

♦ Those who have already borne a child with a biochemical or developmental disorder that can be diagnosed prenatally.

♦ Women from ethnic groups at special risk of a genetic disorder. Black women should be tested for sickle-cell anemia; women of

TABLE 11. RATES OF CHROMOSOME ABNORMALITIES AT AMNIOCENTESIS BY WOMAN'S AGE

WOMAN'S AGE	INCIDENCE
25	1 in 527
30	1 in 476
35	1 in 204
40	1 in 73
45	1 in 23

NOTE: A number of babies with chromosome abnormalities are miscarried, so the rate discovered at the time of amniocentesis is higher than that of babies born with these handicaps. At thirty-five, for example, there is a 1 in 222 chance of a baby being born with such an abnormality, compared with a 1 in 204 chance at the time of amniocentesis; at forty a 1 in 83 chance compared with 1 in 73 at amniocentesis; and at forty-five 1 in 30 compared with 1 in 23 at amniocentesis.

Source: E. B. Hook and D. K. Cross, "Estimated Rates of Clinically Significant Cytogenetic Abnormality (Other Than Down's Syndrome)," *The American Journal of Human Genetics* 31 (1979): 136a.

Mediterranean ancestry for thalassemia, a hemoglobin abnormality; and descendants of Central and Eastern European Jews for Tay-Sachs disease, an enzyme deficiency that leads to brain damage.

♦ Women with diabetes or PET who have been advised to have an induced labor or an elective (planned) cesarean section should have third-trimester amniocentesis.

Amniocentesis also reveals the sex of the baby, which is relevant if there is a history of sex-linked diseases, such as hemophilia or Duchenne muscular dystrophy, where girls carry the disorder but do not suffer from it. In societies where girls have little value and where the birth of sons is of paramount importance, female babies may be aborted following amniocentesis. Sometimes a father insists on an abortion though the woman wants to bear the child. The new power to discover what is going on inside the uterus raises ethical dilemmas and brings with it a new responsibility to wield that power wisely.

If you have amniocentesis, you may want to know the sex of your baby, but not all doctors will give that information. This is partly because they believe that women may seek to abort babies of the unwanted sex. Women themselves often do not want to know the sex because they feel it is more natural not to know and prefer a baby to be a surprise. Others want to have all the information they can. Either way, you have a *right* to know. Whatever can be learned from amniocentesis should not be in a medically restricted category of knowledge.

In 1985 it first became possible to identify with 99 percent reliability fetuses that would develop cystic fibrosis, a disease that leads to severe digestive disturbances and damages the lungs. A child suffering from it has a life expectancy of only twenty years. But it is still not possible to predict which parents carry the defective gene, so the test can help only those women who have already had a child with cystic fibrosis.

Later on in pregnancy, an analysis of the amniotic fluid can also reveal whether the fetal lungs are mature and whether, if born at that stage, the newborn baby is likely to develop respiratory distress syndrome (RDS). This is important information if a baby is very premature. But even then, the results are not 100 percent accurate and many babies diagnosed as not ready for independent life breathe well after delivery.[3]

Amniocentesis cannot guarantee that any baby will be perfect, since it only screens for specific handicaps. Research by the Royal College of Obstetricians and Gynaecologists on late abortions showed that when they were done because amniocentesis revealed a raised AFP level, 6.5 percent of the fetuses were not handicapped in any way and no more than 85 percent of the rest had open neural-tube defects. (This means there was a remaining group of babies with very mild spina bifida which would not have caused any problem.)[4] So there is the possibility that a normal baby could be aborted on the chance that it was abnormal. This is another of the ethical dilemmas associated with amniocentesis.

How Amniocentesis is Done

Amniocentesis takes place in a small room rather like an operating theater, where there is an ultrasound screen that looks like a TV. The test must be done under sterile conditions, or infection can be introduced into the uterus. The woman will probably wear a hospital gown, and if she has not already had a blood test to measure the level of AFP she will have that first. She lies on something like an operating table and an ultrasound scan tells the position of the placenta and the fetus and shows exactly how far the needle should go into the sac in order to get the fluid. Her skin is swabbed with an antiseptic and a paper sheet with a hole through it where the needle is to be introduced is placed over it. She may be given a local anesthetic, though this is not always considered necessary and she should ask for one if she wants it.

A long needle attached to a syringe is then pushed through the skin into the uterus and a little fluid withdrawn. Even in the best hospitals, in approximately 1 in 1,000 cases the needle goes into a blood vessel and has to be withdrawn and another attempt made to get clear fluid. Once the needle is correctly positioned and a quantity of fluid is drawn into the syringe—less than half a demitasse cup— some plastic film may be sprayed on the puncture site and an adhesive bandage put on. Many women say that just as they think the test is going to begin they are told it is all over. Even so, it is normal to feel a bit shaky after it.

If you live far from the hospital, it is a good idea to arrange for someone else to drive you home, and then to go straight to bed for a few hours. Do anything that will help you relax. You could listen to music or read an absorbing book. Spend the next week fairly quietly.

The needle puncture made in the amniotic sac is no bigger than the prick made by a rose thorn. It usually seals over automatically once the needle is withdrawn. Occasionally there is some dribbling of fluid and sometimes there is vaginal bleeding. Two percent of women have some loss of fluid or bleeding.[5] The risk of miscarriage is low—approximately 1 percent—and less in skilled hands. It may be higher for a woman who has had bleeding during pregnancy or who has scars from a previous cesarean section. Miscarriage after amniocentesis is most likely to occur on the third or fourth day.

The test for Down's syndrome entails growing cells obtained from the amniotic fluid. In between 1 and 5 percent of all cases the cell culture does not grow. This is discovered in a week to ten days. The woman is then asked to come for another amniocentesis. This can be an ordeal and she may decide that, since an abortion would now take place later still, she is not willing to have the test repeated.

Ultrasound should always be used with amniocentesis to make certain that the needle does not puncture the placenta or harm the baby. In fact, the baby usually bounces away like a cork in a beaker of water, but ultrasound increases the safety of the procedure. Damage to the placenta can produce an Rh incompatability reaction in the circulation of an Rh negative mother if the fetus is Rh positive, leading to rhesus isoimmunization—the mother's blood manufactures antibodies to the baby's blood, destroying some of its red blood cells and the baby then becomes anemic and jaundiced.

You should be able to have a discussion with a genetic counselor before you decide whether or not to have amniocentesis. If you do decide to go ahead with it, the counselor can then interpret any results you might have questions about.

There may also be things you do *not* want to know. One, as we have seen, may be the sex of the baby. You may also decide you do not want to be told about any deviation from the normal which is as yet not understood and where knowledge cannot help you in decision making. Minor chromosomal abnormalities are quite often detected when analysis is being done for Down's syndrome. Many of us have these slightly abnormal chromosomes and go through our lives without ever discovering it or being hampered by it. If the parents know that a child lacks a chromosome or has an extra one, they are likely to wait in apprehension and watch for any sign of abnormal behavior.[6]

Research has shown, for example, that there are more men with an extra Y chromosome in prison than in the general population. The media picked this up and concluded that the extra Y chromosome made men more aggressive. Subsequent research has indicated that this is not so. (Another theory is that men with an extra Y chromosome are inclined to be rather less intelligent, so they are the ones who get caught!) Imagine knowing that your two-year-old son has an extra Y chromosome. When he has a tantrum in the supermarket—something a great many two-year-olds do at one time or another—would you think that this must be because of his extra chromosome and that he's well on the way toward violent crime? Would it make the tasks of parenthood simpler, or more difficult? There are no easy answers to these questions, but certainly acquiring more and more information does not always lead to greater wisdom.

There are some risks and problems with amniocentesis, and for some women these outweigh the benefits. Women often have marked and sometimes regular uterine contractions immediately following amniocentesis. This can be alarming even if you know that it is normal. There are statistical associations between amniocentesis and bleeding in pregnancy, newborn babies who have some difficulties with breathing, and babies with orthopedic handicaps.[7] In deciding whether or not to have amniocentesis you will want to think through what not having this baby means to you. That cannot be discovered through statistics.

Lynn is forty, with two children, and has decided to have amniocentesis.

If there's something wrong I'd say I can put up with that. I'd have an abortion. It's for the family as much as for myself. They're here already and they've got feelings. I'd get rid of a handicapped baby for their sake.

Karen, whose partner has a brother with spina bifida, has decided against amniocentesis.

We've waited so long to have this baby. We've been trying ten years. If I lost it because of amniocentesis I'd never forgive myself, and if it does turn out that the baby is handicapped, well, I expect—I hope—we'd cope. I know couples where a handicapped baby has drawn them very close. I think our love for each other would give us strength.

Gail had a miscarriage after amniocentesis last year. She is thirty-seven and the risk of having a handicapped baby at her age is only slightly greater than having a miscarriage. She says:

You can't weigh a handicapped baby against a miscarriage. I'd rather have six miscarriages than a handicapped child for life.

Your age, whether or not you conceive easily, your commitment to this pregnancy, your partner's feelings, your acceptance of handicap or the death of a child, and your beliefs about and willingness to have an abortion all need to be considered. This is not something that doctors can do for you.

Having an Abortion

A major problem with amniocentesis is that if the pregnancy is to be terminated it means a late abortion, around twenty weeks. This can be intensely distressing. Women are sometimes told they should be grateful for the opportunity to get rid of a handicapped baby and that, after all, there is nothing to stop them from having another baby very soon afterward. It may be suggested that losing a child in this way is easier than the loss of a perfect child. That kind of arithmetic has no meaning in terms of personal experience. An amniocentesis abortion is the death of a baby and entails making a painful and often heartrending choice.

The abortion is often induced with prostaglandins, and pain-killing drugs are readily available. Even so, it is not an experience that any woman would want to go through. One woman described her abortion as "a hideous mockery of childbirth." The whole process can take eight hours or more. A woman needs strong emotional support during this time and in the weeks afterward. At this stage of pregnancy she is likely to lactate once the abortion is over. A tight bra, reduction of fluids, and cold compresses against the breasts (ice in a large handkerchief or a plastic bag of frozen peas) will help cope with the discomfort.

Another difficulty with amniocentesis is that the interval between having it done and getting the results is obviously a worrying time. Though some results are available in twenty-four hours, others take three or four weeks—sometimes longer. A woman often feels she cannot tell other people she is pregnant and make a social reality of it in case abortion lies ahead. Kathy is thirty-nine and has been trying to conceive for eight years. While she was waiting for the test in the genetics department of the hospital, she said:

> I haven't told my mother I'm expecting a baby. It seems that everyone knows about it apart from our families. They'd get excited—but I daren't tell them yet until I know the result. We want to avoid any disappointment for them. It's all so unreal—weird. I've been wearing especially floppy clothes so they don't notice. The biggest problem was that when I was staying with them I felt so nauseated in the mornings. I ate breakfast when I didn't feel like it and then tried to go to the

bathroom casually so that I could vomit it up. It will be a relief when I can tell them at last—if I ever *can,* that is.

The verdict for which a woman is waiting seems to be a judgment on her ability to bear a healthy baby—even, perhaps, a judgment of her value as a woman. After an amniocentesis abortion she may feel that this developing life had to be destroyed because she is bad and that she carries death and disease deep in her body. This sense of dreadful personal guilt is made more severe if you are cared for by a nurse who has moral objections to abortion.

Everyone needs a confiding friend who realizes what she is going through and accepts the strength of these emotions without trying to argue them away. A woman who has not told people about her pregnancy may keep her termination a shameful secret. And even if she has, there may be no one who can understand the storm of conflicting emotions she feels and the guilt and depression that may grip her for months afterward. Because she has done the "sensible" thing, there may be no recognition of her need to grieve. Friends may say, "How glad you must be that you found out in time!" Relief and gratitude that the abnormality was detected are the only socially acceptable emotions.

In fact, it is usually wise to tell people you are pregnant before amniocentesis. Most babies will be fine, and even when both parents are carriers of some defective gene, there is a three in four chance that it will be good news. And even though it may be difficult to get the emotional support you need if you have to lose this baby, if no one else knew you were pregnant in the first place, you certainly will not receive the help you need.

Amniocentesis is only the first of a whole range of tests and operations that can be done inside the body of the mother. They all raise enormous moral questions—about the quality of human life, about a woman's rights over her own body compared with her responsibility for the fetus, and her personal rights compared with her responsibility to society. In some American states a doctor *must* perform amniocentesis on all women over thirty-five or be guilty of negligence. It has been suggested that, similarly, a woman over thirty-five has a duty to have amniocentesis and to abort an imperfect baby.

Though these investigations and operations involve doctors, they are not really medical questions at all. They concern human values and present challenges we have to meet if we are to accept responsibility for the future. I believe it is wrong merely to be at the receiving end of everything that science makes possible. We have to ask ourselves important questions, and the answers are never easy.

CHORIONIC VILLUS BIOPSY

Chorionic villus sampling (CVS) can be done much earlier in pregnancy than amniocentesis—between the sixth and tenth week. A cannula (a fine hollow tube) is introduced into the uterus through the vagina and cervix, guided by an ultrasound scan, and some chorionic villus tissue is suctioned out. Chorionic villi, projections like miniature ivy roots that stick out from the maternal side of the developing placenta while it is still at a very early stage, dig themselves into the lining of the uterus so that oxygen and nutritional elements can be carried to the fetus. Samples of these tissues can be analyzed for genetic and metabolic defects, including Down's syndrome and other chromosome abnormalities, thalassemia, sickle-cell anemia, and Tay-Sachs disease.

The waiting time for results is much shorter than with amniocentesis, twenty-four hours as compared with two to six weeks. The great advantage of this test is that if you decide on termination it can still be done before twelve weeks. At this stage a suction abortion can be performed, whereas in the second trimester a saline or prostaglandin abortion is necessary, which results in what is, to all intents and purposes, a labor.

Though this may seem an ideal method, there remain many questions about CVS that require answers. One concerns the rate of miscarriage following the test, which in some research units has been estimated in the past to be as high as 10 percent. It is also important to bear in mind that many abnormal fetuses are miscarried, so that when termination is done as early as eight weeks, a number of women with fetuses that would have aborted naturally will have had an elective abortion before this can happen. Other questions concern the rates of pelvic infection, bleeding, and leaking of amniotic fluid, as well as possible developmental abnormalities resulting in low birthweight in babies who go to term after a chorionic villus biopsy.

We do not yet know the answers to all these questions, though research is taking place and the outlook for the future is hopeful.

ULTRASOUND

It took nearly fifty years after the introduction of X-rays for people to realize that they were harmful in pregnancy. Even though warnings about radiation were given in the early 1920s, an authority could state in 1935: "Antenatal work without the routine use of X-rays is no more justifiable than would be the treatment of fractures."[8] Two years later, the director of the Radiology Department at University College Hospital, London, stated categorically that in the hands of a competent operator there was no danger.[9] In one specialized maternity hospital (Queen Charlotte's), two-thirds of pregnant women were having X-rays by 1954, the year new, higher voltage X-ray equipment was introduced.[10] Two years later, Dr. Alice Stewart published her findings that a baby X-rayed in the uterus was twice as likely to die of cancer by the age of ten.[11] It was only then that the warnings were heeded and the rates of X-rays in pregnancy reduced. Since Marie Curie first worked with radium, the dangers of radioactivity had been known, but the knowledge was brushed aside because obstetricians persuaded themselves that the benefits of knowing what was going on inside the uterus outweighed the risks.

Ultrasound was invented during the Second World War and used to detect submarines at sea. By the late 1950s obstetric ultrasound was being used in Glasgow. The principle behind it is that sound waves bounce off solid objects. This produces an image on a screen, or a pulsed beam as in the Doppler ultrasound used for fetal heart monitoring. Ultrasound's great advantage is that it does not have the obvious dangers of X-rays and can reveal more of life inside the uterus.

At present, there is no evidence that ultrasound is unsafe, but there is a great deal of discussion about its possible delayed and long-term risks. Some people are asking whether, since there was such a long delay in acknowledging the risks of radiation, there may not be hidden dangers in the use of ultrasound in pregnancy.

Until follow-up studies have been done on hundreds of thousands of adults who, when inside the uterus, were exposed to ultrasound, how can we be sure, they say, that we are not playing with fire? And if the majority of women and fetuses show no adverse effects of ultrasound, is it possible that some may be especially vulnerable? [12] Whereas it is agreed that ultrasound can be very useful diagnostically —when it is thought that because the top of the uterus is not as high as it should be at that stage of pregnancy the baby may not be growing well, to locate the placenta when it is lying low, or to reveal a congenital handicap—there is no evidence that its routine use to monitor fetal growth is of benefit.

Today most pregnant women in the Western world are exposed to ultrasound in one form or another and many receive a standard scan —usually at sixteen weeks—and at least twenty to thirty minutes of ultrasound in the form of Doppler investigations performed when they go into labor. A good number receive much more than this. Some obstetricians advocate two or three scans routinely in pregnancy, together with fetal heart monitoring in the last weeks. Scans are also used to explore possible abnormalities in the fetus, such as spina bifida and blockages in the gastrointestinal tract, and may be used in addition to amniocentesis for this purpose.

Having a Scan

When you have a scan early in pregnancy, you will be asked to drink a lot of water beforehand and come with a full bladder. This clearly distinguishes the bladder and presses the intestines out of the way of the uterus. Your abdomen will first be greased with mineral oil. Then a probe that emits waves of sound too high for the ear to hear is passed over the uterus. This is completely painless for the woman. The sound is translated into dots, each of which is an echo, on what looks like a TV screen. If you want to see it, ask for it to be at an angle where it will be easy for the operator to explain the different parts to you.

At about six weeks the bag of waters can be seen, with the embryo like a small white moon inside. At sixteen weeks you can see the heart beating and the position of the placenta, which is often low down in the uterus at this stage. The baby's head is a large, white, egg shape. When it twists and turns, the baby is nodding or shaking its head. Sometimes it lifts a hand and starts to suck its thumb. Measurements may be taken from the top of the head to the rump and from one ear across to the other.

With a scan after twenty-four weeks it may be possible to see the baby's sex, though this depends on how the baby is lying. The genitals of girls often look very plump and large at this stage, so it is easy to mistake a girl for a boy. Sometimes a woman is told her baby's sex incorrectly.

You may be offered a snapshot of your baby to take home and stick in the photograph album. The whole process takes about fifteen minutes.

Diana was thrilled to see her baby.

> It was like looking at a tadpole in a tank. The legs were just little stubbles. I was amazed. I couldn't feel anything but it was moving like anything!

Frances was so excited when she saw the image of her baby that she shouted out "Look! He—she's waving to me!"

Because women often enjoy seeing their babies, some obstetricians believe that a scan enables a mother to bond with her child long before birth. The majority of women in the past have managed to love their babies without this extra technological prodding toward mother love. Intrigued as doctors may be with this response, and happy that they can contribute to it, it is insufficient justification for employing a powerful diagnostic technique in the absence of other reasons for doing so.

The ultrasound scan can provide doctors with a great deal of information about the developing fetus. Between sixteen and twenty-four weeks it should be able to give an accurate dating of pregnancy. After that time it is likely to be wrong.[13] It can show that a fetus is, in all likelihood, normal, can detect some fetal abnormalities without the need for amniocentesis—for example, spina bifida, anencephaly, and Turner's syndrome, an intersex condition—and can reveal conditions, such as heart defects, tumors, and skeletal and urinary tract abnormalities that would not be disclosed by amniocentesis. In very early pregnancy it shows whether there is tissue inside the amniotic sac and later on whether the baby's heart is beating, so that it is known whether the pregnancy is continuing. It reveals the presence of twins (or more), and the position of the placenta shows up, so that if placenta previa (the placenta lying over the cervix) is diagnosed, a cesarean section can be planned in advance. It can also diagnose a small-for-dates fetus, though many mistakes are made about this. And it is vital in amniocentesis to guide the introduction of the needle.

But ultrasound also has disadvantages.[14] It often diagnoses a condition—for example, a low-lying placenta or placenta previa, or a malpresentation—that may be present at one phase of pregnancy, but has changed by the time labor starts. Results are not always interpreted accurately, so it can suggest that everything is all right when it is not, or that an abnormal condition is present when it is not.[15] After twenty-five weeks it is very inaccurate in diagnosing fetal maturity.[16] Ultrasound assessment of gestational age is not always as accurate as is often suggested. Sometimes a woman is well aware of when conception must have occurred and knows that the scan gives an inaccurate date.

Jennie was having her second baby at home. She had one scan at sixteen weeks, when she was told she must be eighteen weeks. She described her pregnancy as "perfect." At thirty-seven weeks a transverse lie was diagnosed—the baby was lying across her uterus—and she was ordered to go into the hospital immediately for an induction. "Otherwise the baby may die." She refused, but said she was "absolutely terrified." Two weeks later the baby turned head-down. She went into labor spontaneously at what, according to the scan, was forty-two weeks and delivered a seven pound, six ounce baby who gave no sign of being overdue. If labor had been induced, the baby would have been four to five weeks premature.

In some hospitals ultrasound dating is more reliable than this, and obstetricians do not seek to intervene so readily. A controlled trial in Glasgow revealed a 94 percent accuracy in identifying babies who were small-for-dates at birth when two scans were done, one before twenty-four weeks and another between thirty-four and thirty-six weeks. Nevertheless, this study failed to show any benefit from the routine use of ultrasound in low-risk pregnancies, and the authors concluded that they were "unable to recommend this schedule as a routine screening method."[17]

While the short-term safety of diagnostic ultrasound is clear, there remain questions about its long-term safety.[18] It is not yet known whether ultrasound may produce changes in fetal cells which could sometimes lead to cancer much later in life or whether, through changes in DNA and cell structure, it could affect the health of future generations. In mice, ultrasound alters cells after ten generations of cell division and this persists for up to one hundred generations.[19] If there is even an outside chance of this, it seems wise to avoid a scan in the first twelve weeks, when the tissues of the fetus are at their most vulnerable stage, unless there are pressing reasons to have one. Finding out after heavy bleeding whether you have miscarried or are about to miscarry might be one good reason for some women.

The use made of the information gained from ultrasound, and how this affects the rest of the pregnancy and the way labor is managed, is an issue discussed in medical journals but not much talked about by the general public, or from the woman's point of view. Yet it is an important aspect of ultrasound policy. If it is unlikely to alter care, it is pointless. If the response to the information is anxiety on the part of the doctor or the mother—or both—which cannot be channeled into constructive action, ultrasound has a negative effect on the rest of the pregnancy. If it leads to women being admitted to the hospital unnecessarily or having unnecessary inductions or cesarean sections, the effect is also negative.

Though in Britain the Royal College of Obstetricians and Gynaecologists has accepted a policy of routine scanning at sixteen weeks, there is no evidence that ultrasound is of any benefit when used routinely. This is recognized by the American College of Obstetricians and Gynecologists which has issued a statement that "no well-controlled study has yet proved that routine scanning of all prenatal patients will improve the outcome of pregnancy," and recommends that "at present, only indicated diagnostic studies should be ordered."[20]

If you are advised to have ultrasound, there are some questions you may want to ask.

♦ What information is it expected to provide?

♦ Is this important?

♦ If so, why?

♦ How accurate will it be at this stage of pregnancy?

♦ How will it affect my pregnancy if I do not have a scan?

♦ Will enough be learned to justify exposing the fetus to the possible risk of ultrasound? [21]

You may want to ensure that the results of the scan will be given to you on the spot, and that often happens only if a doctor is present. The technician is normally expected to report to your obstetrician. You may also want to know if a record of the number of scans you have, the intensity of exposure, and the time exposed to ultrasound is kept. Unless records like this are kept, it is impossible to know if there are any long-term effects. You may wish to have an assurance that your partner will be able to be with you. This not only reduces anxiety, but can make it an exciting shared experience.

♦ ♦ ♦ At this stage it might be useful to get out your notebook and, perhaps in discussion with your partner or a friend, jot down your main conclusions. Decide which questions you would want to ask if ultrasound was advised by your obstetrician and make a note of these. ♦ ♦ ♦

DOPPLER ULTRASOUND

Ultrasound is also used to monitor the fetal heartbeat, both prenatally and during labor, in the form of either a transducer pressed over the site of the baby's heart from outside the mother's abdomen and attached to her by a tight belt, or a sonic aid, about the size of a small tape recorder, used intermittently. The other kind of continuous monitoring is done electronically by means of an electrode attached to a screw or clip which is introduced through the mother's cervix and stuck onto the baby's scalp. This kind does not employ ultrasound.

When ultrasound is used for fetal heart monitoring, it often gives information that is misinterpreted, thus producing false positives and false negatives. [22] Women are required to lie down and be still when a trace is being recorded. This can cause compression of the large blood vessels in the lower part of the mother's body, resulting in reduced blood flow to the baby and hence heart-rate abnormalities. It is also often extremely uncomfortable for her to stay in one position like this in order to get a clear reading, and she feels constricted and inhibited. Though this may not matter much for a short time during pregnancy, this kind of stress during labor can affect progress.

The immediate effect of ultrasound on the baby is rarely discussed, but a pregnant woman who is being monitored usually notices that the fetus responds by jumping around. In fact, in late pregnancy this is employed as a test of fetal vitality and the baby's movements often feel quite wild. As with a dog whistle, our ears cannot pick up the sound waves, but for the baby they may be as shrill and powerful as the noise of a police siren. Moreover, the conditions in which most women are examined often prove stressful enough to make the baby move vigorously. One study reported acceleration of the fetal heart rate when doctors merely came to a woman's bedside.[23]

Even in high-risk pregnancies fetal heart recording does not mean that more babies' lives are saved. Studies done on routine heart monitoring show that more babies died in the groups having it than in the control groups that did not have it.[24] Certainly the use of ultrasound in pregnancy, in the words of the U.S. Department of Health and Human Services, "should be limited to situations in which there is an accepted medical reason for the procedure. . . . There is not enough evidence that routine screening benefits either the mother or the fetus."

So, with Doppler monitoring, as with the ultrasound scan, it would seem sensible to keep levels as low as possible, and to agree to be monitored only if there are clinical signs that all may not be well.

GENITAL HERPES

Genital herpes can cause miscarriage and premature birth, and blindness and sometimes death of the newborn baby. It is an infection of the middle and upper-middle classes, not of lower socioeconomic groups. If a woman has had active herpes in pregnancy, a culture is usually taken six weeks before the baby is due and then again two weeks before to check that the disease has cleared. Some obstetricians, however, believe the right point at which to test is once labor has started, and recommend that all women should have this done. Vaginal delivery is usually considered safe if no lesions have appeared in the last eight days. When a culture is positive or there are lesions, a cesarean birth is advised.[25]

If a baby is to be born vaginally, what is important is not whether you have had herpes, but the condition of your vagina *when labor starts,* especially if you have developed herpes for the first time (primary herpes) during this pregnancy. A woman who has had herpes in the past transmits antibodies through the placenta to the baby, so it is very unlikely to get the infection. Even if there is a recurrence of herpes during pregnancy, there is only a 2 to 3 percent chance that the baby will be affected, compared with a 50 percent chance if the mother gets herpes for the first time during pregnancy and has it at the time of birth. This is the real problem: getting an initial attack of herpes when pregnant and having the virus in your genital tract at birth.

Many unnecessary cesarean sections have been performed because women have had a *recurrence* of herpes, when the babies would very likely have already produced antibodies to the virus. However, if you plan to have a vaginal delivery and there is any chance of herpes being present, you should aim for a birth with as little intervention as possible, because a baby can acquire the virus via the puncture site of an electrode clip on the scalp or breaks in the skin made by forceps.[26]

Chemotherapy is given to any baby who may have been exposed to an active lesion, but is only effective before the symptoms are visible. Herpes can also be transmitted after birth from nurses' hands. This is one good reason why you may want to insist that your baby stay by your side all the time instead of going to the hospital nursery.

HORMONE TESTS OR KICK CHARTS?

Because the placenta is the baby's lifeline, obstetricians want to find more effective ways of monitoring its function. One test involves measuring the level of estriol present in the mother's urine. An estrogen hormone produced jointly by the baby's liver and the placenta, estriol is excreted in greater quantities as the baby grows. Since there are usually large fluctuations in the production of estriol at different times of the day, specimens must be taken over a period of twenty-four hours. It is common practice to admit women to the hospital to have the test done, though there is really no reason why a woman should not be able to do it herself if she follows instructions carefully.

As a test, however, the level of urinary estriol is not very reliable in predicting the state of the fetus. For example, a kidney infection can reduce it. In a twin pregnancy it may be lower than anticipated, and even taking drugs such as aspirin or ampicillin can affect the amount present. It is probably unwise to agree to an induction of labor or a cesarean section merely on the evidence of a low estriol level.

Other tests are available and are preferred by some obstetricians: these measure estradiol in the blood and human placental lactogen (HPL), a hormone produced by the placenta itself. Though they are often more accurate, they entail frequent blood tests.

Keeping a daily record of fetal movements is more reliable in assessing fetal well-being than chemical tests.[27] If the placenta is not functioning well enough to provide oxygen and nourishment to the baby, the number and strength of fetal movements decreases. A baby stops moving altogether twelve to forty-eight hours before it dies. Some babies who are perfectly all right, however, have long periods when there are no obvious movements. Perhaps they are just sleeping.

In one research project, of seventy-eight women who felt no movement at all for twelve hours or longer, sixty-six gave birth to babies in good condition one to ten weeks later. Obstetricians decided that the other twelve babies were safer out than in and delivered them. Ten of these were in peak condition at birth and only two were at all stressed.[28]

Obstetricians may prefer chemical hormone tests because they do not really trust women to keep records. Perhaps they suspect that women will cheat, or may not realize when their babies move, or may forget to keep the charts. It is difficult for some doctors to hand over that kind of power to women.

Even though mothers themselves are the best judges of their babies' vitality, and though fetal movement records kept by them are more reliable than other tests, kick charts can cause great anxiety if they are kept only for the purpose of checking whether the baby is still alive. It seems best to limit their use to the very end of pregnancy and only for a part of each day, as a way of getting in touch with the baby and learning its sleeping and waking times and rhythms of activity and rest. Most babies move at least ten times in a twelve-hour period, some much more, but a woman does not notice many of these movements, either because they are slight, or because she is preoccupied and busy doing other things. If you have a good deal of amniotic fluid, it may not be easy to detect separate movements. If you do not have very much, you may feel that the baby is moving all the time. If you are having twins, it will probably feel like a basketful of wriggling puppies.

Some women really enjoy keeping movement charts. Carol said:

> They told me one week I had put on far too much weight and I almost starved myself the next week. Then they told me I had lost weight and they were worried about that. I'd been keeping a kick chart anyway, for fun. It was good to be *doing* something and when the doctor said, "You haven't put on any weight" to be able to say, "Well the baby is kicking a lot. Here is my kick chart."

Other women dislike movement charts. Jane said:

> I never could work out what was a movement and what wasn't, and was always wondering whether I should count it. I got very fraught.

Keeping a Movement Chart

If you would like to make your own movement chart, you will need some graph paper. At the top left of the page write the time you are going to start counting movements, selecting a time when your baby is most active. This is often in the evening. But you may prefer to do it in the morning if you tend to worry at night. Divide the squares by half hours down the page. Across the top of the page write the days of the week and the date. It may look like this:

Time	Aug. 1–7							Aug. 8–14						
	Sun	M	Tu	W	Th	F	Sat	Sun	M	Tu	W	Th	F	Sat
9:30														
10:00														
10:30														
11:00														

Each day you are going to count up to the tenth movement, always starting at the same time. Then darken the square that covers the half hour when you felt the tenth kick. You should feel that kick at about the same time each day, give or take half an hour or so, though the baby may become very quiet in the twelve hours just before you start labor. If you do not notice ten movements in twelve hours, make a note of the number of movements you felt in that time and let your doctor know. Do this if you cannot as a rule feel ten kicks in twelve hours and also if, having previously felt more, you notice now that movements are much less. The obstetrician will probably suggest listening to the fetal heart, perhaps using Doppler ultrasound. The likelihood is that you will be assured that all is well.

The detection of pathology is an important part of an obstetrician's task. But it should not be the only one. What amounts to the constant ringing of alarm bells in pregnancy can sometimes produce the very abnormalities obstetricians are trying to avoid. Even the advice given to a woman in pregnancy can have such an effect. If you are worried about the terrible damage you could do to your baby by smoking or drinking alcohol, it could be that you turn to these things for comfort because you feel so miserable. If you are sick with worry that the baby is not growing properly and you are not putting on enough weight, it is possible that the tension this produces may affect your metabolism and the baby's nutrition in the uterus, bringing about the very condition you are trying to avoid. If you live each day with the threat of raised blood pressure and its dreadful consequences hanging over you, this can actually cause your blood pressure to go up.

Recognition of deviations from the norm is valuable. But an even more important element in the care a pregnant woman receives ought to be support for everything that is going *right*. Many obstetricians have no idea of how to do this. They are expert at tracking down things that might go wrong, but completely at a loss as to how to preserve and enhance the normal.

This is where a woman's confidence and determination to reclaim her body in pregnancy is vital, and is the basis for a positive experience of childbirth.

◆ BEING POSITIVE AND ◆ TAKING ACTION

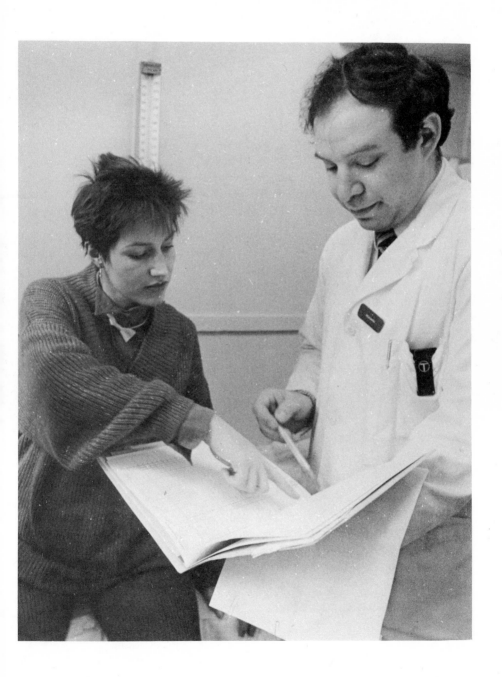

10

◆ SAYING WHAT ◆
YOU WANT

As a pregnant woman you will need special skills to negotiate the
kind of care you believe is right for you, particularly with doctors
who are firmly convinced that they know better. Obstacles may be
put in your way. Information may be hard to obtain. Sometimes you
may feel you are beating your head against a brick wall. To cope
with this, you need to be quietly, firmly, persistently, and imper-
turbably *assertive.*

To be assertive is to make a clear statement about what you think
and want, and set limits on what other people do to you. You appear
confident (even if you don't feel it inside) and can act decisively. Self-
confidence grows out of the practice of assertion.

This is quite different from being aggressive. An aggressor accuses
and attacks other people, intent on destroying the enemy. Aggres-
sion creates adversaries and each encounter is like a battle between
opposing armies, after which you each chalk up the results: win or
lose.

It is incredibly difficult to start suddenly being assertive with
doctors if you are not already accustomed to speaking up and saying
what you want. Yet it is especially important to do this in pregnancy
and childbirth, if only because otherwise they cannot know what you
really want. They may make assumptions about the kind of birth
and the medication you are going to have and the way you want your
baby cared for, because of a set of expectations they have acquired

from medical school, or simply because this is how they have always treated patients in the past. Many women grumble about what happens in the doctor's office or have a quiet weep afterward, but do not make their dissatisfaction clear to the doctor. He can hardly be blamed for not picking up clues as to what a woman wants if her desires are so muted and vague that he can ignore them, or swamp them with his personal style of patient management—whether this is one of fatherly protection, "all pals together," or blind-you-with-science space-age obstetrics—leaving the woman feeling diminished, almost as if she did not exist as a person anymore.

If you get along well with your doctor, you may never have wanted to be assertive, and may question the need for it. It may seem unfriendly to examine what is going on between you and can make you feel very uncomfortable. But how this relationship works is not just a matter of two individuals liking each other, but of how behavior between doctors and patients is *socially* organized.

The relationship between a patient and a doctor is one of unequal power, however kind and friendly the doctor. This is so whether the patient is male or female, but it is especially marked when the doctor is male and the patient a pregnant woman who is anxious to do the best for her baby—particularly if it is her first child.

In Western culture, professionals have largely taken over the role of the priesthood—it is they who now control the dangerous passages through the crises in our lives. They bring their special and often costly expertise both to judge us and to mediate on our behalf with destiny. This occurs in a particularly dramatic way, and one depicted vividly by the media, with heart surgeons, but it also happens, for example, with lawyers, teachers and professors, psychiatrists—and gynecologists and obstetricians. The esoteric knowledge of the professional can be exploited to exert power over a lay person.

The relationship between a woman patient and her doctor is even more lopsided because women are dependent on doctors for the basic control of their reproductive functions: getting and not getting pregnant, staying or not staying pregnant, and childbirth itself.[1] Even a perfectly healthy woman is dependent on them for overseeing her body's normal functions. Gynecologists and obstetricians have become the representatives of women's bodies, with specialist and esoteric information to which women themselves are not supposed to have access. The women's health movement has started to break down these barriers of knowledge, but there are still many women who prefer to trust the doctor and leave all important decisions about their bodies to him.

When a woman and her doctor both accept this pattern, their relationship tends to be friction-free. When either tries to shift the balance toward equality, confusion may result. An obstetrician was talking to me about his feelings of frustration when asking women to make choices between alternatives. Over and over again they would say, "I leave it to you, doctor."

Most obstetricians are as much part of the system, and trapped in it, as their women patients. They sometimes take their superior knowledge so much for granted, and consider the kind of information they have about patients as so much more valid, that medical records appear to have more reality than anything their patients can say about themselves. Ann Oakley reports part of an interview between an obstetrician and his patient in a large, prestigious London teaching hospital.

DOCTOR (reading case notes):   Ah, I see you've got a boy and a girl.

PATIENT: No, two girls.

DOCTOR: Really, are you sure? I thought it said . . . (checks in case notes) Oh no, you are quite right, two girls.[2]

It can be very difficult to start being assertive in medical encounters. It's as if we were preprogrammed to surrender power, abrogate choice, and trust the authority of experts. Taking positive action in our relationships with doctors means that we need to accept what can be a frightening responsibility for the outcome of the choices we make. It also entails acknowledgment of the help and guidance doctors can give us to get the information we want and to weigh the pros and cons of alternative courses of action.

One problem in becoming assertive is that there may be no reward for it. It is unlikely that anyone will say, "Well done," and you may be left feeling that you have committed a grave social error. A doctor who does not usually deal with assertive women may be confused and on the defensive. You will probably notice his discomfort and may be concerned about it. It is vital to prevent yourself from slipping into a passive mode.

Women are brought up to care for others and to be nurturing.

We are taught to be aware of their emotions, to be warm and comforting, and especially to make men feel good about themselves. We smile. We soothe. We admire. There are many good things about this, if men were able to behave in the same way. But they usually do not. They are the executives. They direct and manage. They are too busy with important matters to concern themselves with emotions. Obviously not all men are like this. But most are trained in this style from boyhood. They are taught to dominate, to beat the other guy, and, above all, to be strong.

So feeling sorry for the doctor is a danger signal. Only one step from there and a woman starts to placate, reassure, apologize, and retract whatever she said she wanted. And like the Cheshire cat in *Alice in Wonderland*, in the end only her smile remains. You do not have to make your doctor feel comfortable at the expense of your own discomfort. Though it is important that you recognize and understand them, you are not responsible for his emotions. Let him know what kind of help and support you need. When he gives it, say that you appreciate it. If you feel you are not getting it, tell him how you feel and what you want with greater clarity. If he seems unable to give it, change your doctor. If there is no other doctor but there are midwives, go straight to a midwife. How you go about finding one will depend on where you live. Nurse-midwives are not an accepted part of the health-care system in most parts of North America, and in some places they are not allowed to deliver babies. Midwives who are not nurses often work without the support of the law. Most North American midwives do home births or work in alternative birth centers. Throughout the world as a whole, however, a trained midwife is qualified to give complete care in normal childbirth, without the help of a doctor. She calls in an obstetrician when and if necessary. Childbirth organizations can almost invariably help you find another doctor or a midwife. There is a list of these organizations in Useful Addresses.

It takes courage to move away from the carefully created image of a woman who always understands, sympathizes, and can put herself in another person's place, to the different image of a decisive, go-getting woman who refuses to take no for an answer, who can state her case with verve, stand her ground, and employ a planned strategy to achieve what is important to her. As women, we have been conditioned not to like ourselves this way. But when you are having a baby it is really worth it.

Before you can take control of your pregnancy effectively, you need to discover what your rights are. These are often not clearly defined by law, though childbirth organizations should be able to help you here. You need to know, for example, that it is legal to have a baby at home, though in some parts of North America it may be illegal to have a midwife attend you. In Britain, however, you *must* call a midwife. And if you have your baby in the hospital it may be useful to know, for example, that you can insist on not having your baby separated from you. The baby belongs to you, not to the hospital. There is always a price to pay for not being assertive, and it helps to look at this, in terms both of your feelings at the time and of later consequences. Here is what one woman said:

> In my first labor my nurse told me I needed Demerol [an analgesic drug related to morphine.] I didn't want it so I said so. She said, "You don't realize how painful it's going to get. You can cope now but I shall be scraping you off the walls in two hours' time if you don't have it now." So I let her give me a shot. I think she may have given me another when I was too drowsy to resist at all. When the baby was born, I was so doped that I didn't even remember I wanted to hold her immediately and put her to the breast. I let them put her in a plastic box and wheel her off to the nursery. I bitterly regretted it afterward. I feel I cheated her out of something that was her birthright.

When you are pregnant, there are many obstacles to being assertive. You may be taken by surprise by a decision—to induce labor, for example—and not have considered what you want. Or you may need some information that is difficult to obtain in order to make a decision, and so are left floundering while an obstetrician puts pressure on you to have a cesarean section because your baby is breech, for example, justifying his decision with the blanket statement that "it is safer for the baby." If you don't know what questions to ask, you may feel that you will look silly if you attempt to be assertive, especially if it is your first baby. Suppose, for example, that having read about the advantages of squatting and semisquatting positions for delivery, you ask if you can give birth on the floor in an upright position, but your doctor says that the baby will fall on the floor and may suffer brain damage. Unless you realize that a woman spontaneously bends her knees and crouches down from the standing position as she presses the baby out, and that, with any delivery, someone should be there with hands waiting to cradle the baby's head if necessary, you may feel that you will look foolish in continuing to ask for this. Women are often vulnerable because they are concerned about the effects of their decisions on the baby. That is why emotional blackmail by those who threaten that if you do not obey you can harm the baby is so effective. Get in touch with birth and other consumer organizations that can help you, seek another professional opinion if necessary, and ask whether there have been controlled clinical trials to produce reliable evidence. Then, either stand your ground and refuse the intervention, or, if you can discover a more enlightened obstetrician or midwife, change your caregiver.

Arguing is rarely the most effective way of being assertive. *You do not have to produce arguments at all.* It is enough to say "No, thank you," or "I have decided against it," or "I need time to think about that," or "I want to discuss it with X before I make up my mind," or "I do not give my consent to this," or simply "Please, stop doing that." If you are asked why, you can repeat your statement, add one of the other statements in this list, or say how you feel. Other people may not agree with you, but they must acknowledge the validity of your feelings.

There is great value in repetition—often called the "technique of the broken record." When you repeat yourself quietly but firmly, you cannot be driven off-course. Maggie, for example, has just become pregnant and is choosing her obstetrician. She talked to other women who went to Dr. Z and learned that he insisted on electronic fetal monitoring for each one. Maggie wants to have an active birth and move around in labor. She knows that continuous electronic fetal monitoring usually restricts movement. She wants to know how many of Dr. Z's patients have electronic fetal monitoring.

MAGGIE: Would you tell me the proportion of women you care for who have continuous electronic fetal monitoring? Is it routine for everyone?

DOCTOR: Nothing is routine in my practice, young lady.

MAGGIE: What is the proportion of women who have electronic fetal monitoring?

DOCTOR: It is used when there is a medical indication.

MAGGIE: I see. What proportion of your patients have it?

DOCTOR: You've been reading *books*!

MAGGIE: Yes! And I'd like to know how many of the women you care for actually have continuous electronic fetal monitoring.

DOCTOR (wagging a finger at her):   You can't learn everything from books, you know.

MAGGIE: I'm sure I can't. That's why I'd like to hear what proportion of women receive it.

DOCTOR: I don't have the figures right here.

MAGGIE: I'd appreciate those figures before I make another appointment with you. But could you make an informed guess now?

DOCTOR: Well, I have many high-risk patients with very precious babies. I'd say 85 percent of my patients benefit from monitoring.

MAGGIE: Thank you, Doctor.

The danger point occurred when the doctor accused her of reading books. Maggie could have turned aggressive, retreated shamefacedly into passivity, or started arguing. She did not. She kept cool, agreed with a smile that books cannot teach you everything, and firmly and politely repeated her request. She now knows that at least 85 percent of Dr. Z's patients have continuous electronic fetal monitoring—and thus achieved what she wanted in the interview.

One very difficult thing to deal with is personal criticism. We all have our vulnerable areas. Here again, ideas about what it is to be a woman play a large part. An accusation that you are insensitive, or criticism of the way you care for your children, your personal appearance, or your relationship with your partner may hurt, or at least take the wind out of your sails!

Holly found it difficult to be assertive with her mother, who longed to be needed and involved in every aspect of Holly's pregnancy and birth. She felt there was a risk of her mother taking over the whole experience from her. Her mother worried about her and still thought of her as a little girl who would never be able to look after a baby. Holly decided to be assertive.

MOTHER: I don't want to interfere, dear, but I hope you're not insisting on Bob watching the birth.

HOLLY: Yes, mother. He's looking forward to it. We're reading books together and he's coming to classes with me.

MOTHER: I think you're laying up trouble for your marriage. Your father and I have been talking about it.

HOLLY: Bob feels as strongly as I do that he wants to be there.

MOTHER: You don't understand what birth is like. It's bloody and messy and very, very painful.

HOLLY: No, I agree that I don't really know what it's like. I'm sorry that it was so awful for you, mother, and I know things may be different from how we plan them. We want to be flexible to do whatever we feel is right at the time. But from where we are now, we want to share this experience.

MOTHER: He'll never want to make love to you again!

HOLLY: Bob likes to feel the baby kicking inside me. We feel very close, mother. Much closer than before. And we've made up our minds that this is an important part of the way we express our love for each other. I realize that it wouldn't have suited you and dad, but Bob and I agree that this is how we want it.

Ultimately, assertiveness comes from feeling good about yourself and from a sense of self-worth. Maneuvers designed to express what you do not feel usually seem artificial and strained. But self-confidence can grow from taking the first steps toward being positive and practicing self-assertion.

11

◆ BIRTH PLANS ◆

A birth plan is a concise written statement of your wishes for childbirth and the days following birth, worked out beforehand in consultation with your midwife or doctor. One copy is clipped to your charts; the other you keep yourself. It outlines the kind of care you would like and your general approach to the birth experience. It is not a legal document and has no formal binding power, but it gives everyone an opportunity to understand what is most important to you. It is especially vital to have one if you do not know in advance who will be caring for you in labor, and you may encounter complete strangers. A birth plan should also take into account the care you would like if labor is not straightforward or if there are deviations from the normal—if you have a cesarean section, for example, or if the baby goes to the special-care nursery.

There are those who dismiss birth plans as "shopping lists" that bear no relation to what actually happens in labor, and who say that compiling them gives women false expectations and triggers defensive attitudes, and sometimes outright hostility, in doctors and midwives. This is often true. It happens because we don't yet know how to use birth plans in the most effective way, and there are many misconceptions about what a plan can do and how it should be drawn up.

Let us look first at the arguments against birth plans—arguments any woman might encounter if she raises the question of how she would like the birth of her baby to be:

"Don't plan ahead. Keep an open mind. Wait and see. Then you

won't be disappointed." Superficially praiseworthy—and even caring
—this kind of advice is usually unhelpful. Birth is a major life event,
and for many of us it is also a crisis—even though one we welcome.
It involves often overwhelming emotions, and, especially in the late
first stage, a sense of being a little boat lost in a storm at sea and out
of sight of land, caught in cross-currents, with waves dashing upon
waves. Any woman who avoids thinking through in advance how she
may feel, what she may want to do, and how she wants to be treated
as she goes through this momentous experience is likely to be coerced
and swept along by *other* people's assumptions about what is appropriate, who then make decisions *for* her. Many women who have
suffered a labor like that, even one that was straightforward and
ostensibly easy, look back on it as an ordeal, not only because of the
pain, but because they felt trapped, confused, and totally out of
control—a phrase that occurs again and again in women's birth
accounts. The process of constructing a birth plan—seeking the
information on which to base your plan, considering the advantages
and disadvantages of different courses of action, discussing ideas with
a sympathetic midwife or doctor—can be an important means of
facing up to the reality of birth as a major life event, and of growing
in self-confidence.

Another argument often used against a birth plan is that it sets a
woman up to feel afterward that she has failed. This is often stated
categorically, though there has been no research comparing the birth
experiences and postpartum emotional states of women with birth
plans and those without. This viewpoint derives from an erroneous
idea of what a birth plan is. For it should not be a blueprint of how
labor "ought" to be or how you "should" behave. It is not a description of how a perfect birth would be. Nor is a birth plan a list of
prohibitions to hand to your doctor. It is much more a way of saying
"if such-and-such occurs, then I should like . . ." It is rather like a
plan for a walking or cycling trip—you find out beforehand where
you are going and, since the journey can be modified depending on
how you feel at the time, get information about alternative routes
and consider what action can be taken if the going is tough. It
follows that a birth plan needs to be constructed bearing in mind
that the decision you make in labor may be different from the one
you envisaged yourself making during pregnancy. You may have

thought you would want to eat, for example, and not be able to face food. You may not have wanted an epidural, but find that severe pain leads you to make the decision to have one.

This is not a matter of success or failure, but is an active process of preparation in which you are able to share decision making about your body and retain your autonomy as a human being. One of the problems with some earlier birth education was that it either taught women a brave independence which tended to ignore—and sometimes cut them off from—the help and support a skilled midwife could give, or it instructed women in how to adapt gracefully and gratefully to whatever was done to them, on the grounds that the doctor always knows best. That this is changing now, and that women and midwives are learning how to work together constructively, is at least partly attributable to the new emphasis on prenatal discussion which explores values important to the pregnant woman and acknowledges her right to accept responsibility for an experience in which she is an active birthgiver rather than a passive patient.

Another accusation that may be leveled against a woman who wishes to make a birth plan is that she is thinking only of herself and her own emotional satisfaction, and is ignoring the baby. Obstetricians often consider themselves guardians of the fetus and believe the woman incapable, by reason of her sex, of making rational decisions and, because of a heightened emotional state in pregnancy, prone to flout safety. One obstetrician has pronounced that pregnant women should never be allowed to make or even to share in any decisions about their care because they are "not only emotionally unstable, they are intensely egocentric. . . . In this egocentric state, encouragement to participate can result in a fierce demand to dictate."[1] Here again, there is no research that demonstrates obstetricians are more concerned about babies than the babies' mothers.

The implication is that the mother's and the baby's needs are quite separate and that the woman's physical and emotional well-being has nothing to do with the baby's welfare. Enough is understood now about the feto-maternal circulation to know that the fear that produces hyperventilation can reduce the fetal oxygen supply, and that an excess of catecholamines (hormones that are overproduced in situations of acute or continuing stress) can result not only in prolonged labor, but, because they pass through the placenta into the baby's bloodstream, may also lead to a reduction in the baby's oxygen supply.[2] A woman in labor is not merely a contracting uterus, as she tends to be described in some obstetric textbooks. Nor is the baby only "the passenger." The mother and the child are in partnership.

Another argument against birth plans is that they destroy, or do not permit to develop, a relationship between doctor and patient based on trust. (This means that the patient trusts her doctor—not, as far as I can gather, the other way around.) "Trust," as Michael Klein rightly points out, "can't be mandated by contract."[3] It is true that you need to have a good working relationship with whoever is caring for you. This cannot be guaranteed by rules and regulations, whether they are laid down by the doctor or by you. But is it really a matter of trusting the doctor, or rather of achieving a partnership in which there is mutual respect? A birth plan can be one expression of a good working relationship between equal partners, both knowing what the task entails, bringing their own skills, recognizing those which the other person has, and knowing their limits. This is quite different from a woman having unquestioning trust in her doctor, and from the mystique that blankets a relationship in which the doctor assumes an almost priestlike role.

Caregivers are sometimes very anxious about birth plans. You may find you need to reassure them about why you want to make one. You can explain that you are flexible, will accept intervention if you consider it necessary, and are glad to have advice (even if your conclusions may be different from those your doctor would come to).

Of course there will be occasions when a woman will make a decision the obstetrician or midwife considers wrong, or one that later proves to be wrong: she elects to have an epidural and has an otherwise unnecessary forceps delivery; or she decides on home birth and has to be transferred to the hospital during labor; or she refuses the offer of an episiotomy and has a third-degree tear; or she declines continuous electronic fetal monitoring—and, tragically, the baby dies. It is a very common psychological response in such situations to blame someone else. The woman blames her caregivers. The obstetrician blames the woman—and often the midwife, too.

When a woman accepts responsibility for a decision, she also accepts responsibility for the outcome of that decision, and it cannot be shifted to the obstetrician. This is one reason why the making of birth plans needs careful discussion about the degree of responsibility that is sought and the way in which it is to be shared between the woman giving birth and those helping her. It also means that she must have honest information, in terms she can understand.

In practice many women find that they are subjected to crude emotional blackmail. A woman is threatened, for example, that if she does not "toe the line" and deliver in the hospital, or agree to induction because she has reached forty-two weeks, she is risking the baby's life. (Home birth and induction are both subjects of a good deal of obstetric bullying.) A particular decision may introduce an unacceptable risk to the baby, and it is for the woman to consider the pros and cons of this in the light of her own beliefs and values. Ultimately, this is not a medical but a moral decision. No one else has the right to take that responsibility from her if she makes the decision to accept it.

So the main issue concerning birth plans is that of responsibility and control. Are doctors willing to return to women the control of their bodies in childbirth? Are women confident enough to accept responsibility for their bodies and for their babies?

In Britain hospitals are increasingly designing their own formal birth plans and asking women to state their preferences in advance. In some ways this is a sign of progress in communication and of a genuine effort to create a better environment for birth. But many hospital birth plans tend to ignore or to trivialize these fundamental questions of responsibility and control. They provide instead a framework within which selected choices are invited: "Do you want to wear your own nightie or a hospital gown?" Or they request approval for a nowadays customary procedure: "Do you want to hold your baby immediately after birth? Please check the appropriate box." Birth plans can be employed merely as a facade for the insidious institutional control of the whole birth process.

The concept of consumer choice is useful for women having babies when it makes us think about our priorities and compare what we want with the services offered. But it can be misleading when it suggests that we have a choice when there is really none but the most trivial, or when it gives an entirely false impression of the degree of courage and initiative women have to find if, in making their own informed decisions, they insist on choosing something not already on the set "menu" presented by the medical system.

As hospitals come to treat childbearing women as "consumers," there is a danger that the ethics, the management style, and even the advertising techniques of competitive business will be introduced, and birth plans run the risk of being used as a softening-up treatment and a sweetener to obtain what the drug companies call "patient cooperation," conditioning women to put their trust in the professionals who control the birth place.

The creation of a birth plan can be an educational process for all concerned. It stimulates dialogue with those caring for you and prepares the way for a working partnership in which they understand your priorities and are aware of your hopes and fears. It brings out into the open exactly what you expect of your birth companion, whether this is your partner or someone else of your choice, and helps you to talk together about what you want and expect of each other. And it enables you to focus on your role in birth in a positive way, triggering an active search for more information and a deeper understanding of the whole experience.

When you reach the end of this book, you will have a lot of ideas on which to base your own birth plan. But even at this point, you can begin to think about the more general issues, such as where you want to give birth, who you want to attend you, and who else you would like to be with you to share the experience.

YOUR BIRTH COMPANION

One important issue to consider is the person you want to be with you to share the experience.

The father of your baby may be your best birth companion. A woman often says that it was his hands she sought, his strength on which she relied, and even that she does not know how she could have gone through it without him. For many couples it is a peak experience in their lives, and one they would not have missed sharing together for the world. Yet sometimes another woman best fills that role, and the mother should have the freedom to choose who she has with her in labor, and whether it is just one person or several.

Discuss everything in your plan with whoever is going to be your birth companion. This person needs to understand not only what you want but the *way you think* about these subjects, so that you can relax, sure that if necessary he or she will say, "Hold on! Can you ask her about this first?" or "I think she wanted to manage without that," or "I know she'd like you to help her."

There have been various studies that show the importance of a birth companion, someone concerned exclusively with supporting the woman in labor, not only because of the psychological benefits but also because of how this affects physiological function, helps the birth process unfold more naturally, leads to less intervention, and increases the physical well-being of both mother and baby.[4] In Latin American countries, fathers are rarely present, so it was decided to investigate the effect of having a woman companion, not specially trained, befriend each woman laboring in a Guatemalan hospital. One interesting aspect of this study was that the women did not even know their companions beforehand. Even so, their friendship had a remarkable effect. Labors were much shorter; there were twice as many obstetric interventions (including oxytocin augmentation of uterine action and cesarean birth) in the labors of mothers who had no companion, and twice as many complications during labor (including meconium staining and fetal distress). When she had a companion, the mother responded more positively to the sight of her newborn baby and cuddled and talked to it more in the first hour after birth. Fewer babies needed to be brought back to the hospital in the first six months of life.

So there is a strong case to be made for having a companion with you in labor, even if this is not the father of the baby; and if he does not seem to be the right person to give you the best emotional support, or is unable to be with you, you may choose to have someone else, or another woman companion as well. Some women feel support is best when they have a group of people to whom they feel close, but unless you are very sure that this is what you want, it is probably wise to limit the number of people around you, if only because you need to focus on your own experience, not theirs, and should not feel that you are having to put on a performance for them.

Your Other Children

In traditional cultures, children are often present during birth. A Zulu chief explained to me that it is an important part of children's education about the precious nature of life to witness both birth and death. When I was doing anthropological research in Jamaica, I saw children running in and out of the room during labor or curling up in bed beside their mother. In Mexico and other parts of Latin America, the other women present at the birth, helping and encouraging, often have their own children with them.[5]

In the same way that children see the preparation of food and cooking going on around them, and are aware of the skills and rhythms of household tasks, so in Third World cultures they see the preparation for birth and the heavy work of labor and become aware of the skills and rhythms in the group of women attending a birth. This probably results in a more realistic and informed attitude about

More parents. Live in next street. Baby of same age

Another parent. We swap things, babysit for each other

Family doctor

Health Visitor

Occasional cleaning lady, baby minder. Straightforward because I pay her

Her son. Runs errands, takes messages, plays with the baby

SUPPORT GROUP

birth-giving than that of many young women and men who grow up knowing nothing about birth except what they have read in books and magazines or seen in the occasional film. Though there has been little systematic study and follow-up of children present at birth, such evidence that does exist suggests that this is usually a positive experience for them.[6]

Robbie had seven people with her for Jason's birth: her husband Robert, two midwives, a male friend who took photographs, the godfather-to-be, another woman friend and her three-year-old daughter, and Robbie's own four-year-old, Peyton. She had previously had a cesarean section for "failure to progress" and was deter-

Fellow parents who live next door. We have their 2-year-old to stay if they go out, and ours loves to stay with them at night

My mother does all the things that I hate doing. I daren't argue about it

The little person this is all about

Me with my support plan

Our 2-year-old. Loves playing with the baby. 'Sings' to her, but 10 minutes is enough

Teenager. Takes the baby for a walk after school in good weather. Amuses her at home in early evening while I concentrate on the toddler

Husband. Super cook and washer-up. Takes over completely when I need rest

mined to give birth vaginally, at home if possible. In Britain no obstetrician would have assumed that she needed a cesarean the second time around, but she was in the United States where most obstetricians take it for granted that once a cesarean, always a cesarean. So if she wanted an autonomous birth, her only option was to labor at home and hope that she did not need to go to the hospital.

The labor lasted three days, during which she walked, squatted, rocked by the fire, crouched, knelt, slept when contractions stopped, ate, sang, danced, lay in a hot tub "in silent bliss," and sometimes at night walked around outside and counted the stars. She valued having friends and her older child with her to share the experience:

> Together we proceeded to perform the incredible feat of pushing out a ten-pound baby. One friend held the camera, the midwives held my legs and my perineum, another friend held the watch, another the oxygen mask and Peyton held her doll and yelled, "Come quick! The baby's head is coming!"

Now that's support!

THE PLACE OF BIRTH

One of the biggest decisions you must make is *where* to have your baby. This does not have to be the conventional hospital setting. In most places there are other options, and you may want to explore alternatives to the hospital. Everything else that happens, and the relationship you have with those caring for you, is affected by your choice of birth place.

Birth at home

You may be thinking of having your baby at home. This means that you will be cared for by a midwife, though in many countries a family practitioner may attend you, too. The pros and cons of home birth vary in different areas according to back-up services available, and, of course, the skills and personalities of the individual midwife and doctor. But in general terms, planned home birth, as distinct from accidental out-of-hospital birth, is safe for a healthy woman whose pregnancy has been straightforward. British studies show a perinatal mortality (stillborn babies and those who die shortly after birth) of between 4 and 5 per 1,000. The babies who die are usually those who suffer from congenital handicaps. In Britain and North America this perinatal mortality rate is half or less than half that of babies born in a hospital. It is comparable to the perinatal mortality rate in Scandinavian countries and the Netherlands, where birth is safer than anywhere else in the world.[7]

Planned home births produced the smallest proportion of low-birthweight babies. In a British study, 2.5 percent of home-birth babies weighed less than 2,500 grams (5½ pounds), compared with 18 percent delivered in a hospital.[8] Babies born at home usually start life healthy and vigorous. It is possible that more babies would survive birth if hospitals had never taken over childbirth.[9]

Many obstetricians are implacably opposed to home birth, however. It is true, as they usually point out, that many more mothers and babies survive childbirth today than in the bad old days when nearly every woman had her babies at home. But when two statistical trends occur at the same time, this does not prove that one is the cause of the other. A perinatal epidemiologist has pointed out that many more people have TV sets than fifty years ago, when perinatal mortality rates were higher. But no one suggests that the rise in TV ownership has caused the reduction in the perinatal mortality rate.[10] Many changes have occurred over the last fifty years, all of which have contributed to better social conditions, improvements in women's health, and safer childbirth: smaller families, readily available contraception, abortion when a severely handicapped fetus is diagnosed, more awareness of the effects of pollution—and its reduction in many areas—and increased public education about health. In Britain the perinatal mortality rate started to decline during the Second World War. This was well before most women had their babies in a hospital and before the introduction of modern technology such as electronic fetal monitoring. It was a time when women were cared for by midwives, rather than doctors, many of whom were away in the armed forces, and when a system of food rationing, and the distribution of welfare orange juice, vitamins and milk, made available to the vast majority of people, and to pregnant women in particular, better and more wholesome nutrition than they had ever had before.

Since 1973 in Britain, as a consequence of a policy of hospitaliza-

tion for all (about which women were never consulted), the proportion of out-of-hospital births that are accidental and unplanned has
become larger. As a result, the mortality rate for home births appears
to have risen compared with the mortality rates for hospital births.
However, the following are classified as home births: deliveries in
taxis; the concealed births of babies to frightened teenagers, some of
whom did not even know they were pregnant; births following illegal
late abortions; those resulting from massive and sudden hemorrhage;
and premature delivery of babies born long before a woman expected
to go into labor. These *unplanned* (it might be better to call them
"uncared-for") births skew the statistics and result in uninformed
generalizations about the risk of home birth.[11]

Holland still has a relatively large proportion of home births, 34.7
percent in 1981, for example. The perinatal mortality for home
births there was 3 per 1,000 in 1979. One study revealed that
women who had home births experienced "significantly fewer complications during pregnancy, delivery or puerperium than among
those who had their babies in hospital. Morbidity was also lower
amongst babies born at home." The study suggests that it is a
responsible decision for a normal healthy women given the right
kind of antenatal supervision to have her baby at home.[12]

If you decide that you want to give birth at home, it may be
difficult to find a doctor who will agree to it. Doctors have most or
all of their training in hospitals. Many have never seen a truly natural
birth without any intervention, and the absence of an institutional
support system arouses anxiety. They are also often concerned about
the attitudes of colleagues and of those higher up in the medical
hierarchy. Even British general practitioners who have done home
births in the past are increasingly nervous about agreeing to them,
because they feel they are out of practice. In the United States,
physicians worry about malpractice insurance and possible litigation
if things go wrong. Medical insurance companies refuse to insure a
family practitioner who does home births, and some refuse to insure
any doctor who works with a midwife. So having a baby at home
may mean that you have to forget about doctors and choose a midwife. As already mentioned, she may be able to call on a doctor if
necessary, but because doctors are so frightened of home birth, this
may not be possible.

An overwhelming advantage of home birth is that you control the territory in which birth takes place, and those helping you are guests in your home. You can move around just as you want, eat and drink, take a bath, or go out for a walk—do whatever you feel like doing. You can have just your partner and the midwife with you, or a group of friends and family to whom you feel especially close, without having to ask permission. Your other children can be there, too, and because it is home, can go in and out of the room freely. As one woman explained:

> Last time, the hospital atmosphere was very unsupportive. There were a load of routines and different kinds of interference which were never explained and I didn't have any choice about it. I'd already labored happily six hours at home, but from the moment I stepped inside that hospital I became a patient. Labor turned into an ordeal. Next time I want to be able to do whatever I feel like—eat when I want, labor in the bath, have the room dark, and groan and moan and yell and not be told over and over again that I need an epidural.

For two other women the reasons they chose home births were slightly different. One said:

> I chose home birth mainly because it was a way I could get a VBAC [vaginal birth after a previous cesarean section]. No doctor in the area where I live would consider it. I feel, too, that birth should be a normal part of family life, and siblings are not allowed in the case rooms at either of the hospitals here.

The other woman focused mainly on the baby's birth experience.

> I am concerned to make it as good as I can for the baby. The decisive thing was that I don't want my baby taken away from me at all, not even for a pediatric check or anything. I don't want any kind of drug going through the cord into the baby either, or in my breast milk afterwards. I'd like the delivery to be gentle and the baby always to be handled lovingly. The only way I can get that in this city is at home.

The disadvantages of home birth are that it may be difficult to find a doctor or midwife to attend you and even if you do you may be uncertain of his or her skills. In the United States and Canada, a midwife may have no medical backup, a disadvantage if problems develop. You cannot have an epidural at home, and since this is the most effective form of pain relief, it is vital that you have other nonpharmacological ways of handling pain. Similarly, at home you cannot have a cesarean section. If your labor is prolonged, or the baby's heart rate shows it is under special stress, or you bleed heavily afterward, you have to be moved to a hospital. Rarely—but it does happen sometimes—a baby has to be transported to a special-care nursery.

For more about home birth consult the Further Reading section at the end of the book or contact the home birth organizations listed under Useful Addresses.

♦ ♦ ♦ Think through the pros and cons of home birth from your own point of view. Make a note of the questions you would like to ask to get further information. If you decide that you want to give birth at home, work out a strategy for achieving this. ♦ ♦ ♦

Birth Centers and Birthing Rooms

A birth center is rather like a small hospital, but one that does births only. As a general rule, it encourages natural birth without medical intervention, has a warm, homey atmosphere and offers family-centered care based on the principle that birth is not a medical procedure but a natural physiological process in which a woman benefits from loving human support. A birthing room is a labor-delivery room within a hospital in which the same principles of care apply.

Birth centers are of two main types, either part of a larger hospital or separate. Those outside hospitals may be within the medical system. Or they may be completely outside that system, having grown out of community-based self-help movements or the initiatives of independent midwives.

Because birth centers are for natural births only, there may be very careful screening before a woman is admitted to one. Any whisper of difficulties and she is transferred to a hospital. Some birth centers won't take women over thirty-five, or even those having a first baby, for example. Many are not happy about accepting a woman who smokes during pregnancy.

In those birth centers that are not in hospitals a woman must go to the hospital if there are complications. Some midwives—including most nurse-midwives—have hospital privileges or work with a doctor who has them. Others do not.

In Britain small maternity units corresponding to birth centers are called general practitioner hospitals. Community midwives work in such hospitals and GPs can send their patients to them, though women believed to be at special risk have to go to a consultant unit, which is staffed by midwives who work in a team with obstetricians.

In a birth center a woman usually labors and delivers in the same room. This tends to look like a motel bedroom, but she can bring her own cassette tape recorder, pictures, and other familiar objects she wants to have around her. Many of the rooms are quite cozy, with curtains, patterned wallpaper, hanging plants, a rocking chair, a carpet on the floor, and soft lighting. The bed is usually the kind that can be turned into a delivery table, but is more often used to allow the woman to get into a semiupright position with good back support and something to hold on to.

For women who have no serious problems in pregnancy, and who therefore do not need a high level of sophisticated care, births in this type of maternity unit—even when they are far from a hospital—are as safe as in units with a great deal of technological equipment for obstetric intervention. Since most GP units are an integral part of the National Health Service in Britain, much of the research has been done there.[13]

A midwife and family doctor actually provide better care for low-risk women than specialized obstetricians. In a system with midwife care and home visits, women have fewer inductions, are less likely to be admitted in false labor, have less need of drugs for pain relief (and are more likely to have none at all), have fewer forceps deliveries, and are less likely to have a perineal wound. Their babies tend to start to breathe earlier than those born in high-tech units and breast-feeding tends to be more successful.[14]

The idea behind hospital-based birth centers and birthing rooms is that there should be quick and easy access to obstetric skills and equipment when necessary. The problem is that in birth centers in large hospitals the transfer rate tends to be very high, mostly on the principle of "just in case." Even though a woman may have gotten through the fine mesh of the screening process to be admitted to the birth center in the first place, there is a strong probability that she will be "wheeled down the hall." In some hospitals, the caregivers she has chosen can stay with her. In others, a different staff takes over at this point. From a woman's point of view, it is obviously much better if she has the same people with her throughout. On the other hand, when it is simple for the staff to transfer a woman to high-tech care—or even introduce it into the birthing room itself— while they still remain in charge, this is likely to happen the moment the midwife or doctor feels anxious that the labor is going on a long time, there is a lull in the activity of the uterus, or the baby is not lying in a perfect position.

So one of the things you will probably want to find out if you are interested in a birth center or birthing room within a hospital is the policy that controls the care given there. Is there a time limit on the first stage of labor, so that if dilation progresses slowly, or you come to a point when nothing seems to be happening, you are automatically moved? And will this in turn mean that you encounter a sudden staff change and have to cope with strangers just when everything seems to be going wrong? Or is there a flexible policy that takes into consideration a variety of labor patterns which do not all conform to the textbook norm? If the staff has access to high-tech intervention, such as the kind of electronic fetal monitoring that entails putting a clip on the baby's scalp, intravenous drips that stimulate the uterus, and epidural anesthesia, in what percentage of women using the center or room are these techniques employed? The answer to this question, if it is accurate, will give you a clear idea of the amount of intervention a woman hoping for a natural birth can anticipate. If a woman is transferred to another part of the hospital when there appear to be deviations from the normal, can her midwife continue to attend her, even if responsibility is taken over by the high-tech team?

If a hospital has only a few birthing rooms (or only one), you may find that when you happen to be in labor they are already occupied and you are then forced to use the ordinary labor and delivery rooms. This does not matter a bit if the only difference between the birthing rooms and the rest of the hospital is one of interior decoration. It matters a lot if hospital policy and the attitudes of your caregivers are different.

In some hospitals the attitudes and atmosphere of the birthing rooms or birth center have permeated the rest of the maternity ward, changed practice—reducing intervention, substituting emotional support in place of pain-killing drugs, and lowering rates of episiotomy and forceps delivery. In fact, in some British hospitals midwives would rather *not* have special birthing rooms because they believe changes need to take place throughout the hospital, and that they should not be limited to those women who want natural birth and are classified as low-risk.

You cannot tell for sure whether a hospital has the atmosphere you are seeking simply from the presence of birthing rooms. Decor and furnishings are an insufficient guide to attitudes. There are hospitals where women are offered flowery curtains, patchwork quilts, a special birthing bed or chair, and soft music, but where all this is merely a facade for interventionist obstetric practice. In a commercial system, where medical care is another commodity competing in the open market, some hospitals provide these pleasant rooms to persuade women not to have their babies at home, in out-of-hospital birthing centers, or in rival hospitals. Such competition may be a force for change, but it can also result in mere window dressing, with no real change in attitudes.

♦ ♦ ♦ Make a note of the questions you want to ask hospital administrators about the facilities available in your area. It is a good idea to jot down the actual phrases you want to use and, in case replies are vague, any follow-up questions aimed at getting more specific answers.

You will probably want to talk to women who have had babies in these places, too. Decide what you want to focus on in your discussions with them and make a note of these subjects. ♦ ♦ ♦

Here are some women's reports on the birthing rooms and birth centers they were considering.

DEE (in the Midwest)

The hospital has a birthing room. You can have up to four people with you, including your other children. If you want your children there, they must have an adult to look after them, and this must be someone other than your support person. They don't usually do shaves and enemas. You can walk around during labor and use the shower. Demerol is given if drugs for pain relief are needed, but no epidural is available. Intravenous drips, oxytocin, electronic fetal monitoring, and forceps are not used. After the birth, my partner could stay for up to twenty-four hours. However, very few births take place in the birthing room—last year only 3 percent of all vaginal births.

FRANKIE (in California)

This is a community-based birth center in which lay midwives work. Most of those having their babies there are very poor Mexican women. The birth center offers a package of prenatal care, nutritional counseling, care during birth, and contraceptive advice. There isn't any emergency equipment to deal with complications. It is an ordinary house, with small birthing rooms, and there are usually not more than one or two women in labor at the same time. They are encouraged to move around in labor and can give birth in any position they like. The baby's father, other children, and relatives and friends can be there for the birth.

KATY (in London)

The hospital has a new birthing room which is very beautifully equipped and looks luxurious. There is TV, stereo, a bidet, indirect lighting, a rocking cradle. Electronic fetal monitoring is used for about twenty minutes after you are admitted and then for fifteen minutes every hour. You may have an intravenous drip in your arm. The baby's father or one other person can be with you. You can walk around when the fetal monitor is not being used. Analgesia is often given, but epidurals are not done in this room. The couple can have up to two hours with their baby after the birth.

BIRTH CHAIRS AND BEDS

Another option that may be available is a special birth chair or birthing bed. This is often rather like a dentist's chair and allows you to be in an upright position for delivery—if it is tilted at the right angle or has a squatting bar in place at the time. There is, however, no question of completely free movement, and you are more or less fixed and immobilized in it. Still, it is a great advance on the narrow, cold slab of the delivery table with its stirrups (in which a woman's legs are fixed wide apart) and its hand and shoulder restraints. In fact, most of these chairs and beds have stirrups too, but you don't usually see them when taken on a conducted tour. The firms manufacturing them are careful to point out that they can be quickly adapted to enable the staff to do obstetric operations and perform a wide range of maneuvers. At least one birthing chair also has shoulder restraints, so that the woman is firmly fixed in a position and cannot move away from the obstetrician's hands if a painful intervention is done.

Many women who have used birth chairs, especially if they had to lie on a delivery table for a previous birth, say that it made it much easier to push the baby out. They were more comfortable and it was good to be face-to-face with those caring for them, rather than lying on their backs staring up at powerful lights.

Most birth chairs are designed for the mother to sit, well supported, legs apart and knees bent. The mechanism to change the angle and the position of the footrests may be under her own control, but is often constructed to be controlled by attendants. If a chair is available and you think that you will want to adjust it yourself, look to see if you will be able to reach the control buttons.

Some chairs are very narrow so that it is difficult to spread yourself and to tilt your pelvis, for example, to adopt a position in which one knee is bent while the other leg is extended. It can also be hard to straighten your legs, which you may want to do in between pushes. If you get a chance, it is a good idea not only to look at what is available, but actually to get on it and find out how it feels as you act through part of the second stage of labor. Imagine that you have a bad backache, or that you are very uncomfortable with the baby's head like a huge melon pressing against your anus, and think how

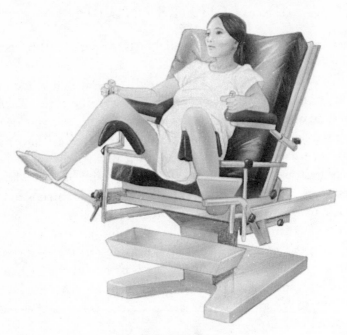

A Birth Chair

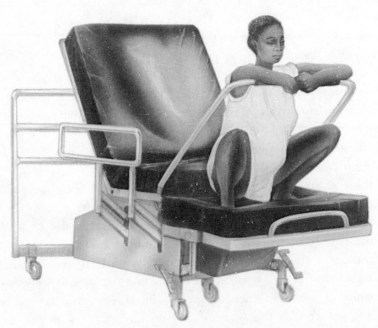

A Birth Chair with Squatting Bar

you may want to move then. Or imagine you have cramp in your leg and see if it is easy to extend your leg and foot, press your heel down on the foot support, and rub your calf with one hand. Check also whether you are able to bend forward easily, rounding your lower back, to see the top of your baby's head and stroke it if you wish. Some chairs are designed so that it is difficult to move your back freely—the molded plastic fixes you in one position. There is one well-known chair in which it is impossible to rock your pelvis unless you press your feet into the footrests and stand up, gripping the sides of the chair. Two obstetricians have reported that women who are in birth chairs for a long time tend to have edema of the vulva, a condition they rarely met before birth chairs were used.[15] They claim that this necessitates a large episiotomy, which heals poorly. So they insist on a woman being horizontal while she pushes—thus negating the whole idea of the birth chair—that a woman should be upright, in a physiologically correct and comfortable position. There have also been reports of heavy bleeding. Both edema and bleeding result from the immobility of the pelvis when the woman's position is fixed, with her buttocks and thighs pressed against a hard, unyielding surface. So it is important to be free to move.

You should also investigate the material covering the chair. Does it feel pleasant to the skin? Many women get very hot in the second stage of labor. Will the material feel comfortable if you are already hot? Is it slippery? Find out whether your body will be in direct contact with it, or whether a sheet, a towel, or a pillow can be used as well.

A birth chair or bed is usually placed under a bright light for delivery. It is distressing for a woman to have a light shining in her eyes throughout the second stage. Will it be possible to give birth in soft light, or at least to have a bright light only on your perineum? Ask to see how the lighting can be modified.

♦♦♦ If you will have the choice of using a birth chair or bed, make a checklist in your notebook. These are some of the items you may want to cover.

♦ Does it permit an upright position?

♦ Can I get into a squatting position if I wish?

- Is there freedom for pelvic movement?

- Is there comfortable support for the back?

- Is there something at the right height and angle to hold on to while in different positions?

- Are the controls in a place where I can reach them and operate them easily?

- Does it permit a variety of angles for back and leg support?

- How is the texture of material used for covering?

- Where is the lighting? Can it be modified? ♦ ♦ ♦

There may be other equipment you would like better than a chair or bed. If it is not provided by the hospital, you may be able to bring it in yourself.

A large beanbag chair or floor cushion can be comfortable to sit up against or to lean forward onto in a kneeling position if you have a backache. You can use it either on a bed or on the floor.

A low stool gives support for a squatting position. It can be the kind used by a small child to reach the sink, or the sort of stool the hospital provides to climb on to a high bed or delivery table. Or it may be a special birth stool, shaped like a horseshoe or boomerang, similar to those used by midwives throughout the Middle Ages. Some of these have a back. They limit mobility of the pelvis, and some are so high that you cannot squat. Choose one that does not slip on a tiled floor; rubber knobs over the feet can make it more stable. A stool should not be used on a delivery table. You don't feel safe and you could fall.

If you choose a stool, your support person can sit behind you on a higher chair, legs apart, cradling you against his or her body. Or you can have a big cushion or a wall behind you so that you can lean back between contractions.

A towel or sheet knotted to any strong bar, so that you can pull on it from a squatting position, may feel right. Fifty years ago women often gave birth pulling on a strip of material tied to a door or a bedpost. Or you can sit on a bucket with a towel fold on the

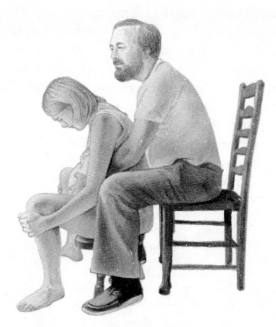

BIRTH STOOL WITH SUPPORT PERSON

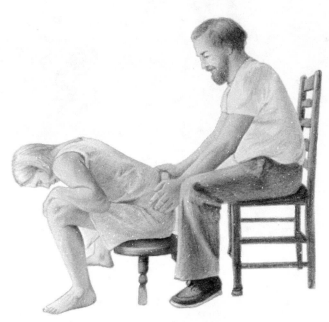

ANOTHER POSITION USING A BIRTH STOOL

rim under your buttocks. Many women find it easiest to push when they are sitting on the toilet, and this position is similar.

In the second stage of labor, a woman often feels she needs to get her feet planted firmly on the floor. She feels most secure this way and physiological coordination comes most naturally. She may want to grip a piece of furniture that is handy or hold on to the person who is helping her. In many British hospitals women can now give birth on a sterile sheet on the floor. Sometimes this is placed over a mattress. In this way the woman is not fixed in one position. She can move freely, changing position whenever she wants. The midwife

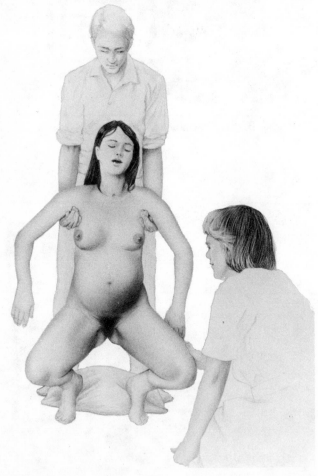

SUPPORTED SQUATTING POSITION FOR THE SECOND STAGE OF LABOR

kneels or sits beside her and delivers the baby from the front, back or side, as the mother wishes.

Freedom of movement is important to give the best chance of a spontaneous vaginal delivery, especially if labor is difficult and the second stage long and drawn out, with the baby in an awkward position, or with a tight fit between the baby's head and the maternal pelvis.

Expensive equipment is not necessary for comfort in childbirth. Nowadays, an elaborate birth chair is often provided as if it somehow guaranteed the right conditions for a natural birth. It doesn't. Some-

VARIATION OF SUPPORTED SQUATTING POSITION

times it seems to be available mainly to deflect any further questions women may have about natural birth. It's as if the hospital is saying: "Look at the amount of money we have spent to provide the latest model in birth chairs. This is evidence that we encourage women to give birth naturally. What else can you want?" The answer to that is *freedom of movement*. Most hospitals have a very long way to go before this is achieved.

◆ RIPE WITH CHILD ◆

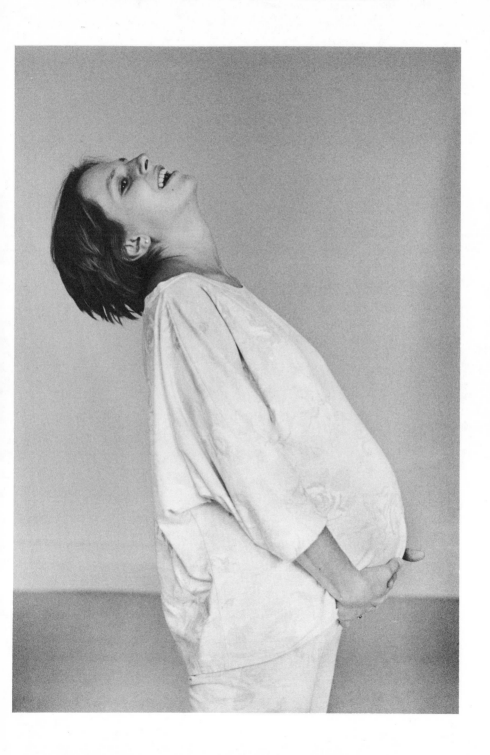

12

◆ GETTING IN TOUCH ◆ WITH YOUR BABY

You may alternate between imagining your baby in every detail and thinking that a mass of moving limbs can't possibly be a baby at all: it must be an octopus or a basket of kittens. On quiet days it may feel like an awkward bump, or you may even forget all about it. Then there is a sudden burst of activity and you are fully aware that there is a living being there waiting to burst into the world.

Pregnancy is a time not only for getting ready for childbirth but also for preparing to be a mother, with all the powerful emotions this involves. Some women prefer to leave these emotions to take care of themselves.

I'm too busy for introspection. I hope I'll be an adequate mother. But with the heavy load of teaching I'm doing this year there is no time now.

Other women enjoy this emotional journey to motherhood.

I don't think I could ever be a "Madonna mother," calm and tender all the time. But I'm sure I can be a stimulating mother and the baby will be fascinating to watch grow and develop. Sometimes I panic that I have no maternal instinct. Then the baby moves, I put my hand on the bump and it feels magical and I realize I shan't have to struggle to produce the right emotions. They're all there!

A woman needs time to get in touch with her baby and with her changing self, to dream and let fantasies play around the idea of the coming baby. This is not self-indulgence, nor is it time wasted. It is an important part of preparing for your new relationship with another human being.

LIFE BEFORE BIRTH

The ancient Chinese dated an individual life from nine months before birth. Today, a new science of perinatal psychology is developing which explores the influences on a baby that can operate prenatally, during birth, and immediately following delivery.

To some women this may seem another burden placed on them, a duty to make contact with the fetus, concentrate on it, and consider its needs—at the expense of their own. This imposes additional stress on pregnancies which are often stressful anyway. A woman has her own needs, her own priorities and rights, and they are not all subsumed by the fact that she is going to have a baby. This is one compelling reason why the exercise of choice about what she does in pregnancy is vital.

On the other hand, increased awareness of the baby inside, making contact with it, is for some women an enhancement of pregnancy.

It's one of the things I enjoy about being pregnant—feeling the baby move and talking to it. It's a different rhythm of living. Usually it's all rush and go. I've calmed down. I'm turned inward.

Even for a woman who can't afford time to slow down—who is, for example, especially busy in her job, perhaps trying to clear the decks in order to take maternity leave—a break in her hectic life when she focuses on the baby can be refreshing and restful. For some women that break provides a luxurious interlude in the last three months of pregnancy.

The fetus cannot respond to stimuli until it has developed a nervous system which makes this possible. Conciousness demands something else again: the nerve pathways that allow the cerebral cortex (the part of the brain necessary for thought) to function are not connected till after the beginning of the twenty-eighth week of pregnancy (dating it from the first day of the mother's last period).[1]

Reflex activities, however, start long before that (see table 12). They occur spontaneously and can also be stimulated by touching the fetus. As early as thirteen weeks the fetus moves its tongue and can swallow. In another week lip movements begin and it is capable of facial expressions.

From about ten weeks the amniotic fluid in which the fetus is lying flows into its open mouth and by at least fifteen weeks it can distinguish different tastes. Amniotic fluid contains traces of sugar, various acids, protein, mineral salts, and fat.[2] Taste preferences seem to be already established in the uterus, since studies done with newborn babies reveal that they suck more quickly when fed sweet fluids and sucking is slower and they grimace when fed fluids containing quinine or citric acid.[3] Babies also prefer sweet to plain water. Not only do they suck more strongly, but their heart rates speed up.[4] They like plain water better than salt water and are very quick to notice salt, even in low concentrations.[5]

What the Baby Can Hear

Already by ten weeks the vestibular (balancing) system is functioning, and the fetus can orient itself in space. In the mid-1970s medical researchers examining the results of studies of fetal response to sound concluded: "It is clear that long before birth, the fetus can hear and respond to sound and that the uterus is not a soundproof chamber."[6] Since that time, the ultrasound scan and fetal heart monitor, whatever disadvantages and hazards they may have when used routinely in pregnancy and birth, have produced increased understanding of life inside the uterus, of what the fetus can hear, and even its preferences.

The ear is the only part of the body to reach adult size while the baby is still inside the uterus. At twelve weeks the nerve endings necessary for hearing develop. By twenty weeks the complex, fluid-filled labyrinth of the inner ear is formed and the baby responds to various kinds of sound, though until about thirty-two weeks this sound is not transmitted in the same way that it is after delivery. The fetus can respond to resonance, however, long before it can hear

TABLE 12. FETAL BEHAVIOR [20]

8 weeks   The embryo starts to make tiny movements and may get hiccups, but the mother cannot feel these yet.

9 weeks   The embryo starts to kick.

10 weeks   The embryo moves more than 12 percent of the time; also begins to make breathing movements, and now or in a couple of weeks starts to drink amniotic fluid.

11 weeks   Movements become more vigorous and the embryo occasionally jumps as if startled.

12 weeks   In experiments, if the lips are stroked with a straw the fetus closes its mouth and swallows.

13 weeks   Bouts of hiccups most frequent at this stage of pregnancy. When the fetus hiccups, it does so 26–28 times a minute.

16 weeks   By now the fetus has developed a sense of taste. In experiments it doubles its swallowing rate if amniotic fluid is artificially sweetened. If a bright light is shone on the mother's abdomen, the heart rate speeds up and it turns its head away.

18 weeks   Movements are first felt by the mother now or within the next three weeks.

20 weeks   In experiments, if a rod is put in its hand, the fetus grasps it and moves its arm up and down.

22 weeks   From now on the heart rate speeds up when the fetus moves, and it also begins to make definite sucking movements.

25 weeks   The fetus may get excited at loud, sudden noises; become quiet when the mother speaks softly; and fall asleep when she walks around and it is rocked in the cradle of her pelvis.

27 weeks   The fetus makes strong breathing movements now.

28 weeks   At about this time the brain has developed to the point where it can be assumed that there is consciousness.

29 weeks   The baby responds to sound by moving more and its heartbeat gets faster.

30 weeks   The baby's experience of its own heartbeat seems to be important from now on for establishing a response to rhythm after birth.

33 weeks   From now on there are two states of sleep: rapid eye movement (REM) or active sleep, which in adults is dreaming sleep, and deep, non-REM sleep.

37 weeks   By now the baby moves in some way at least every 10 minutes. Some of these movements cannot be felt by the mother because it is breathing activity, which occurs in spurts.

39 weeks   During quiet sleep the baby often makes mouth movements at 10- to 20-second intervals. In active sleep the baby moves every 0.5 to 2.5 minutes and makes sucking and other mouth movements for 5 seconds to 3 minutes. At this stage of pregnancy the baby spends 95 percent of the time asleep.

---

clearly. This may be why fetal movements and increased heart rates are recorded at four to five months when music is played. Babies at this stage can distinguish between different kinds of music, becoming more active when Beethoven and Brahms are played and calming down in response to Vivaldi and Mozart.[7] Even when the baby does not actually move to music, its heart rate changes. Loud sound produces a quicker heart rate. Babies probably cannot hear anything below forty decibels.[8] As David Chamberlain, chief clinical psychologist at the Anxiety Treatment Center in San Diego, who has done a great deal of work on consciousness at birth and on birth memories, points out: "This puts many of the sounds in the baby's natural environment clearly within audible range."[9]

The baby inside its mother's body can also pick up the frequencies of human speech. In fact, it appears to store speech patterns learned from its mother. Babies move their bodies and eyes in a pattern that is synchronized with the speech of whoever is talking to them. They do not do this if presented with a gabble of speech sounds, only with language.[10] They respond this way whether the language is English or Chinese.[11] So it seems that in the last months of pregnancy, once hearing is developed, the baby, though lying in water in which sound is picked up differently from sound carried in the air, is already tracking human speech and becoming accustomed to the tones and rhythms of the language spoken by its mother.

A newborn baby can recognize its mother's voice. Given a choice between her voice and another female voice the baby will opt for the mother's. In one experiment babies under three or four days old were given a rubber nipple to suck that did not provide milk.[12] By changing their sucking rate the babies could get the recorded voice of their own mother reading a Dr. Seuss story or the same story read by another woman. In less than twenty minutes the babies learned how to get their mothers. If there are other children in the family, the fetus almost certainly hears and responds to their voices, too. Young children's voices are even higher pitched than the mother's and because two and three-year-olds are usually in close proximity to the mother, sitting on her lap, being cuddled, climbing over her—and can also be very noisy—it would be surprising if the fetus did not become familiar with the sound of its siblings' voices. In my own experience, the newborn can often be comforted by the sound of its siblings' voices and becomes quietly attentive.

The baby also practices muscle movements that, once it is born, produce a cry—and for each baby that cry is as unique as a fingerprint. To anybody who has not had a baby, different babies' cries may sound very similar, but any mother knows she can pick out her own baby's cry amid a dozen or so others. That cry has been rehearsed already in the uterus and was in turn derived from her speech pattern.[13]

Within a few minutes of birth a baby turns its head in the direction of a sound, particularly that of the human voice, and prefers the high-pitched sound of a woman's speech to the lower pitch of a man's.[14] Many people spontaneously speak at a higher pitch when talking to new babies. In a tape recording of one of my own children's births, my husband first speaks to me in his normal voice and then turns to his newborn daughter and says, in a noticeably higher-pitched voice, "Hello! What are we going to call you, little one?"

The fetus can hear the churning of the mother's digestive system and the pulsing of blood through her arteries and veins. There is also the steady drumming of her heart beat. The beat of the human heart seems to be particularly comforting to newborn babies. In a well-known study, the sound of a heart beating at seventy-two beats per minute was played to babies in a hospital nursery.[15] There was a control group of babies who did not hear the sound. The babies crying in the two nurseries were recorded and their milk intake and weight gain were measured over a period of four days. The babies in the control group cried nearly twice as much as those in the heartbeat group. Twice as many babies in the heart-beat group as in the control group put on weight, though each set of babies was taking approximately the same quantity of milk. Those who were soothed by the sound of the heartbeat seemed to be able to make better use of the food.

When the heartbeat was speeded up to 128 beats per minute, none of the babies like it and they all started crying. So it is not just any noise that works, but a specific sound to which the baby has become accustomed in the uterus and which represents closeness to the mother and security with her.

In late pregnancy many women discover that it is possible to affect the baby's behavior, to send a message so that it moves or quiets down, for example. The baby may get into a position that is uncomfortable for you, with a foot sticking in your ribs. Try shifting your position or pressing a hand firmly over the baby's back to get it to roll into a different position. A very active baby who is twisting and dipping, turning and bumping, can often be calmed by a hand cupped over its buttocks, by slow, deep breathing, or with soft music. A baby often seems especially active just as the mother is trying to go to sleep, and she learns that changing her position, cradling its back between her hands, and telling it to quiet down seems to soothe it. A woman may also discover that the baby reacts to certain kinds of sound, apparently excited by some, becoming still and even going to sleep in response to others.

She may be aware, too, that her own emotional state affects the baby. If she is feeling lazy and soporific as she lies in the sun on a beautiful summer day, movements often slow down and become spaced farther apart. If she grabs a few minutes to rest during a very busy day, however, the baby is likely to be churning around as if it were aware of all the rush and bustle and the host of things on her mind.

When women start to relax and breathe slowly in childbirth classes, babies usually move energetically at first. This seems to be a response to the mother starting to let go of the tensions she felt about getting to the class—leaving work on time, making a meal, organizing the family, making sure her partner is ready, maneuvering through traffic to get across town, and so on. When she has settled down into rhythmic, full breathing and feels relaxed, the baby slows down, too.

A healthy fetus moves a lot right up to the time of birth, though mothers' awareness of movements varies a good deal. One woman may consistently record few movements and another always record a great many. Movements change at different phases of pregnancy, too. When they are first felt at eighteen to twenty weeks, they may feel like small nudges, like bubbles popping, or as if a bird has fluttered its wings inside you. Later, they turn into obvious bumps and knocks. From nineteen weeks the baby begins to make breathing movements as if in rehearsal for breathing after birth. These movements get stronger and occur more often, until by twenty-seven weeks they form a regular rhythm of activity.

Until twenty-four to twenty-six weeks the baby has enough room to turn complete somersaults. Within the next four to six weeks it usually turns head down (termed vertex or cephalic presentation) into the position for birth. The head is the largest and heaviest part and usually fits neatly in the cavity of the bony pelvis. Because it is a tight fit, it stays there.

From that stage on, the baby can switch from side to side, rotate its head and swing its whole body round, but can no longer change position so that it is bottom down.

Sleeping and Waking

Already by the fifth month of pregnancy the baby has its own pattern of sleep and waking. In the last three months of pregnancy, there are some times when the baby seems to exercise strenuously, and others when it is alert and there is a potential for movement in response to sound, the mother's change of position, or hand pressure on the abdominal wall. It is particularly in this state of waking that she can get in contact with her baby. It corresponds to the "quiet, alert" state psychologists have described in the newborn baby, a time when the baby catches the parents' attention and they can have a conversation with the baby.

Sleeping periods are of two distinct kinds, too. During REM sleep rapid eye movements occur. This is dreaming sleep. Non-REM sleep is deep sleep in which the heart rate is slower and the eyes do not move. At thirty weeks a baby spends its entire time in REM sleep. By thirty-three to thirty-five weeks this has been reduced to 67 percent of the time, by thirty-six to thirty-eight weeks it is 38 percent, and at forty weeks, when the baby is ready to be born, only half its time is spent in REM sleep.[16] The fetus often moves during REM sleep, apparently in response to a dream. The authors of this research believe that dreaming sleep is important for the final development of the central nervous system and, in later life, for its maintenance.

The definite waking and sleeping cycle of the last few months of pregnancy is often similar to the pattern of waking and sleeping that exists following birth. The undrugged baby usually has a period of alertness after delivery. It lasts for an hour or two, but then the baby sleeps much of the time for the next three to four days. As the mother's breast milk comes in there are more frequent waking periods and there tend to be one or two prolonged waking times during the twenty-four hours. A baby who kicked regularly every evening while inside the uterus is likely to have an evening waking time afterward. One common waking period is between 8.00 P.M. and 11.00 P.M. For many babies it is longer than that. Just as the mother wants to have some peace and quiet at the end of the day, the baby wakes up.

♦ ♦ ♦ When you are in the last ten weeks of your pregnancy make a note of the times when your baby is most active over a period of a week. See if any pattern emerges. ♦ ♦ ♦

Harriet's baby, Dan, is now five months old. Looking back to what she learned about him before he was born, she says:

In the morning he was quiet, though I may have thought that because I was so busy and didn't notice when he moved. Early afternoon was a kicking time. But he kicked more after six in the evening. Sometimes he kicked so much that I felt quite bruised under my ribs. And now he always sleeps solidly in the morning, which lets me get on with things. Then he likes a playtime after lunch, has a nap after that, and then his main waking time is from about six in the evening till about 10:30. It's very difficult to get him to settle before that. I start the evening meal before he wakes up and David finishes it. Then I eat while he holds Dan. Then I hold him while he eats. We switch the record player on and sometimes we put him in the baby sling and we dance! Our evenings are very energetic!

Movement Clues

There are several distinct kinds of movement you may be able to distinguish in the last months of pregnancy. One is the body roll: the baby turns from one side of the abdomen to the other, and then perhaps back again. At the height of the action there is a momentary pause as your abdomen is pushed out by the hard curve of the baby's back. It sticks out like the shell of a giant turtle. Another movement comes from the feet, which you may feel kicking up under your ribs on the left or right side. The baby's body is on the opposite side to where you can feel the kicking. If you are aware of these foot movements, you can be sure that the baby is head down and anterior, that is with the back of its head toward your front. The firm, melon-shaped curve at the front is the baby's back. This is an excellent position for the baby to be in when labor starts.

The baby is born with a reflex to bend its knee up when pressure is applied to the sole of the foot. In late pregnancy the walls of the upper part of the uterus become thicker as part of a process in which the lower segment gets thinner and muscle fibers are drawn up into the top of the uterus. The baby's feet are pressing against this strong wall. When the uterus contracts, as it does regularly, pressure is exerted on the feet. This encourages the baby to make the stepping movements you feel as kicks. They help the baby to curl up in a ball, with limbs flexed, back rounded, and its head forward on its chest. This position has a mechanical advantage in labor because when the uterus tightens it can press the ball of the baby's head down through the open cervix and the curve of the birth canal.

You may also feel the baby bouncing its head. This only happens when it has engaged—that is, it has descended into the pelvis with its head like an egg in an eggcup. The baby is born with a reflex to lift its chin when pressure is exerted against the top of its head. Your pelvic floor muscles lie across the outlet of the bony pelvis beneath the baby's head. Every now and again the baby bounces its head against them, using them rather like a trampoline. For you the sensation is one of tingling in your vagina as if you were being tickled or having a very mild electric shock. With this head movement the baby helps itself wriggle deeper into a good position for birth, head tucked firmly against the cervix, the part of the uterus that is going to open in labor.

You may also sometimes experience quick staccato movements. They may be hiccups. Or they may be the rapid movements of the baby's head from side to side in order to find again a thumb or finger it was sucking but has lost for a moment. After birth, this rooting reflex helps the baby find the nipple.

By the end of pregnancy the baby rarely goes ten minutes without moving in some way, simply practicing breathing movements—which you cannot feel—or bending or stretching an arm or leg, waving, kicking, turning or rolling from one side to the other—and the bigger the movement the more likely you are to feel it.[17]

The Baby's Position

As you get near the end of your pregnancy, you can determine how your baby is lying by feeling the different parts of its body through your abdominal wall. The medical term for this is "palpation." The next time you see your obstetrician or midwife ask to be shown how to do it.

Here is how you can find out how your baby is lying in a way that is rather different from the medical method but may work well for you. Empty your bladder first, as this makes it easier to feel the different parts of the baby. Lie on your back propped up with pillows. Now have a look at the curve of your abdomen. Can you see any obvious bumps? Look especially at your navel. If it is popping out, you can be almost certain that, for the moment anyway, the baby is in an anterior position, with its back well to the front. If there is a slight dip around your navel or it is level, the baby is probably sideways. If there is a saucer-shaped dip, the baby is probably posterior—lying facing your front. The space is the gap between its legs and arms. Exhale fully and relax completely so that your muscles are not tense and you can feel through them with your hands.

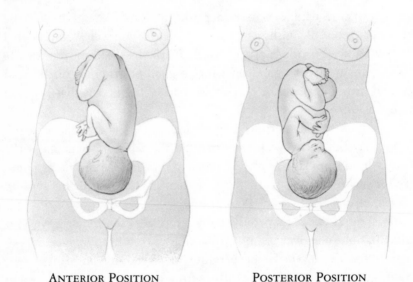

ANTERIOR POSITION   POSTERIOR POSITION

In the last few weeks your baby is most likely to be lying head down with its back more or less toward your front. So feel first whether the feet are under your ribs on the right or left side. Moving your hands slowly and deliberately, press in firmly. A foot feels rather like a small doorknob or the round knob on an old-fashioned brass bedstead. You can often coax it to move by pressing it hard with your finger. If the baby is awake and it really is a foot, it will be drawn away and then, perhaps, come back again. You will probably be able to feel an obvious foot shape and hold the baby's foot in your hands. If you cannot find the foot under your ribs but can feel kicking in the lower part of your abdomen, it is very likely that your baby is head up in the uterus in the breech position.

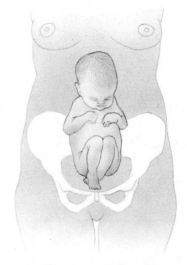 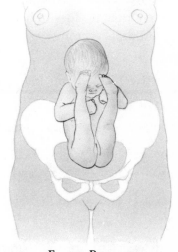

COMPLETE BREECH   FRANK BREECH

If you feel kicking all over your front and have a saucer-shaped dip around your navel, the baby is probably posterior at the moment, its back lying against your back. If the head has not yet dropped down into the pelvis, the baby may shift between an anterior and posterior position several times during the day. If the head has engaged, however, you may start labor with the baby in this position, and your contractions will press the head around into the more favorable anterior position. This often takes a long time. The mother gets a backache because the hard back of the baby's head is pressing against the small of her back. With patience the baby almost always turns. But if it has not turned, it can be born in the posterior position. This is a rather more difficult delivery as a wider part of the baby's head is coming through the birth canal. Obstetricians often turn the head with forceps, a *ventouse* (vacuum suction machine), or manually.

Both the head and the bottom are hard. But the head is round like a ball, whereas the bottom is flatter. To distinguish the head from the bottom you can try palpating what you think is the head. Place your fingers on each side of it and try to bounce the bump between your fingers. The head moves like a cork floating in water. The baby's bottom will not move. When the head is up under your ribs, it may feel rather like a small upturned saucepan sitting there uncomfortably. If the baby is head down and engaged, you may not be able to feel the head at all because it is deep inside the pelvis.

Here are some clues to help you decide whether or not the baby's head has dropped into your pelvis. The head is likely to be engaged if

♦ when you stand you feel as if there is something heavy between your legs.

♦ you are uncomfortable sitting down quickly on a hard chair.

♦ you get an occasional buzzing feeling in your vagina as the baby bounces its head against your muscles.

♦ you feel pressure against your bladder and have to empty it more often.

♦ it is easier to breathe than it was a few weeks earlier as there is less pressure against your ribs.

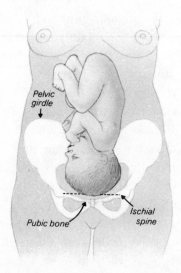

Pelvic girdle

Pubic bone

Ischial spine

- the baby is no longer leaping about so much.

- you can feel the feet under your ribs.

- you have located the baby's head in the lower part of your abdomen on previous occasions, but now you can't find anything you can identify as a head.

You can also use your hands to check whether the head is engaged. Place them just above the pubic bone on either side of the part of the baby's body you can feel there. Then walk your fingers in from the outer edge toward the middle. If there is a space at the bottom where your fingers can meet, between the rounded curve of the baby and the edge of your pubic bone, the head is not yet engaged. If there is no space at all, the head has engaged and the part of the baby's body you are tracking with your fingers is probably the shoulders.

Even if the baby is not engaged when you are lying down, it may become so when you stand up. You can feel it drop like a large orange and press against your bladder and vagina. Second and subsequent babies often do not engage until just before you start labor, or even after it has already begun.

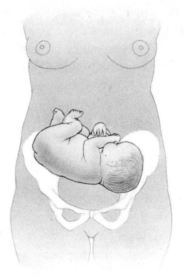

TRANSVERSE POSITION

Sometimes the baby never fixes in one position. This often occurs when a woman has already had several previous pregnancies. In late pregnancy the baby then often lies across the uterus. If the baby is fixed in this transverse position during labor, it cannot come down the birth canal, but it usually turns and is head down by the very end of pregnancy, slipping deep into the pelvis when strong contractions start.

If your partner or a friend is feeling the baby's position, guide their hands and put your hands over theirs to give them confidence to press firmly enough and to show them the degree of pressure that feels comfortable for you—and don't forget to talk to the baby at the same time.

DREAMING

Especially at the very beginning and the end of pregnancy, many women find they dream a good deal. These dreams may be very vivid. Some women dream in color, having only dreamed in black and white before. Many say that themes are repeated in different forms on several occasions or that they have various versions of the same dreams. Sometimes these are disturbing.

The baby is often represented as a baby animal—a kitten or puppy perhaps. Or it may be turned into a part of the body that has dropped off or been amputated. Sometimes it is a tooth that is extracted. This is not surprising, as during pregnancy it feels to the woman as if the baby were part of her own body—and birth brings with it the necessity of separation.

Water is an age-old symbol of birth. Sometimes dreams involving water express fear of birth and its danger, but they can also convey a sense of fulfillment.

Many women have dreams about being in the hospital; sometimes these are nightmares. One woman who had previously had a distressing labor and then been separated from her baby, who was in the special-care nursery, had repeated dreams during her subsequent pregnancy of being tied down on the delivery table, with doctors and nurses wearing devils' masks and her baby locked up inside a glass bottle.

Some dream of a machine that has started and cannot be stopped, a vivid symbol of the feeling a pregnant woman often has that she is taken over by doctors and the hospital system. Some have dreams of being trapped, behind a locked door, for example, perhaps because they feel powerless in the hands of professionals or trapped by the pregnancy itself.

Women who already have children often have nightmares in which one of them is harmed because of their own negligence or inattention. "I am going through the yard gate," Carole said, "and my two-year-old is running in front of me and suddenly she darts right out into the road. There is a screech of tires, a scream. The car stops. Her body lies there." A woman often feels guilty that, with a new baby on the way, she is not giving enough love to the older child and her sense of guilt is expressed in dreams like this.

When a woman wakes in the night, she may put it down to pressure on her bladder or the baby's movements, but these physical causes of waking can mask the stimulus of powerful and disturbing dreams. It seems simpler to explain this sudden waking in physical terms than to dredge up to the surface of consciousness exactly what happened in a dream. But sometimes tracking these dreams down and recollecting them can help to pinpoint anxiety which has been unacknowledged. It is often useful to do this so that something can be done to defuse the anxiety.

It may be a matter of getting hold of more information, achieving better communication with caregivers, talking through something that is on your mind with someone close to you, or sharing with other women who have gone through a similar experience.

♦ ♦ ♦ You may want to jot down any pregnancy dreams you feel throw some light on your hopes and fears and on things that are important to you about the birth and the baby. ♦ ♦ ♦

MATERNAL EMOTIONS

When a pregnant woman is very frightened or angry, stress hormones flood into her bloodstream and through the placenta, so that her baby is transfused with them, too. Most women notice that when they are alarmed, furiously angry, or highly aroused in any way, the baby jumps around a great deal and may go on being restless for an hour or more after they themselves have calmed down. Stress hormones seem to send an alarm signal to the baby to speed up its heart rate and provoke what feels to the mother like agitated behavior.

But this is not the only way in which the baby may respond to our own violent emotions. If a woman is under great stress, other metabolic changes occur, too. Her breathing, her heart rate, blood pressure, and state of muscle tension are all affected, and this in turn may affect her fetus.

Fear triggers a physical fight-or-flight reaction. Blood flows to the large muscles so that we can resist attack or escape. It is a primitive response that is maladapted to modern life, because we can do little or nothing about any of the things that threaten us. In a pregnant woman, the fight-or-flight reaction occurs at the expense of the blood supply to the uterus, so that the baby gets less oxygen. Most babies are pretty tough and can cope well with isolated incidents of this kind, but if the mother is under prolonged stress the baby's oxygen supply may be reduced for a long period.

Some psychotherapists claim that this can set up a pattern of emotion in the baby—panic, helplessness or depression, for example —which may stay with a person throughout life. They say that reliving incidents in our prenatal life and birth, with the pain and terror we felt then, can enable us to understand these feelings and cope with them better.[18]These psychologists believe that though the brain is important for memory retrieval, memory *storage* may take place through the whole cellular chemistry of the body. When people replay painful experiences that happened in the uterus or during birth, these memories, they say, can be picked up by the conscious mind and turned into words. Once they have become words, adults understand themselves better and use the experience to grow emotionally.

"A cynical part of myself," a British psychoanalyst remarked, "says that all this is just a useful symbol. But it is one everyone understands . . . we can all think back to being in a little capsule with one portal of entry, totally helpless and dependent, and then struggling out through a narrow exit."

Knowing that the baby is a feeling creature, already learning inside the uterus, and that it can receive messages and even, in a rudimentary way, send messages to you, means that bonding between you both can start long before birth. When you begin a relationship with your baby during pregnancy, the whole process unfolds gradually. It is not, as it now sometimes seems to be in the delivery room, a sudden demand to bond and prove that you have the appropriate maternal feelings.

Being in touch with the baby inside has practical implications, too. Not only do you become aware of your baby's rhythms of sleep and waking and the pattern of its movements, but you are probably the most reliable guide to your baby's well-being. Though many hospitals still rely on hormone tests of urine or blood to discover if the placenta is working properly in late pregnancy, when mothers themselves keep kick charts they are often more accurate in predicting problems than any chemical tests.[19] (See chapter 9 for how to make your own kick charts.)

♦ ♦ ♦ Bearing in mind the stimuli to which the fetus is known to respond and the ways in which your emotional state may affect the baby, think now of other things you could do to get in touch with the baby inside you. Some of these may affect the baby through changes in your feelings, muscle tone, and breathing; others through changes in posture or through sound. Here are some different activities you might choose:

♦ Practice deep relaxation

♦ Breathe slowly and completely

♦ Sing

♦ Play music

♦ Walk energetically in the fresh air

♦ Dance

♦ Exercise with pelvic movements

In your notebook jot down any other things you may want to do that could directly or indirectly affect your baby. ♦ ♦ ♦

There are obvious hazards resulting from the new knowledge that babies in the uterus can feel and hear and that they have a developing awareness of their mothers and of the world into which they are going to be born. One of the psychologists at the Toronto Congress of Perinatal Psychology said that if the woman didn't want to be pregnant or hated her pregnancy, "the child gets the message of fear and rejection and may feel that she isn't wanted, that she doesn't belong on the earth, through her entire life." That kind of statement ignores the power of mammalian biology to provide a good deal of protection to the fetus through the exquisite mechanism of the placenta. In seeking to emphasize the closeness of the relationship between the mother and baby before birth, and criticizing the old idea of the uterus as a safe haven, it goes to the opposite extreme. This is likely to be just as inaccurate. It is also a heavy burden to place on the mother. An involuntary, biological, instinctual power is ascribed to women in order to deny their rights as individuals and render them powerless. If we have this influence on our unborn babies through our blood and hormones, it seems that the baby must be at the center of all our thinking, and that we dare not express our true feelings. It can make pregnancy a kind of imprisonment. A woman is trapped with a being who has taken over her body and whom she is never allowed to ignore or forget. She has a duty to be happy twenty-four hours a day, not for her own sake, but because if she lets herself be depressed or anxious, or so she is told, she can damage her baby irreparably. If the child does not turn out well, it is all going to be *her fault*.

To be able to nurture and enjoy her baby spontaneously, in pregnancy as well as after the baby is born, a woman needs to be nurtured and cherished *herself*. If she feels secure and confident, supported by people who love her, and has a chance to get to know her baby in her own time, without feeling that she has to put on a performance, she spontaneously cares for her child in exactly the right way.

CLOSENESS TO THE BABY
AFTER BIRTH

When the baby is born, you may feel that at last you can belong to yourself again and be happy to put the baby down in the crib whenever you can and rediscover your own identity. But something else may happen. Even though you were weighed down with the baby in the last weeks of pregnancy and were looking forward to being able to reclaim your body, once the baby is born you may miss having it inside you and feel empty. If anyone insists on taking the baby away —even if only into another room—you experience an intense feeling of loss. It is only when the baby is close and in your arms that you feel really whole again. These powerful feelings serve an important biological function. They ensure that newborn babies are cared for, cuddled, and fed and that the mother does this not just out of duty but because she *longs* to do so.

As a woman gets to know her newborn baby, she is caught up in a demanding and unremitting process. Babies need their diapers changed and their bottoms wiped. They have to be fed regularly and in the early weeks like to feed and suck ad lib. They may bring up milk and burp and fill their diapers again just after they have been changed. And when they need you—for food or comfort—they cry, and go on crying until that need is satisfied.

When you think about this in advance, or if you watch other parents taking care of *their* babies, it may all seem rather offensive. You may hope that you can organize your life differently and regulate things so that your day does not revolve around the baby in such a demanding way. But the strange thing is that when you have your own baby, wanting to be separate and in control gives way to the pleasure of closeness with the baby—finding out what the baby wants and enjoying his or her dependence on you.

This change in your feelings affects decisions you'll make about whether, for example, you want to nurse your baby or give formula; to have the baby in your own bed or in a separate room; to cuddle the baby close in a sling against your body or put him down in a baby carriage for lengthy periods of time.

Most new mothers enjoy the feeling of the baby close to them, the smell of her skin, the rounded curve of the head, the firm weight of the little body in their arms. Even though a woman thought she had no maternal instincts she usually, given half a chance, can't help falling in love with her baby.

One way of preparing yourself for this experience and getting in touch with your feelings is to take time to think, and, perhaps just as important, to *dream* and have fantasies, about holding, cuddling, and feeding your baby. Think how it would feel, for example, to have your baby close to you in bed at night, a tiny hand gripping your finger, the weight of the baby's head in the crook of your arm and the firm, rounded buttock in your hand, or to have the baby sucking at your breast, attached firmly as a limpet. Here is how some women imagine their feelings about the coming baby.

A bit like the feeling I have with my cat. I like stroking her, she is so soft and furry and she purrs with pleasure. I have never thought of myself holding a baby but I know I enjoy cats and other baby animals.

Sometimes it is almost as if Pete's like a baby. When we are relaxed I hold his head in my arms like that. It's not . . . passionate or sexy or anything—just very gentle and tender. Yes, I can see myself being like that with a baby.

I can't help watching women with their babies. I'm curious. It's not the techniques of fixing a diaper or whatever, but how they touch their babies. Maybe that's a way of learning how to do it myself. I've never been around babies much. But now I can't help noticing them everywhere and I stare, I know I do. It's a kind of learning.

One way of enjoying closeness and getting in touch with your baby is to have some quiet time, a dream time, each day when you let your thoughts form, shape, and reshape themselves about the pregnancy, the baby, and the birth. Ten or fifteen minutes is enough, though some women get to like this space in their otherwise busy lives so much that they stretch it to half an hour. They tell other people they are having a rest. The point of this is not so much to rest physically as to make space for you and the baby together. It is the beginning of tuning in to the life that is to be, the first communication with your child, while it is still small enough to fit into the palm of your hand.

Some pregnant women are reluctant to do this in case they do not hold on to the pregnancy or there is something wrong with the baby or it dies. They feel that to allow themselves to bond with the baby while it is still inside them is dangerous. But even if this baby should not stay with you, even if there should be a miscarriage, for example, or if later you were to lose the child, there will have been someone with whom you have been in touch, whom you feel you have begun to know, a real little person to whom you have given yourself. The hardest thing of all is to grieve when you do not know exactly who you are grieving for, when the person you grieve for has no identity. Women whose babies have died at birth and who have not seen or held them often say this.

It may be that your partner, too, can make some quiet time to be with you and your developing baby. There is no need to talk. But once a couple has begun to enjoy this quiet space, other things happen. You may find that you stroke the gentle curve of your body in which the baby is cradled and talk to the baby. Do whatever you feel like doing.

After each time of dreaming you may want to jot down your thoughts. They won't all be beautiful ones and it probably won't be great literature. Avoid censoring what comes. You are simply recording what is in your mind as you get more in touch with your feelings and in touch with your baby.

13

♦ ON THE THRESHOLD ♦ OF THE UNKNOWN

Every birth is an adventure. However many times a woman has done it before, she is setting out on a new experience which can bring unforeseen challenges.

♦ ♦ ♦ When you get to the last weeks, take time to write in your notebook some of your impressions of this stage of your pregnancy —both emotional and physical. Describe the good feelings and the bad. Pick up any doubts or fears you have about the birth or afterward. Write about your feelings for the baby in these weeks. You may want to write, too, about your hopes for your child and about how you want to be as a mother.

It is easy to forget many of the thoughts and feelings you now have once the baby is born. Writing about them now can give you an important record of these final weeks of pregnancy. ♦ ♦ ♦

For a woman having her first baby, the whole process may seem mysterious and awesome in its magnitude. She wonders how she will cope with the pain, what contractions will feel like, how it will be when the baby's head slides out of her and pops like a pea out of its pod, whether she has any maternal instincts, and if, afterward, she will ever be the same person again. Excitement, hope, curiosity, and astonishment at the creative power expressing itself through her body are mingled with often only half-voiced fears and doubts about her own strength, ability, and intrinsic worth.

Even when a woman already knows exactly what is involved in childbirth and has firsthand experience of being a mother, and thus is much more relaxed and pragmatic in her approach, she may still be not completely confident that she can cope with *this* labor and *this* baby.

A woman who already has a child may be much more tired than the first time around because she is busy nurturing her family and has little time to nurture herself. She often feels that this pregnancy is being crowded out—that she has no chance to concentrate on or enjoy it. It is as if this particular baby cannot be special because she is swept up by everybody else's demands on her energy.

For a woman having her first baby who takes time off from work outside the home, the last weeks of pregnancy can bring an unaccustomed space in her life and a feeling of leisure, though it will be short-lived. On the other hand, some women are beset with worries about getting behind with work and how they are going to cope with a baby and a job afterward.

A woman on maternity leave discovers herself in a different world from that of her colleagues. As she becomes more and more baby-oriented, with prenatal visits, childbirth classes, and getting everything ready, it may seem that real life is going on at work without her. It can be frightening to change identity so swiftly, and she may be anxious that she will never again be able to define herself as a capable working woman. The big question that seems to confront her is how she is going to fit the baby into her life. In fact, whatever she does, her life is never going to be the same again!

By the end of pregnancy a woman longs to see and hold her baby and, like a child waiting for a birthday or Christmas, feels the suspense mounting and is impatient to discover what she has been given. But even then, eager anticipation is often mixed with anxiety and a feeling that she is not yet *ready*.

Whereas one woman thinks in terms of "being delivered," another thinks of "giving birth." The very language used about birth reflects different attitudes to the whole process. When a woman is "delivered," it implies that her role is passive. When she "gives birth," she has an active role in creating new life. The first woman perceives her labor mainly as something that has to be endured for the sake of the baby, and the actions of the obstetrician who performs the delivery as of primary importance. The second sees her caregivers as peripheral to the main task of giving birth, which, if everything turns out well, will be hers alone, and she looks forward to it as a fulfilling experience. Yet very much wanting birth to be natural, to bring satisfaction and fulfillment, can impose its own stresses. If you are the sort of person who sets clear goals for yourself, the last weeks are a time in which there is often a shadow of something like stage fright. As the day when labor must begin draws nearer, you may wonder if you will make a fool of yourself. You imagine yelling, swearing, or pleading for pain-relieving drugs even if you have decided in advance that you do not want them. You may worry that you will not live up to some predetermined, frequently self-imposed standard and will disappoint your partner, your childbirth teacher—or yourself.

"He expects such a lot of me!" Sybil said. "He's read all the books, religiously been to classes. I feel I've got to put on a star performance."

"We've delayed having this baby until everything was just right —our careers, the house, and so on," Alison told me. "We plan to have only one child and it matters a great deal to us that everything goes right—that I have natural childbirth, no medication of any kind, and nurse the baby on the delivery table."

For both of these women the script is all there. Now each feels it is up to her to play her part superbly well. No wonder that women under this kind of pressure are anxious that they will fail! Goal-oriented education, which puts the emphasis on success, conditions us to approach childbirth as an athletic contest we are determined to win. And if it turns out that labor does not measure up to this predetermined goal, we then run the risk of feeling inadequate and guilty and of being unable to enjoy the early weeks of motherhood.

Childbirth is not the kind of event in which you can dictate what happens or know in advance exactly how you are going to feel or what you are going to want to do. Like other life processes that involve dramatic physical change and intense emotions, it cannot be planned in detail ahead of time—only *lived*. For above all, it is an experience to which you bring not only your rational, planning self, but your whole being. When you make your birth plans, it is important to remember this.

If you try to stick closely to some blueprint of how it *ought* to be and how you *should* behave, not only are you likely to be disappointed, but you can actually make it harder for yourself to live in the moment and let your feelings flow. The strength of the uterus, the whole powerful process of birth, is such an intense experience that if you try too hard to control it, you may end up feeling like you are on a runaway horse, desperately struggling to hold on to the reins and pull back.

Think carefully about what you want, plan ahead, learn all you can, make your wishes clear to those who are giving you care, negotiate changes when routine practices do not match your priorities— but then, when labor starts, *give* yourself to the experience of birth.

YOUR BABY'S POSITION

At the very end of the pregnancy, you will probably become aware of the different positions in which the baby lies—pressing against your ribs or the small of your back, bouncing against your vagina as if it were about to fall out, or leaning against your bladder. These physical changes in late pregnancy, which result from the baby dropping lower and settling itself into a position for birth, may mean that you feel almost full to bursting, and there is hardly a moment when you are not conscious of the imminent arrival of your baby.

By thirty-six weeks many babies, especially in first pregnancies, have engaged in the pelvis in a position ready for birth. Others have not; they are still changing position. This is likely if it is your second baby, and still more usual if you have had two or three babies before, because the uterus will have stretched with each pregnancy and is not such a tight fit for the baby. Sometimes a baby lies in a transverse position—right across the uterus—with the bottom on one side and the head on the other. You may be worried, because when a baby is transverse during labor it gets stuck and has to be delivered by cesarean section. But in practice this rarely happens, because the baby's head is the heaviest part and when labor starts the baby nearly always rolls over with its head down in the cervix. The official name for all this is "unstable lie," and it sounds ominous. In fact, all it means is that the baby is not fixed in one position.

Coaxing a Breech to a Vertex

Most babies are head down in the uterus by sometime during the seventh month. Others remain stubbornly bottom down, though when they have not yet engaged in the pelvis they can still move fairly freely into different positions. But when a baby engages in a breech position, and gets more or less fixed in the pelvis, it is not going to disengage and somersault over unless you, or your doctor, take active steps to change the position. And even then, it may fit the available space in your pelvis more comfortably sitting up, so it may turn back again.

Both ends of the baby have to be born anyway, of course, but the head dilates the opening better than the buttocks, and the problem with a breech is that if the body is born but there is still not enough room for the biggest part, the head, there can be a delay at delivery, during which the baby can be short of oxygen. That is why babies are often delivered by "forceps on the after-coming head" or by cesarean section.

If your baby has started to go down into the pelvis as a breech, there are ways you may be able to persuade it to turn. Wait until this point is reached, or the baby may simply go back again immediately—being inside the pelvis restricts movement.

First feel with your fingers exactly how your baby is lying. You can get help with this from your doctor or midwife. With a breech baby you will feel the head like a coconut against your midriff. Leg movements occur in the lower part of your abdomen, unless the baby is lying with its feet by its shoulders, in which case it is splinted by its own legs and does not move much at all.

To coax the baby to change position you first need to tip it out of the bony cradle of your pelvis. Choose a time during the day: there is no point in doing it and lying down afterward, because the baby may then turn back. Start by lying with your hips raised and bottom high, head down, for twenty to thirty minutes. A large, firm bean-bag, or even two pillows piled on top of each other, will allow you to be reasonably comfortable in this odd position. Make a depression for your tummy and lie on your front. The baby's back and head are its heaviest parts, and since you want the head down and the back forward for it to be in the best position, it is good for you to be on your front rather than your back, and to reduce the pressure against your abdomen. Slightly bending your knees, so that your bottom is even higher, will probably help. A bed and plenty of pillows, arranged so that you kneel up on the side or end of the bed, with your head on a pillow on the floor, can also be used. You may have other furniture that you can adapt for this purpose.

Once you have been lying in this position for some time the baby will tip free of the pelvis and may start to move. Keep your head down and bottom up, and with your hands check the position of the head. Can you still feel it pressing against your diaphragm? It may, of course, stay that way. But often the baby will somersault over and suddenly the big, round lump in your middle is gone, and instead you can feel smaller lumps under your ribs, often to one side only—the baby's feet. If this happens, have someone help you get up (you may feel a bit dizzy), and then keep standing and moving around for the next hour or so—perhaps go for a long walk—to see if you can fix the baby in your pelvis head down.

When a doctor helps you do it, you adopt a head-down position for twenty minutes, and the doctor then grasps the head and buttocks through your abdomen and turns the baby, usually in the direction of its nose. (It must be done carefully or the placenta can be pulled away from its moorings.) This procedure is preferable to a cesarean section, but many doctors no longer know how to do it.

Coaxing a Posterior to Anterior

What if your baby is head down, but with its limbs to the front? You can tell if this is so because you feel all the movement at the front, there is a saucer-shaped dip around your navel, and the hard back of the baby is pressing against your sacrum (the bone where your pelvis joins your spine) so you probably have a backache (though bad posture can cause this too, so you cannot be certain just from this). When the baby is anterior, a woman's navel usually sticks out like a button in the last few weeks. When the baby is posterior, it still looks like an ordinary navel.

Doctors do not attempt to turn posteriors to anteriors, except internally with forceps or manually just before delivery. But in some peasant cultures midwives have traditionally coaxed babies round with massage, and there is no reason why you should not try this yourself. If you have a small pelvic inlet, the baby may need to enter the pelvic cavity in a posterior position, but can turn around, sometimes with a bit of persuasion, into a better anterior position for birth.

Wait until the head has negotiated the pelvic inlet, because the baby will be moving around all over the place before then anyway. Moreover, if you can persuade the baby to turn around, it will help to fix the head in the new position if it is inside the pelvis like an egg in an eggcup.

To change an anterior to a posterior, wait until your baby is awake and moving. In this way the baby may help you. Now get on all fours with your tummy hanging down. First feel how your baby is lying. Can you find the back? It may be to the back and difficult to feel at all. It is often on your right-hand side, but tilted toward your back. Sometimes it is in a similar position on your left. See if you can get the palm of your hand around it. Rock your pelvis up and down a bit. Then, once you can feel the back, grasp it firmly, as if it were a kitten you were trying to slide along the sofa so you could sit down, and little by little press and stroke it toward the front with a deep scooping movement, every now and again rocking your pelvis. Because the back is heavier than the limbs, there may be a point at which it simply falls forward. And that's it! Now either stay upright for an hour or so or, if you do lie down, avoid lying on your back, or the baby may turn around again immediately.

Sometimes a baby will not turn, but does move from an extended position to curl up into a ball, and that is an improvement too.[1] Sometimes, even if you manage to turn the baby successfully, it goes back again. You may need to repeat the maneuver at intervals before the baby fixes as anterior. Some babies will not turn, and then you will have to wait for strong contractions in labor to press the baby into a more compact ball and rotate it into a good position. If given enough time, seven out of ten babies rotate to the anterior during labor.

One disconcerting thing about prenatal examinations is that a woman is expected to lie on her back for her abdomen to be palpated.

The result is that her baby may roll around to a posterior position. This is why your doctor may find the baby is posterior, whereas when you are lying on your side, turned over toward your front on all fours, or standing, you may notice that the smooth, firm sweep of the back is toward your front, which means the baby must be anterior. This is a good reason for deciding to adopt upright, forward-leaning, and all-fours positions in labor.

♦ ♦ ♦ Once you are in the thirty-sixth week of your pregnancy, note down any observations you have about your baby's position and any changes in it. Get help from your doctor or midwife if you are uncertain.

If you decide to try either of these ways of coaxing the baby to a different position, record what happened. ♦ ♦ ♦

CHANGES IN YOUR BODY

The physical changes of pregnancy are so powerful, and in the last few weeks so inescapable, that for many women it feels like they are on the edge of a new state of being, as this familiar body starts to open in order to push out into the world another living creature.

Once the baby has dropped into the pelvis, it often feels to the pregnant woman as if her insides were being slowly but inexorably sucked downward; that not just the baby, but everything is slipping lower, ready to drop out. When the baby has engaged, the head presses so low that it feels like a coconut swinging between your legs. You may have a fantasy of waters bursting and everything happening in the middle of the local supermarket.

The physical sensations experienced during the last weeks of pregnancy are not so much painful as odd. You may not be able to get completely comfortable in any position. At times it feels as if you are lumbering around like a tank. On good days it is more as if you were a ship in full sail.

There are advantages—even some pleasures—in occupying a larger space than usual. Though it is rarely talked about, the magnitude and splendor of advanced pregnancy may bring with it a sense of power. The woman moves with the great globe of her uterus pressing under her rib cage and down against the muscles slung across the base of her hip bones, the skin stretched taut over her abdomen, a huge curved dome, with the baby safely inside, rolling and kicking beneath it like a dolphin playing. Other people move away, giving her space. They may be considerate and caring, awed, or perhaps just fearful that labor will start and they will have to deliver the baby.

If you already have children, you will find they react to your changed shape very differently from adults. They play on the bump, lean against and poke it, and climb and crawl over it. They sit or lie on it, knock, press, and prod it. They may talk to the little creature inside. The baby is already part of the family!

The sheer weight carried around in the last weeks of pregnancy tends to make a woman very tired at the end of the day and ready for an early bed. At a rough guess there are seven to nine pounds of baby, one and a half to two pounds of placenta, one and a half to two pounds of amniotic fluid, two pounds of uterus, a pound or more of extra breast tissue, two pounds of extra blood, two to two and a half pounds of water in the tissues, and about eight to nine pounds of personal body fat, for a total of twenty-five to thirty pounds.

When you go to bed, it may be hard to find a position in which you can easily drop off to sleep. You can shift pillows around to support a leg, cradle the bump, or press against an aching back. Even so, once off to sleep you may wake to discover that the baby is sky diving against your bladder, and there are frequent trips to the bathroom. Some babies move so much, even in the last weeks of pregnancy when they must be short of space, that they wake their mothers constantly with a foot protruding under the ribs or a belly roll like a tidal wave.

The pressure against the pelvic floor muscles, which support the bladder, rectum, and uterus from underneath, is so intense at this stage that they may be stretched. When you cough, sneeze, or laugh you may wet your pants. Hormones released into the bloodstream have softened and loosened your body for birth, but made daily life more complicated. This softening has its positive aspect, too, for it brings a sense of physical succulence and richness. The accordianlike folds of the vagina are thick and full now, ready to open out as the baby's head presses through. The cervix is being drawn up into the main body of the uterus and is also softening like a ripe, squashy fruit about to ooze its juice. The breasts are veined and full, ready to give thick, creamy colostrum. The uterus is tightening intermittently, as if preparing for its task in labor. This may happen so often, and contractions become so strong and regular near term, that you think you must be in labor, though in fact, it is just an energetic rehearsal.

Labor can start in several different ways. You may notice you are having contractions that become stronger, longer, and closer together over a period of some two hours. Anything less than this and it is best not to decide you are in labor. You may be aware that the mucus plug has come out, and that you have passed a pink "show" —much like the very start of a period—but this can happen a couple of weeks before you actually being labor. Or your waters may leak or break in a rush. And this again may occur before you feel any contractions, though they usually start within five to eight hours.

PREMATURE RUPTURE OF THE MEMBRANES

If the waters leak before labor starts and the baby, though viable, would be very premature, doctors are agreed that they should try to keep the pregnancy going as long as possible. Steroids may be given to the mother in order to help the baby's lungs mature and so avoid the respiratory distress syndrome common in very premature babies. (However, it is possible that steroids may make the baby less able to resist infection after birth.) If the membranes rupture when the baby would be premature but not dangerously so, doctors disagree about what should be done. Some admit the mother to the hospital for bedrest, and wait and see. Some believe in performing amniocentesis to assess the maturity of the baby's lungs, and if the signs are good will then induce labor.

When the membranes rupture near term, many doctors believe that labor should be induced if it does not start spontaneously in twenty-four hours, or twelve hours, or whatever is the particular time limit they impose, because they are concerned that pelvic infection or infection of the baby may result. So a woman is usually told to go into the hospital immediately, is put to bed, and lies around hoping against hope that contractions will begin.

This is not a good way to start a labor. It introduces stress and anxiety because something seems to be going wrong, and even though you are feeling completely healthy you are immediately transformed into a sick person.

The possibility of premature rupture of the membranes is one of the insidious worries in some pregnant women's minds in the last weeks of pregnancy. They are often told by their childbirth teacher and by the doctor that if there is any leaking of water they must take immediate action and go to the hospital because of the risk of infection. Infection, however, is sometimes the *cause* rather than the consequence of the premature rupture of the membranes, and it seems to start in the underlying layer of membranes, not in the outside layer.[2]

The usual treatment when membranes rupture prematurely consists of antibiotics and, after some hours of hopeful anticipation, induction of labor. Occasionally, the membranes seal up again spontaneously after an initial leak. This sometimes happens if the leak was in the hind waters, above the baby's chin, rather than in the forewaters, which form a bubble below below its head. No one knows how the membranes can seal over again. But once you have started to lose water, it usually goes on flowing.

If induction is proposed, there are several things to discuss with your obstetrician. There is no need to take it for granted that from now on everything is abnormal and the whole thing must be treated as a medical crisis. It would be useful to know whether or not your cervix is ripe and partially effaced (drawn up into the uterus). There may be evidence of this already in your records, so it may not entail having another vaginal examination. If the cervix is not ripe, labor that is started artificially is likely to last longer than spontaneous labor, and there is an increased chance of it ending in a cesarean section.[3]

On the other hand, it is important to bear in mind that when the interval between rupture of the membranes and delivery exceeds twenty-four hours, vaginal examinations increase the risk of infection. A Dutch study reveals, however, that infection is no greater *when no vaginal examinations are performed.*[4] Occasionally, as we have seen, the membranes seal themselves over again and a woman does not go into labor for some days, the membranes rupturing anew once labor has started. There is a strong case to be made, therefore, for waiting expectantly, having no vaginal examinations, and taking your temperature every four hours to check if there is any rise which could indicate that you have an infection. It is also a good idea to smell the amniotic fluid every time you change your pad, since the very first sign of infection is an unpleasant odor. A prophylactic course of antibiotics will further reduce the chances of developing an infection. Provided that you do not become feverish and that the water remains clear and odorless, there would seem to be no good reason to induce labor. The membranes may have ruptured early merely because there was a weak spot in them, as sometimes happens at the end of a pregnancy in which there was amniocentesis.

Leaking of the waters is not, after all, such a bad way to start labor. You have warning that something is about to happen soon and can make preparations. Nor, if labor starts naturally, does it mean that it is likely to be longer, more arduous or more painful, though doctors are trained to treat the premature rupture of the membranes as an abnormality and often want to intervene.

Thinking ahead to how you would want to cope if this happened can help you retain your own autonomy, share in the decision making with your doctor, and stay calm, relaxed, and looking forward to your labor.

◆ THE WAY BIRTH IS ◆

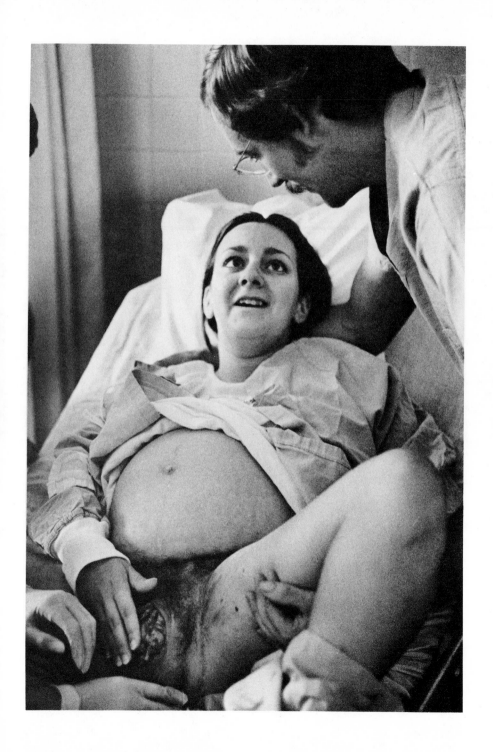

14

◆ THE JOURNEY THROUGH ◆
LABOR

Before you set out on an unfamiliar journey, it helps to have a rough idea of the territory you are going to cover, the challenges you may meet on your way, and the steps you can take to cope effectively with them. Though each labor is different, there is a common unfolding pattern to childbirth, and it is important to be aware of this so that you are prepared for the various phases as they follow each other and are not shocked by sudden changes in the feelings you are experiencing. It is vital that your birth companion understand these things, too, in order to give you strong and confident support.

Each birth is in some ways like a theatrical production. There is a lead-in which is rather like a prologue, a first scene which serves to introduce the plot and characters, then increased concentration and involvement in the action as the plot thickens, often interspersed with intervals when nothing much seems to be happening and you can take a break, and finally a build-up of excitement to the grand finale—the birth of your baby.

Though the medical view of labor is that it is divided into three stages—dilation of the cervix, expulsion of the infant, and delivery of the placenta, much like a three-act play—you may experience many phases within the first and second "acts" which have different, and even contrasting, moods and kinds of action for which you need to be prepared.

However enthusiastically you start out on labor, there are often times when morale drops and you feel tired and irritable, times when you feel bewildered and anxious about what is going to happen next, and occasions when there is fear, doubt, frustration, or insecurity. Learning how to deal with these negative elements is important if you are to be well rehearsed for your part in the drama of birth.

The pattern of labor outlined in table 13 is divided into four columns showing what is happening in your body, how you may feel, what you can do to help yourself and how your birth companion can best give support in each phase. There are no rules here for you to follow—but this description of how birth is for many other women will help you gain from their experience.

LABOR REHEARSAL

In the last six weeks of pregnancy it is a good idea to talk with your future birth companion about his or her role in helping you. This may be your partner, a family member, or a friend. Whoever it is, they should understand the kind of preparation you have been making for labor and, if possible, have attended at least some classes with you. It is important that they are confident and calm, and this is made easier if they understand what is happening, what you are trying to do, and how they can help.

From the preceding outline select some phases in labor and first talk about and then act through what you might do and the help you would want in these circumstances. To simulate a contraction, your partner can take hold of a little flesh from your inside thigh (not over a varicose vein) and squeeze it gradually tighter and tighter over a period of thirty seconds or so, then gradually release it for another thirty seconds. Breathe and relax into it. Start with some fairly easy contractions and move on to difficult ones. You may find they make you feel angry, frustrated, irritable, trapped—all emotions that may flood through you in labor, too. How can you handle the next contraction better? What do you want your helper to do? (In labor, fortunately, your companion will have both hands free and will not have to act the part of the uterus as well!)

Include in your rehearsal different ways in which you might start labor. Imagine one that starts slowly, one that begins with the waters breaking, or one with contractions only two minutes apart. Imagine having a short, sharp labor; a long drawn-out, tiring, backache labor; an induced labor; even a surprise birth without anyone else there to help—and so on. Talk about how you feel and what your needs are. You might want to say, for example, "It would have been better if you had massaged me *here*" or "I wanted to be quiet." It may help to say, "I need from you . . ." (and finish the sentence by telling your helper what is most important for you). There are other phrases that may be useful, too: "I am afraid that . . ."; "I hope . . ."; "I want you to give me . . ."

Your support person will approach the birth with expectations and doubts of their own. It can be useful to bring these out into the open also and to discuss them. Here are some phrases that may help to express these: "I know that . . ."; "I'm not sure that . . ."; "I shall be glad if . . ."

There are, of course, many other ways in which you could talk about feelings and I do not mean this to be a formal exercise. But some discussion like this can help you get on the same wavelength.

As you do this, include as much practical action as you can. For example, if you want to go to the bathroom, do you want your birth companion with you? If so, what would you like him to do: hold your shoulders, your feet, your hands—or just be there? If you take a shower, do you want your birth companion to stay with you? (If so, a man should bring bathing trunks.) Does it help to be held? Is it important to maintain eye contact? You have cramp in your leg; what do you want done about this? You are thirsty, what do you want? You have slipped too low against the pillows and want them more upright. You are hyperventilating or tensing up your legs; how can most effective help be given?

You may find that labor is very different from what you expected and that some things you practiced beforehand are irrelevant. The point of these rehearsals is to establish a close working partnership so that, whatever happens, your birth companion is sensitively responsive to your moods and you are intimately in touch.

HAPPY BIRTH DAY!

TABLE 13. THE PATTERN OF LABOR

PHASE	PHYSICAL SIGNS	HOW YOU MAY FEEL	HOW YOU CAN HELP YOURSELF	WHAT BIRTH COMPANION CAN DO TO HELP
Prelabor—the last few days of pregnancy	Some thinning out (effacement), ripening, and possible dilation of cervix. Increased and stronger Braxton-Hicks contractions. Baby's head may engage in pelvis. May have "show"—like beginning of period.* May have loose bowel movements. May have low backache.	Anticipation. Exhilaration. Some self-doubt likely: Am I going to be able to cope? Surge of energy—nesting instinct.	Prepare everything needed for birth. Get regular rest and sleep. Exercise. Gentle massage of nipples will help cervix ripen.	Make sure you can be reached easily at all times. Take over some household tasks. Give emotional support. If woman likes it, stroke and play with one nipple at a time to help ripening of cervix.
Early first stage	Cervix is being drawn up and thinned out. 1–5 cm dilation. "Show" if have not had it before.* * If steady bleeding occurs, call the doctor.	Excited. Confident.	Have light meal—soup, omelette, bread and honey, banana, grapes. Relax in bath. Alternate rest and activity if daytime. Get some sleep if nighttime or you need it.	If things start slowly, have meal together in relaxing setting, go out to a restaurant, or invite friends in.

Stage			
	Contractions get longer, stronger and are at regular intervals, 5 minutes or more apart. They may feel like indigestion, cramps, period pains, or an elastic band pulling in around your lower abdomen. Waters may break with slow leak, or pop so that water streams out.	Do some cooking that takes a long time—bread, meringues, slow casserole. Empty bladder every 1½ hours. If not sure that this is labor, try completely different activity—if in bed, get up and do something; if up, rest or watch TV. If contractions are strong enough not to be able to talk through them, start slow, full breathing. Relax.	Choose distracting activity together—watch a film, do light gardening or cooking, invite friends in, or go out and visit friends, play scrabble or cards, take a walk. Help her relax. Stay calm, confident, loving. Make sure any phone numbers needed are handy, there is money to make calls, and if using car there is gas in tank. Help with household tasks. Rub her back or stroke her abdomen.
Late first stage	5–8 cm dilation. Contractions get stronger, longer, closer together, till every 2–3 minutes and lasting 60 seconds or more. Waters may go.	General sense of everything getting faster and more intense. Feel you want to concentrate on labor. Get more serious. May become apprehensive, discouraged, impatient, irritated. May feel tired. Go to hospital or birth room if not already there. Discuss birth plan with doctor or midwife. Focus concentration during contractions. Drop shoulders and relax as each one starts. Welcome each contraction with slow breath *out*.	Help her relax. Use touch, stroking, firm holding, or massage. Put cold cloth on her forehead between contractions. Rest warm cloth or hot water bottle against lower abdomen, between thighs, or over lower back. Offer ice water and ice chips. Breathe with her if this helps.

PHASE	PHYSICAL SIGNS	HOW YOU MAY FEEL	HOW YOU CAN HELP YOURSELF	WHAT BIRTH COMPANION CAN DO TO HELP
Late first stage *continued*		May feel trapped. May vomit.	Breathe more lightly if you need to over peak of contraction. Give long breath out as contraction finishes. Doze between contractions and relax completely. Use aerosol water-spray or small spray bottle to freshen up. Move around and change position as often as you wish. Empty bladder every 1½ hours. Suck ice chips, sip liquid, or suck on sponge. For backache, try hands and knees position, walking, side-lying, kneeling, or sitting forward.	For backache: use strong counter-pressure, ice wrapped in cloth, or hot towel. Help her change position so leaning forward. Help her move and walk around.
Transition: bridge between first and second stages	8–10 cm dilated Contractions powerful, every 1½–2 minutes and lasting 90 seconds, or almost continuous.	As if tossed in a storm at sea. Restless, increased irritability, sense of time lost.	Welcome each contraction with a long, slow breath out. Then breathe in, and follow this by breathing as lightly and quickly as you want.	Stay with her. You are her anchor in a stormy sea. Remind her that transition, though intense, is short.

Physical signs	Feelings	What she can do	How to help
Some contractions may have double peaks.	May not want to be touched.	Concentrate on one contraction at a time. That particular one will never come back again.	Give her information. Remind her of baby, signs of progress, "not long now."
Concentrated pain around cervix as final tissue is pulled up over baby's head and baby is pressed down through cervix.	May be forgetful and even forget you are having a baby.	Relax buttocks and pelvic floor like heavy hammock.	Encourage and reassure her.
Cramp in legs.	Find it difficult to relax completely and keep breathing rhythms.	Walk around, change position for comfort.	Speak simply, and clearly.
Feel hot—then cold—then hot.	May want to give up.	Use any rest times for complete relaxation.	Be responsive to her mood.
Cold feet.	May be frightened because everything is overwhelming.	Blow out if feel urge to push and attendant says not to push yet.	Breathe with her if this helps.
Drowsiness.	May feel urge to push.		Maintain peaceful atmosphere.
Shaking.	May fall asleep between contractions.		Place hot water bottle between legs, at feet, in small of back; or she may prefer ice in towel for back pain.
Flushed face.			Help her change position. She may get stuck and uncomfortable in one position.
Hiccups, catch in throat, belching, involuntarily holding breath, grunting, groaning on breath out at end of contraction—all signs of pushing urge.			She may appreciate massage, stroking, firm holding, having her back rubbed. If she is shaking, firm massage of inner thighs may help. Use whole palm of each hand, fingers pointing down; massage from tops of inside legs to knees, stroke back lightly over tops of legs, in continuous rhythmic movement.
Waters may go if they have not gone before.			Offer sips of ice water and ice chips; vaseline or lip salve for lips.
May begin to feel pressure against rectum.			She may like to be sponged down with cool or hot water.

PHASE	PHYSICAL SIGNS	HOW YOU MAY FEEL	HOW YOU CAN HELP YOURSELF	WHAT BIRTH COMPANION CAN DO TO HELP
"Rest and be thankful" interval	Full dilation. Contractions often become weak or fade away for about 20 minutes, sometimes longer.	Sense of peace. Anxiety because no contractions felt if told to start pushing.	Rest. Close eyes. Enjoy lull	Relax. Wait patiently. Brush her hair back from her face, offer cologne, and freshen her up for pushing. A shower may feel good. Reassure her that all is well. Give encouragement. Play soft, relaxing music.
Second stage	Urge to push gets stronger as the baby comes lower. Contractions may be farther apart. Degree and timing of pushing urge may vary with each contraction. 1–4 urges, coming in waves, during each contraction. A little blood may appear when pushing; may have small bowel movement.	Cheerful, excited. Amazed at power of pushing urge, as if *being* pushed rather than pushing. May feel very tired and doze between contractions. Completely absorbed in what you're doing and not concerned about surroundings.	Right time to push is when *you* want to; you should push only as and when your body tells you to; hold breath only as long as you need to. Do whatever you feel like doing. Change position often for comfort; try kneeling, crouching, squatting, on all fours, supported standing squat. Relax perineum, buttocks, legs.	Encourage her by saying "Open up" and "Good"—*not* "Push"—with contractions. Remind her to breathe again as soon as she can after involuntarily held breath. Rest hot cloth over anus and perineum if she finds it helps her relax pelvic floor muscles. Help her change position so that upper part of body is raised. Most comfortable position is right. If progress is slow, help her squat. Support her in different positions: stand, kneel, or sit behind her to support her back.

	Feels like grapefruit in anus—then this changes to tingling, stretching, heat around vagina, as head presses against perineum. Feels like "ring of fire." Crowning. Birth of baby's head—then whole body slips out.	Renewed determination as you see and feel baby's head. Burst of energy. Interest turns to baby. Feel cannot stretch any more without popping. Relief—astonishment—joy—gratitude—ecstasy.	Touch top of baby's head before it is born. *Breathe* out baby. Put hands down to feel whole head when it has slid out. Reach out arms for baby and do whatever comes naturally. Let feelings flow.	Sponge her with cold water between contractions; offer ice chips. Remind her to open eyes to see birth. Adjust delivery mirror so that she can see her perineum. Tell her when head can be seen. As head is about to crown, breathe with her, mouth open, to enable head to be born gently. Watch birth. Welcome baby! Let feelings flow. Kiss, embrace, stroke, hold each other—whatever comes spontaneously.
Third stage	Delivery of placenta and membranes in 45 minutes or so. In 5 minutes if injection given to stimulate uterus. Contractions milder, further apart. Bleeding should only be about half a pint. May be uncontrolled shaking.	Completely engrossed in baby, or may need time to come to terms with power of experience, recover from shock and reality of birth. Excited, tired.	Express love, triumph, wonder, feelings that well up. Relax, hold, and enjoy baby. Watch for when baby opens eyes. Push to expel placenta; ask to see it if interested.	Hold and enjoy baby. Help baby on to breast when he/she begins to root for nipple. Put warm blanket over. Hold in arms.

15

◆ DEALING WITH PAIN ◆

A central issue for many women is how they are going to cope with pain. Most women have pain in labor but find it manageable. Some, however, have more than they can handle without help. If you understand *why* you are experiencing pain, then you can make plans about how to deal with it. Pain is most likely

◆ if the baby is a very tight fit for your pelvis—cephalo-pelvic disproportion (CPD). The baby's head is not hard bone all over: the skull bones are in sections which are pressed toward and can even slide over each other. Since the uterus squeezes the baby's head (its largest part) as if it were a ripe grapefruit, fitting it to the outlet available, a woman with small bones can often bear a large baby, but the process may be painful.

◆ if your uterus is short of oxygen. Though some researchers do not accept this as a cause of pain, it is possible that cramplike discomfort occurs when the uterus is not getting enough oxygen. Any muscle aches when insufficiently oxygenated. If there is not enough time for the uterus to become oxygenated between contractions, they may hurt a great deal. Breathing slowly and fully between contractions, and at the beginning and end of each, oxygenates your blood and this oxygen is carried to the uterus.

◆ if your cervix is slow to open. The baby's head presses through the cervix as if a tight sweater were being pulled over it.[1] Your cervix is very flexible and can open up more and more, given time, but it can be tough going.

♦ if the baby is in an awkward position. Though breech (bottom first) labors are not often especially painful, if the baby is head down but lying with its back toward your own back, the crown does not fit over your cervix, and the back of the head, the occiput, presses into the small of your back, causing backache. Labor with a baby in an occipito-posterior position like this may be painful and tiring because it can take a long time for the contractions to turn the baby's head into the correct anterior position.

♦ if the uterus is not working efficiently. Contractions are huge and painful, but because there is incoordinate uterine action the cervix does not dilate. No one knows why this happens, but sometimes it is because the baby is lying awkwardly.

How we feel about what is happening in our bodies is just as important as what is occurring physiologically. Negative feelings can intrude on childbirth and make it more painful

♦ if a woman is afraid, very anxious, angry, or frustrated, demanding a great deal of herself and struggling to keep control of a labor that she finds confusing and muddled. Emotions can help or hinder labor and reduce or increase the perception of pain.

♦ if a woman is sure that labor is going to be excruciatingly painful, she may get into such a state of tension that the slightest touch hurts. It is an unfailing recipe for a painful labor. Grantly Dick-Read, who introduced the concept of natural childbirth, taught that ignorance produces fear, which leads to tension, which creates pain. Yet knowing what is happening to you and what other people are doing to help—even knowing how to help yourself— though important, may not be enough. Any emotions that prevent you from feeling free and acting spontaneously can sharpen pain and make it intolerable. This is why it is important to think in advance about the emotional aspects of birth.

♦ if labor is very long (twenty-four hours or more) and the woman is suffering from lack of sleep. It can be difficult to cope with a normal eight- to twelve-hour labor if you have inadequate sleep the night before. Labor demands energy and stamina. This is why it is important to be well rested when you start. If you are having your baby in the hospital, avoid going in too soon. Many more women go in too early than too late. You are at risk of having labor accelerated with synthetic oxytocin (Pitocin), as well as a whole range of other interventions, simply because you have gone to the hospital before you needed to.

♦ if a woman is in the hands of people she does not like or trust. The environment for birth has a great deal to do with the amount of pain she feels. When she feels trapped in a situation in which she is controlled by others, she cannot do simple, easy things to handle discomfort, and the pain feels more severe.

♦ if a woman has not allowed herself to believe that labor might be painful. Then any pain experienced can be overwhelming. Pain is a normal part of most labors. It usually occurs only during contractions, and for much of the time is slight at the beginning and the end of the contractions, but strong as they reach their peak. Each contraction is followed by a rest period of about five minutes early in labor, one minute or less as she approaches full dilation of the cervix. Many women have no pain at all as they are pushing the baby out, though the feeling of the head like a grapefruit against the anus and then pressing through the vagina is often alarming. If you hope to have your baby without drugs, it is important to be able to accept the idea of pain.

♦ if a woman has not learned and *practiced* ways of handling pain herself. She is then left at the receiving end of powerful sensations she can do nothing about. Breathing, relaxation, changes of posture, movement, massage, focused concentration, visualization (picturing what is happening inside your body), meditation, self-hypnosis, acupuncture and acupressure, hypnosis—all these can help you handle pain in a constructive way.

♦ ♦ ♦   Look back over the list. There is something you can do about most of the causes of pain, so go through each item one by one and work out ways to prepare yourself. You may decide, for example, that in case the baby is posterior you need to know and practice in advance positions, movements, and massage for dealing with back-ache labor. Since it is often people closest to a woman who are anxious that she should go to the hospital once labor seems to have started, you can discuss with your partner the disadvantages of going in too soon and plan things you could do together early in labor. You may decide that you need to set aside more time to rehearse labor and ways to handle pain, and arrange a regular half hour each day to do so in the future. If you have been avoiding thinking about pain, the time has probably come to talk about it with some women who have had babies recently and find out exactly how they felt and what helped them most. You can also think back to the last time you had pain—period pains are a good example, or if it is not your first baby, how it felt in your previous labor—and note what helped you cope best, or things that in retrospect you wish you had done. As you watch TV, read, or sew, you can prepare for the sensation of the baby's head on your perineum by sitting on the floor with your back straight against a wall, the soles of your feet together near your buttocks, and feeling your pelvis wide open. Be aware of the space in your vagina and imagine the weight of the baby's head like a coconut ready to drop. Or try squatting, feet well apart and back rounded as you hold on to something steady, and visualize yourself completely open. ◆ ◆ ◆

PAIN-RELIEVING DRUGS

In an obstetrically directed birth, the doctor decides when and if drugs are necessary in order to control pain, and the patient does not have the freedom to cope with pain in any way she wishes. Pain is reduced or eradicated by something done *to* her rather than something she does for herself, and drugs are used as a first, rather than a last, resort.

When powerful pain-relieving drugs are employed, a woman becomes dependent on her caregivers for their administration, for the constant monitoring of her condition and that of the baby, and for any other procedures that may be needed as a consequence of drug use. The more effective the medication, the more interventions she is likely to have. Strong drugs can interfere with the action of the uterus and slow down labor, so measures may have to be taken to stimulate the uterus. This may entail further intervention to monitor the fetal heart rate and the use of other drugs which act as antidotes to those given for pain relief. If a woman cannot feel her contractions, the decision may be taken to accelerate labor or to lift the baby out by forceps.

Analgesics (pain-relieving drugs) and anesthetics (pain-eradicating drugs) are often recommended by obstetricians because they enable them to have more control over the birth process. One obstetrician explained that having anesthesia in labor is like having local anesthetic for a dental filling, and, "just as a pain-free non-squirming relaxed patient enabled dentists to perform their task smoothly, so did an epidural give rise to a relaxed, manageable and accessible mother."[2]

On the other hand, drugs for pain relief have a definite place in childbirth—especially when there are deviations from the normal and a woman is in severe pain. There is no need for any woman to prove her womanhood by laboring without drugs when she is experiencing more pain than she is prepared to cope with. It is often claimed that supporters of natural childbirth do not approve of any drugs. The founding father of the natural childbirth movement, Grantly Dick-Read, expressed a very different point of view when he said: "To tolerate suffering when it can be relieved is no less brutal than to insist on suffering when it is not present. . . . The administration of anesthetics and analgesics should have definite indication in obstetrics as it has in every branch of medicine or surgery."[3]

In considering the benefits and hazards of different kinds of anesthesia, these are some of the things you should ask your doctor or midwife:

◆ How is it given?

◆ What effect will it have on me in the lowest dose available? In the highest dose available?

◆ What effect might it have on the progress of labor? Does this depend on the time when it is given? The dosage?

◆ What effect is it likely to have on the baby? Is this dependent on timing and dosage? If so, how?

◆ Are any long-term side effects experienced by the mother? If so, what are these?

◆ Could there be long-term side effects for the baby? If so, what are these?

◆ What alternatives are available?

◆ Is this method of pain relief available at any time in the twenty-four hours?

◆ Can it be given so that, if everything is normal, its effect wears off by the time the second stage starts?

◆ Is there a higher incidence of forceps delivery with this kind of anesthesia?

◆ What do you see as the main advantages of this form of medication? The main disadvantages?

You will obviously not want to ask all these questions at one time, and the answers you get will probably make some of them unnecessary. But they are useful questions to keep in the back of your mind during any discussion about drugs.

DRUGS USED IN LABOR

Sedatives (for example barbiturates) may be offered early in labor. They cause drowsiness and if the latent phase is long, may enable you to get some sleep. A disadvantage is that they often lead to disorientation and once the active phase starts a woman may be struggling to cope with contractions that prove overwhelming, since each time she is roused from heavy sleep. Sedatives should not be given within four hours of delivery as they depress the baby's respiration.

Antihistamines (for example, Phenergan) and *tranquilizers* (for example, Sparine and Valium) are used to calm the mother. Tranquilizers reduce anxiety and some are used, like antihistamines, to treat nausea and vomiting as well. One disadvantage is that they may make the woman feel drunk and out of control. They can also produce dizziness and blurred vision. They should not be given within four hours of delivery because they cause respiratory depression and poor muscle tone in the newborn and lead to feeding difficulties. They may be used alone or in combination with narcotics.

Narcotics (for example, Demerol) may be offered once dilation of the cervix is progressing well. The dose should be related to the woman's weight. They have the effect of muffling pain, but also cause confusion and can make a woman feel powerless to cope actively with labor. Sometimes there are vivid dreams or hallucinations. The effects of these drugs last three to four hours. The problem is that when given too soon, these drugs stop dilation, but since they pass through the placenta and into the baby's bloodstream, they should not be given within four hours of delivery. This is yet another reason why narcotics are not the best answer to pain in labor. Moreover, breakdown products build up in the baby, who thus suffers more from the depressant effects on the central nervous system than the mother, and the baby's breathing is depressed for longer than the pain relief works for her. An antidote can be injected into her, or into the baby after birth if breathing is slow to start. It is not known if this has any long-term effects on the baby.

General anesthesia

This sends the woman to sleep. It eradicates pain, but is the most hazardous method of pain relief for her and the baby because of the risk of inhaling vomit, the fourth most common cause of maternal death in the United States and Great Britain.[4] It is used for cesarean deliveries, especially when done as an emergency, and occasionally for a difficult vaginal delivery or the birth of a second twin.

Ketamine is one fast-acting general anesthetic, the effect of which lasts only five to ten minutes, which is also used intravenously in smaller doses for pain relief instead of narcotics. It can produce confusion, unpleasant dreams, and hallucinations. It should never be used with sedatives or barbiturates. Though its safe use in obstetrics has not been established, it is claimed that when it is used to reduce rather than eradicate pain, it has no side effects on the baby.[5]

Regional anesthesia

This kills pain in one area of the body only. The great advantage of this method is that the mother is awake and aware and ready to greet her baby. There are many types of regional anesthetics.

Paracervical block involves injecting into the cervix an anesthetic similar to that used in dental surgery. Pain relief lasts for one to two hours and works well in seven out of ten women. The anesthetic passes through the mother's bloodstream to the baby, causes temporary slowing of the fetal heart rate, and may have subtle neurological effects on the baby in the period after birth.

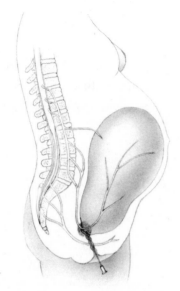 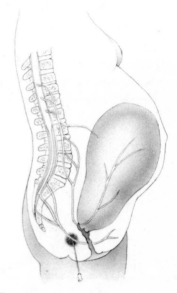

POSITION OF THE NEEDLE FOR A PARACERVICAL BLOCK

POSITION OF THE NEEDLE FOR A PUDENDAL BLOCK

Pudendal block entails anesthetic being injected inside the vagina. It anesthetizes the area around the vagina and between the vagina and anus, and may be used just before delivery. The effect lasts for about an hour. If it gets into the baby's bloodstream because delivery is not immediate, it can cause respiratory depression.

With *spinal anesthesia,* anesthetic is injected into the fluid around the spinal cord. Pain relief lasts for one to two hours. There is loss of sensation from the level of the breasts down. This means a greatly increased chance of forceps delivery since the woman does not feel an urge to push the baby out. Because the pelvic floor muscles are slack from anesthetic, the baby's head may not rotate into the correct position for birth, and as a result may get stuck. This is called deep transverse arrest. Spinal anesthesia can be used for a cesarean birth.

The anesthetic has an indirect effect on the baby through changes in the mother's metabolism and may also be present in the baby's bloodstream, resulting in subtle neurological changes in the period after birth. A major problem with spinal anesthesia is that after the birth a woman may have a crashing headache, which can last as long as eight days, so that she cannot sit up or even shift position as she lies in bed. This occurs because of an escape of cerebrospinal fluid. If the headache is severe, a blood patch can be done by injecting her own blood into the puncture hole, which forms a clot and closes it.

A *saddle block* is a form of spinal anesthesia in which the only part anesthetized is an area in the pelvis corresponding to the shape of a

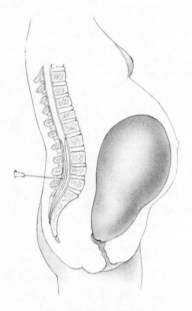

POSITION OF THE NEEDLE FOR A SADDLE BLOCK

saddle, which includes the lower abdomen, buttocks, perineum, and inner thighs. The effects and side effects are similar to those of a spinal anesthetic. It may be used for forceps deliveries and lasts for one and a half to two hours.

Extradural anesthesia does not entail entering the fluid around the spine; the injection stops short at the dura, a wall of tissue between the vertebrae and the spinal canal. There are two main types: caudal and epidural.

Caudal anesthesia is given by an injection just below the sacrum, the bone in the small of the back. There is less paralysis than with a spinal and no risk of postpuncture headache. But the chance of forceps delivery is high for the same reasons as when a spinal is given. There is also a possibility that the injection may be given to the baby instead of the mother if the head is low, resulting in a slowing of the fetal heart rate and respiratory depression at birth. Otherwise, any neurological effects in the baby are slight. A single dose lasts forty-five minutes to an hour and a half.

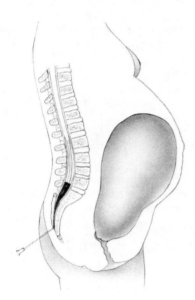

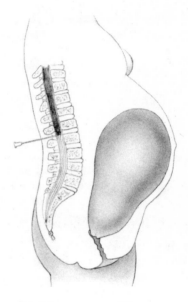

POSITION OF THE NEEDLE
FOR CONTINUOUS CAUDAL
ANESTHESIA

POSITION OF THE NEEDLE
FOR CONTINUOUS LUMBAR
EPIDURAL ANESTHESIA

Epidural anesthesia is given by injection at a point slightly higher on the back. It uses less anesthetic than a caudal and can be done so that it anesthetizes only the area where pain is felt. Pain relief lasts for one to two hours. If done expertly, a woman may retain feeling and some movement in her legs; however, many women lose all sensation.

With one kind of epidural, a *continuous lumbar epidural,* a fine plastic tube (a cannula) is inserted in the lower back between the vertebrae and into the epidural space around the spinal cord, and left in place. Additional anesthetic can be given through this when needed. With all epidurals, a small test dose of the anesthetic should always be given, and the effects noted, before the full dose is intro-

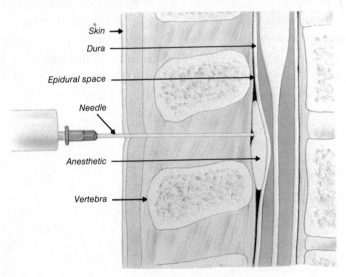

Skin

Dura

Epidural space

Needle

Anesthetic

Vertebra

NEEDLE INJECTING ANESTHETIC INTO
EPIDURAL SPACE, OUTSIDE THE DURA.

duced. If the anesthetist seems to be spending a long time setting up the epidural, it is because great care must be taken. It may take half an hour to forty-five minutes to give it.

The pros and cons of epidurals

For a woman who decides that she needs the help of drugs, an epidural is the most effective way of achieving complete relief from childbirth pain—and, indeed, possibly from all sensation, while remaining mentally alert. Even so, for two or three women out of every ten an epidural does not block all pain. It either does not work at all, or relieves rather than eradicates pain, or there are "windows" in the area the drug is intended to numb, often resulting in one-sided pain.[6]

Since an epidural service is available in most modern obstetric units, it may be worth discussing epidurals in more detail so that, depending on the circumstances and how you feel at the time, you can make a decision about what you want.

Some advantages of an epidural are that

♦ the baby is likely to be minimally affected by the drug, which is usually bupivacaine, a cocaine type of drug.[7]

♦ the woman's mind is unclouded to welcome her baby.

♦ when forceps or any other operative procedures are employed, no other method of anesthesia has to be used.

♦ when used for a cesarean birth, the mother is able to be awake and to see her baby immediately. She does not have the unpleasant aftereffects of general anesthesia. If her blood pressure is very high, an epidural reduces it to a safe level.

♦ when a woman is in pain and hyperventilating, the relief from pain that comes from an epidural restores the balance between acid and alkaline elements in her blood, and also in that of her baby.[8]

Some disadvantages are that

♦ the woman's blood pressure may drop excessively, making her feel faint, sick, and giddy. Sometimes it plummets and other drugs must be given to raise it again—one reason why an intravenous drip must be set up first. An IV is an inconvenience to the woman and limits her mobility.

♦ it tends to make the second stage of labor longer.[9] This is a problem when obstetricians impose set time limits on the expulsive phase, and a woman may end up with a cesarean section for this reason alone.

♦ once an epidural is given, a woman may become a passive patient and receive further interventions she had hoped to avoid. Because she cannot empty her bladder voluntarily, a catheter is inserted to draw off urine. She must have an intravenous drip in her arm so that any negative effects of the drug can be immediately counteracted with other drugs. She receives continuous electronic fetal monitoring. If contractions slow down and get weaker, as they often do after an epidural has been given, a uterine stimulant may be used in the intravenous drip to force her uterus to contract more efficiently.

♦ the chances of forceps delivery are greatly increased.[10] This is partly because the woman may not feel the urge to push and so is unable to work with her body to get the baby born, and partly because the normal tone of the pelvic floor muscles through which the baby descends, its head rotating into the correct position for delivery as it does so, is destroyed by an epidural, so the baby may get stuck.

♦ occasionally the needle punctures the dura (the membrane that encloses the spinal cord). This can result in escape of spinal fluid and a very severe headache after the birth—so bad that the woman has to lie flat and still for several days. If the drug solution is injected into the spine following accidental dural puncture, the result is a spinal anesthesia, not an epidural. Since a much larger dose of anesthetic is used for an epidural, introducing it directly into the spine may lead to a sudden dramatic drop in blood pressure, difficulty in breathing (or, very occasionally, inability to breathe) and, very rarely, cardiac arrest.

♦ after the birth, a woman who has had an epidural may have a greater blood loss than otherwise, and may have difficulty emptying her bladder for some hours or days. Approximately three women in ten report this bladder problem. The urinary catheter may need to be left in place. The woman sometimes also experiences dizziness and ear-popping.[11]

♦ it may have some harmful effects on the baby. Bupivacaine crosses the placenta into the baby's bloodstream within ten minutes and, after the baby is born, cord blood levels of the anesthetic are 30 to 40 percent of the mother's blood level.[12] It is often claimed that an epidural has no effect at all on the baby. It is true that it does not produce the problems with breathing and limpness that can result from Demerol, but it may have a more subtle effect on the baby's behavior. The baby may be less responsive to the human voice, may have decreased motor maturity (muscle tone and strength), and may be more irritable than babies of mothers who have no drugs. Various orienting and alerting skills tend to be depressed for as long as six weeks after birth.[13]

In spite of the many articles in medical journals about epidurals, most studies are uncontrolled surveys. One obstetrician has summed up the state of current knowledge and its implications as follows:

> We have no way of knowing which of the reported results are really due to the epidural, and which are non-causally associated. In the absence of a randomized controlled trial, we are left with the uncomfortable realization that any differences reported might be due to differences in the women who choose to have or not to have an epidural, in the type of prenatal preparation they may have had, in the support they may have received in labor, or in other confounding variables which may influence the results rather than to the procedure itself. . . . However, even if strong evidence were available, it could only give us the statistical probabilities of various outcomes. Pain, suffering, enjoyment, control, sense of accomplishment, all have different meanings and values to each childbearing woman. She must weigh the available evidence according to her own value system, her own unique experience.[14]

A woman may very much want to give birth naturally but be unable to do so, and be enormously grateful for the relief from pain an epidural can give. Maggie, for example, went to childbirth classes and was enthusiastic and confident about having a natural, unassisted birth. Unfortunately, she was overdue and her doctor was worried about whether the baby was still growing. She was induced fourteen days after term. She told me about her labor (her baby was in a posterior position).

> Contractions began two minutes apart, like they were testing me or trying to break my resolve. At the end of three hours I'd gone from two to three centimeters. I was vomiting, sweating, and shaky. My legs would no longer let me walk. I was put on a Pitocin drip. I now admitted that I was at the end of my

tether. I had good rapport with the medical staff and felt I could trust them. They didn't mention an epidural. I said I wanted one.

I was given the anesthetic quickly by a kindly anesthetist who was sympathetic to my feelings. The fear and tension were soon gone. I felt waves of almost euphoric (and slightly sexual) passion with each contraction. After about four hours I suddenly began to PUSH. The anesthetic was wearing off, I could feel pressure and contractions but no pain. The doctor and midwife were concerned that I should deliver normally and avoid episiotomy and forceps. Because of the anesthetic, I needed to be guided but it was no time before I could put my hand down and feel the baby's head just awaiting birth. I delivered my daughter with no assistance but lots of encouragement quietly and considerately given. I had a little skin tear which was sutured immediately while I held my baby and looked into her eyes.

In the months leading up to labor, I prepared myself intensely and determinedly for a natural delivery and refused to even entertain the idea that anything might go wrong or be beyond me. I had to cross the barrier of anger and frustration before I could peaceably accept it. But my epidural made it possible for me to enjoy what would otherwise have been an exhausting, painful, and distressing labor.

HANDLING PAIN
WITH YOUR OWN RESOURCES

Wendy Savage, the feminist obstetrician, offered this perception on the differing attitudes men and women have on pain in childbirth:

Men, who are not going to actually physically give birth, but are onlookers and bystanders, have the feeling that they have got to *do* something about the pain, about the way labor is progressing, whereas women, who know that they will probably go through this experience, even if they have not already been through it, understand that it is a very important part of how a woman functions in life, and that there are worse things in life than pain, and that to go through the process of pregnancy and labor and be in control of it is a very important part of a woman's self-esteem.[15]

Since no pain-relieving drug is entirely free of risk, you may want to consider nonpharmaceutical ways of achieving pain relief. One anesthesiologist claims that 30 percent of women can benefit greatly from what he calls "psychological analgesia," 10 percent of them requiring no drugs at all and another 15 to 20 percent needing fewer drugs because of their previous preparation.[16] And even those for whom pain is not diminished do not suffer in the same way because pain is not compounded by fear and anxiety.

For many women the pain of normal childbirth is qualitatively different from that of injury. It hurts, but that is a side effect of a creative process, the powerfully working uterus. It is pain with a purpose. But even this pain can be shattering if you simply struggle to endure it.

Techniques for handling pain are not an end in themselves. They are a way of changing your level of consciousness—being in a state of what I call "focused concentration" and what Michel Odent describes as "being on another planet."[17] It probably does not matter what you call it as long as you realize that it is not a question of doing exercises or of distracting yourself from pain, as is often suggested, but of going along with the experience and adapting yourself to the incredible power of your uterus.

Rhythmic, controlled breathing, relaxation, and focused concentration are all ways of meeting pain and working with it, instead of trying to fight or escape from the sensations of labor. You will need to learn these in childbirth classes, as they are almost impossible to learn from a book. Whatever classes are available in your area, remember that good ones are not concerned only with pain prevention or the reduction of sensation. Other methods—hypnosis, for example—may do this better. In a childbirth class you should find that as you learn how to work with your body and trust it, you become more self-assured and ready to start out on the exciting experience of birth with courage, confidence, and energy. Classes teach you how to adjust yourself to your labor, whatever kind it may be, and how to understand what your doctor or midwife is trying to do to help you, as well as providing a sort of map for childbirth, so that at any point you can take your bearings, tell approximately where you are, and see where each part fits into the whole process. You will usually learn specific breathing and relaxing techniques, and how to adjust your posture and make special movements to help you handle contractions.

Many women who have been to classes would say that to have anesthetics for normal childbirth is a bit like offering someone who is enjoying climbing a mountain, or a runner about to win a race, a whiff of something to ease the pain. Aching muscles are indicative of the hard work the body is doing and are part of the task in which you are totally involved as you concentrate on "riding over" each contraction with controlled breathing and neuromuscular release. There is something enormously rewarding in the rhythms of labor, even above the joy of bringing new life into the world. When you really start to swim with the waves of contractions, it can be a deeply satisfying experience. I remember feeling myself—and I am a far from athletic person—"Oh, this is one sport I can really do!"

In classes you learn, with your future birth companion, how to relax while keeping your breathing rhythmic during powerful contractions. This is often done by "lifting" breathing over the crest of each wave, allowing it to get quicker and lighter if you can no longer breathe slowly with comfort. One way of doing this is to visualize a spiral staircase. When you are at the bottom of the staircase, the breathing is slow and full, as if in big circles. When you need to, you go up the spiral into the smaller circles of quick, light breathing, ascending your spiral as far as you feel you need to go for that particular contraction, and then drop down again into slow, full breathing as it comes to an end.

Relaxation is sometimes taught as a drill, contracting the muscles of the left arm, right leg, right arm, left leg, both legs, and so on, and releasing them on command. That kind of teaching is unrelated to the actual patterns of muscle contraction in stress situations, and does little to help us become aware of how and why we tighten up. The new way is to teach relaxation as part of an increased and more positive and pleasurable body awareness, closely linked with breathing.

One of my own approaches to relaxation is called Touch Relaxation, in which the warmth and pressure of your partner's hands become the signals for relaxation and release. To feel how this works, contract some of those muscles most likely to tighten at different stressful phases of labor: in your shoulders, back, neck and throat, abdomen, inner thighs, feet, buttocks, pelvic floor, and so on. As you deliberately hold the tension, note which other muscles have contracted at the same time; observe also whether this tension has affected your breathing and, if so, how. At the same time, your partner should notice how you look, so that he or she is aware of your appearance when tense. Have your partner rest his hands firmly over the contracted muscles and then release these muscles as if flowing out toward his hands. Your partner can feel the release of tension and so knows that the message given has been effective. Even someone who lacks confidence about helping you realizes immediately that this works.

You will discover that certain kinds of touch are particularly effective. For many women firm foot holding is useful, or your partner can use massage, stroking, or holding to encourage relaxation. In labor your partner can sit holding your shoulders, breathing with you during difficult contractions while maintaining continuous eye contact. The emotional support and encouragement this gives is an advance on the kind of exercises in which a woman is supposed to fix her gaze on a spot on the wall while her partner stands by, timing contractions with a stopwatch.

Women were once prepared for the second stage of labor by being encouraged to tone and develop their abdominal muscles, and went into training in order to hold their breath for long periods. We now know that such gymnastics are not only irrelevant, but can sometimes, as in the case of prolonged breath holding, be dangerous. There is no advantage in being able to hold your breath for ten seconds or longer, and this practice may reduce the oxygen concentration in the blood available to the fetus, especially if you are also lying flat on your back, with resulting pressure on the inferior vena cava (the big blood vessel in the lower part of your body).

A major change is also taking place in the way in which breathing and posture for the second stage are taught. My own teaching focuses on the idea of the "unforced second stage," and aims to help women be aware of and respond to the surges of desire to push which come like waves within each contraction, rather than training them to push for as long, as hard, and as often as they can. The result is a less strenuous and more rhythmic, spontaneous way of handling contractions, without the need for cheerleaders urging the woman: "Push! Come on! Don't waste your contraction! Push! Push!" Your partner can remind you to think of yourself opening up, to keep your mouth soft and relaxed, and to release the muscles around your vagina. Each push is followed by shallow breathing until the next wave of desire to push builds up, when your breathing spontaneously becomes more staccato, culminating in the next automatically held breath as the baby moves down your vagina toward birth. (This kind of breathing and relaxation, and the gentle approach to the second stage, is further described in my books *Pregnancy and Childbirth* and *Women's Experience of Sex*.)

In many classes you can also learn the skills of visualization, which enable you to link actively created, vivid pictures in your head with the feeling of opening up and letting go, a much more effective way of tuning in to your body in childbirth than performing exercises.[18] I often describe the fanning-open of the tissues of the perineum as similar to the petals of a peony unfolding, for example, with the baby's head like the hard bud in the center.

Focused concentration is another important element in handling pain with your own resources. Listening to your breathing is one way of doing this. Each breath in and out sounds like a wave washing on the shore, and focusing on the sound and image of the waves enables you to become more positively aware of your body. Some women find that it helps to make "affirmations"—simple positive statements, or sometimes prayers—as they go through labor, not only to reduce the sensations of pain but to have a positive effect on the body's energy and coordination through the power of the mind: "I am strong . . . I accept the healthy pain that will birth my baby . . . My cervix is dilating more and more." An Orthodox Jewish woman I know said over and over again, "Gates of Jerusalem, open for me!" (And they did!)

A woman who has her sexual partner sharing the birth experience with her may find not only that the very fact of her lover's presence and emotional support gives her strength, but that being held, stroked, and embraced releases tension and enables pain to become a

sensation she can go with, and even enjoy. There are good physiological reasons for this. Though it may seem that making love is the
last thing a woman would want to do when she is in pain, you may
have noticed that erotic arousal can temporarily obliterate the pain
of a toothache or headache, for example. Many women have found
that lovemaking can ease both premenstrual tension and menstrual
pain. This is not only because it helps them to relax, but because
they feel suffused with a feeling of peace and satisfaction that, though
difficult to describe, somehow softens pain; though it may still be
there in the background, it seems unimportant. This is because
sexual arousal stimulates the release of natural pain-killers in the
body which are chemically related to opium.[19] As you become more
and more sexually excited, these endorphins pour into your bloodstream to change what may seem like sheer, overwhelming hard work
or an endurance test into a thrilling experience in which pain is there
but no longer dominates you.

Sexual arousal in childbirth also releases estrogen into your circulation. This helps the uterus to contract effectively, speeds up labor,
and if uterine action has been uncoordinated, can get your uterus
working better and enable the cervix to open more easily. When
there is more effective uterine function, with the upper part of the
uterus thick and the lower part soft and opening, pain is reduced,
even though contractions get stronger.

For many women, the whole of childbirth is a psychosexual experience. The energy produced by the uterus, the feeling of the baby's
head pressing down and all the tissues fanning out and opening up
—these sensations are in themselves felt as sexual, and produce the
same joyous feelings that might come from being held and caressed
by a lover. Endorphins and estrogen flood through the woman's body
to coordinate the action of the uterus and to change her perception
of pain.[20]

Many other techniques have now been introduced into childbirth
education, which, either directly or indirectly, contribute to the
relief of pain. Acupressure (shiatsu), for example, can be very helpful
when incorporated into other ways of giving comfort and finding
harmony with what is happening in your body. There are specific
points on the feet, buttocks, and wrist, where firm pressure can help
a woman cope with labor pains, and this can be linked with massage.

Teachers who have attended my workshops in body awareness in childbirth often use these techniques with their childbirth classes. Others have studied shiatsu, and sometimes acupuncture, too, and have a systematic approach based on the oriental philosophies of healing.

Most acupuncturists who work with women in childbirth, however, say that it is wrong to see acupuncture simply as a means of pain relief. They usually ask that you start treatment during pregnancy because they are concerned to help your body work harmoniously and to establish the right physical conditions for a positive experience of labor.

Ice massage is similar to acupuncture. It not only produces local constriction of blood vessels and makes the area numb, but can relieve pain for a long time after these effects have disappeared.[21] In labor it is sometimes useful over the lower back.

Transcutaneous electronic nerve stimulation (TENS) which involves intense stimulation of the skin is another way to relieve pain. Two pairs of electrodes are connected to a small battery-operated stimulator and the woman controls the electrical impulse herself, producing sharp bursts of pulsed buzzing as the pain increases. The electrodes are supposed to be taped into position on either side of the spine. In fact, it is worth experimenting with them at different sites; sometimes having a pair on the thighs, feet, or at other points on the body is still more helpful. In two Swedish hospitals where TENS was tested in childbirth, 44 percent of women said they had good or very good relief from pain using this method, another 44 percent had some relief, and 12 percent said it did not help them.[22]

Hypnosis, whether it is the kind you use on yourself or powerful suggestion introduced by someone else, can also be helpful for some women in childbirth. Though it can work satisfactorily without being practiced beforehand, it is best to start hypnosis about halfway through pregnancy; you then discover well in advance whether you are a good hypnotic subject, and can become confident that it is an effective technique. It provides complete relief from pain for approximately 20 percent of women. And many others discover that it takes the edge off pain and reduces the quantity of pain-relieving drugs they require.[23]

Yoga, which involves breathing techniques, and positions in

which the pelvis is wide, can also increase your trust in your body and bring the strength that comes from self-confidence. Try to find yoga classes especially designed for pregnant women, since the positions, movements, and types of breathing used during labor need to be related to the specific stresses you are feeling then. The teacher should have a good understanding of the physiology of childbirth, and know how it feels to be in labor.[24]

There are many other nonpharmacological ways of relieving pain, giving comfort, and increasing psychophysical coordination in childbirth: the use of heat (hot compresses; a hot water bottle tucked in the small of your back, between your legs, or over your lower abdomen; warm water, either floating in it or having it flowing over you.[25]); distraction techniques (such as slowly counting backward from ten); or what appears to be the opposite of this, the removal of all external distractions and being in a quiet, darkened room where you can surrender yourself completely to the enveloping experience without any interruptions;[26] or rhythmic sound, in the form of music, singing, or chanting—it is said that one of the queens of France gave birth singing the Magnificat!

You will probably think that some of these methods could not possibly be right for you, but there is good evidence that every one of them works for some women. Pain is diminished, energy is released, and everything the woman is feeling in labor is coordinated into a total experience which has pattern and meaning for her. There are many alternatives to using drugs for pain relief, and it is wise to select several you think would suit you, so that if one approach is insufficient other methods can be used to reinforce it. This sense of flexibility and the opportunity for choice can be empowering and may itself contribute to the reduced perception of pain.

♦ ♦ ♦ At this stage it may be a good idea to look back over all the methods of handling pain described in this chapter and note down some thoughts about each. Do you need to find out more about any of them? If so, how will you do this?

Then write about your own preferences, thinking both in terms of a labor that is going well, and also how you would want to handle pain if the going proved difficult.

Which methods, from your present vantage point, would you

decide against? Make a note of these and the questions you want to raise with your doctor or midwife about each of them. Discuss this with your birth companion, too, as it is important that this person understands exactly what you want. ♦ ♦ ♦

For a woman expecting her first baby, the question of how she is going to manage pain tends to loom large in her thoughts. But the second time around, she is often more concerned to negotiate beforehand to avoid all the irritating interference which is itself a cause of pain, so that she can give birth in her own way, in her own time, and in peace.

16

◆ OBSTETRICALLY ◆
DIRECTED BIRTH

The idea behind obstetric direction of labor is to improve on nature and get control over what can sometimes be an unpredictable, painful, long, drawn-out, and occasionally even disastrous process. One obstetrician who takes this view writes:

> The natural childbirth groups fail to understand that the practice of medicine consists of the recognition and correction of the shortcomings of nature—nature is a bad midwife. Childbirth has become safer because of increasingly sophisticated methods of diagnosis and treatment. With the illogicality of women these are the very procedures they wish to discard. . . . They insist that birth is a natural phenomenon but, equally, so is death.[1]

Kieran O'Driscoll, in Dublin, believes that complete obstetric control in labor, as distinct from a wait-and-see attitude, reduces the amount of intervention needed later, makes the mother more comfortable and, in his hospital, cuts down the number of forceps and cesarean deliveries to an impressively low 10 and 4 percent respectively. He aims at a labor lasting not more than eight hours and promises each woman that she will not be in labor for more than twelve hours. If the rate of dilation of the cervix falls below the norm, labor is speeded up with a synthetic oxytocin drip. (Called Pitocin in the United States, Syntocinon in Britain, these are artificial forms of the hormone that makes the uterus contract.) Four out of every ten women having their first baby receive uterine stimulation of this kind.[2]

The Dublin approach is probably obstetrically directed labor at its best, with one-to-one nursing care and careful explanation to the woman of everything that is happening. But a good deal of obstetric management is at a much inferior level, and in O'Driscoll's words, labor "is made even more arduous for mothers by the introduction of invasive procedures practiced in the name of the child, often with scant evidence as to their real value."[3] Failed inductions that end up in cesarean sections are a case in point. The routine use of Demerol and epidural anesthesia is another, for "benefits . . . are reaped almost entirely during the first stage of labor and the price paid largely during the second stage."[4] That price is an increased chance of forceps delivery or cesarean section. All these things turn a normal physiological process into an obstetric emergency.

So there is high-quality obstetrically directed labor, with each woman having her own personal midwife and continuity of care, on the one hand, and on the other a type of autocratic and invasive obstetric management which routinely interferes with the natural process of labor and introduces unnecessary risks.

INDUCTION

Doctors have been intervening in childbirth ever since theories about labor based on the laws of mechanics were developed, and methods of manipulating the fetus and enlarging the birth canal were devised in the hospital schools of Paris in the early sixteenth century. But they were often spectacularly unsuccessful. The practice of chemically controlling labor has become common only in the last twenty years, following the invention of synthetic oxytocin. And it is only in the last five years or so that vaginal tablets of prostaglandin gel have been used to soften and ripen the cervix and start labor.

Some obstetricians have definite rules as to which women should have labor induced—for example, those with breech babies or who are diabetic and at thirty-six or thirty-eight weeks; anyone who is two weeks over her expected date, or, depending on the obstetrician, ten days, or even one week. Some insist that all women who are over thirty-five should be induced on the expected date, or even earlier. A slight rise in diastolic blood pressure to ninety may also be an indication for induction. You can ask about your doctor's policy on induction. A rate of more than 10 percent is high.

Induced labors have disadvantages. They tend to be more painful, so induction starts a process in which powerful pain-killing drugs may have to be given. These in turn slow down labor and may lead to a forceps delivery. Induced labors are more likely than spontaneous labors to end in a cesarean section.

When synthetic oxytocin is used, the fetal heartbeat should be continuously monitored in case strong contractions are making labor too difficult for the baby and insufficient oxygenated blood is flowing through the placenta and umbilical cord into its bloodstream. Again, the combination of an intravenous drip and continuous electronic fetal monitoring prevents a woman from moving around freely.

The introduction of prostaglandins means that now more women can have their labors induced and still have a chance of vaginal delivery, because they soften the cervical tissue and make it easier for it to stretch. Even so, prostaglandins fail to induce labor in two out of every three women if the cervix is not naturally ripe.

After an induced labor, the baby may be discovered to be immature. Though a scan at sixteen weeks helps to date pregnancy, babies are still sometimes hurled into the world before they are ready. Doctors often warn a woman that she must be induced because otherwise the baby will be too big to pass easily through her pelvis, but then find that it is of average, or even below average, weight.

You do not have to agree to induction unless you are convinced that there is a strong reason to go into labor as soon as possible. Social reasons for induction—that your doctor is going away on holiday or your mother is coming to stay, for example—are no justification for interfering with the birth process.

Induction can be beneficial if a woman has severe preeclampsia or any other condition in which it could be dangerous for the baby to be left inside longer, because it is not being nourished well in the uterus. One sign that the baby is not growing—which you can observe yourself if you stand on the scales at the same time each week—would be that you were losing rather than gaining weight. Otherwise, the safest course of action is to wait patiently, keep a record of fetal movements, and look forward to the spontaneous onset of labor.[5]

In up to 12 percent of pregnancies the bag of water bursts at some time during the hours or days preceding the start of active labor, and amniotic fluid leaks out.[6] As already mentioned, induction because of premature rupture of the membranes is usually unnecessary. The chances of infection can be much reduced by not having vaginal examinations until labor is well under way, and even then having as few as possible.

♦♦♦ Make a note of anything else you want to find out about induction and acceleration of labor—for example, other women's experiences of it, and the standard practice of hospitals in the area. Your childbirth teacher is a good resource person, and you may want to do some further reading.[7] ♦♦♦

LABOR BY THE CLOCK

Obstetric management goes along with high-technology childbirth. But one simple technological invention, often overlooked because it is ancient, forms the basis of all the intervention that takes place—the clock.

The progress of dilation per hour, the number of minutes between contractions and the length of each, the time from 2 centimeters to full dilation (10 centimeters), and then from full dilation to delivery, the time the head is on the perineum, the time of active pushing, and the timing of the third stage—from delivery of the baby till delivery of the placenta—are all watched and scrutinized, often with anxiety, and recorded on the labor chart.

Yet, obstetric management aside, time is often also important to the woman in labor. Women ask: "How long will it be?" "When will the baby be born?" "How long will contractions like this last?" "When do you think I will go into the second stage?" "How many more hours of this?" These are all questions that caregivers cannot answer honestly or with any precision unless they manage labor with aggressive intervention. It means they often feel under great pressure from the woman to help get the labor over with.

But it is not such a simple matter as women wanting labor to be fast. Some women cope well with a tumultuous labor lasting only a few hours but are shattered by a long one. Others are shocked by a short, sharp labor they feel has run away with them, but can handle well a longer, more slowly unfolding labor—especially if they have some way of alleviating the backache often experienced in this kind of labor.

With any labor longer than about six hours, women are often made anxious by those caring for them about the time it is lasting. This anxiety makes labor more difficult and, by triggering the production of large amounts of the stress hormones epinephrine and norepinephrine, can interfere with its progress. There is a kind of timelessness about a labor that is going well, whether short or long. The woman is immersed in the reality of her own experience, and nothing else matters.

FETAL MONITORING

The baby's heart rate can be monitored intermittently by hand with a fetoscope (a special stethoscope), by Doppler ultrasound, or electronically. With electronic fetal monitoring (EFM), electronic signals are picked up and fed into a computer that measures and records them, producing the results on a long, continuous tracing.

On the printout—the cardiotocographic tracing (CTG)—the

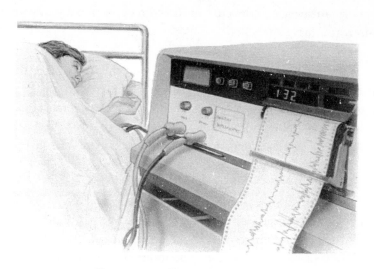

ELECTRONIC FETAL MONITORING

upper line records the baby's heartbeat, while the lower line shows the baby's movements. The normal fetal heart rate is between 120 and 160 beats per minute, but the time between heartbeats varies (the "beat-to-beat variation"), so the line zig-zags. Normally, there is a variation from 5 to 10 beats per minute, but if the baby is asleep or drowsy from narcotic drugs received from the mother's bloodstream, it may be less. When the baby kicks, or when the mother has a vaginal examination or shifts position, the heart rate may speed up.

In some labors it is sensible to have continuous monitoring—for example, if

♦ you have an oxytocin intravenous drip producing very powerful and frequent contractions.

♦ labor starts more than three weeks before the baby is due.

♦ there are signs that the baby has not grown well in the uterus and is likely to be frail.

♦ you have any serious problem during pregnancy such as diabetes, severe preeclampsia, or a very high temperature.

♦ there is meconium in the amniotic fluid.

♦ abnormalities are discovered on listening to the baby's heart rate intermittently.

One advantage of EFM is that it gives you the reassurance that all is well with the baby—provided the machine is working properly and your baby conforms to a norm. But machines cannot always be relied on, and babies sometimes look as if they are in trouble but turn out to be in good condition at birth. Another advantage of EFM is that it allows you and your birth companion to know when contractions are coming and be ready to adapt to each one.

There are two main types of monitoring machines. With the external monitor two tight bands with discs on them are taped to your abdomen, one for recording the baby's heartbeat and the other the pressure of the contractions. The internal monitor has a probe in the shape of a small wire screw like a miniature corkscrew (or a clip like a staple), which is fixed to the baby's scalp, and a pressure balloon (a tube filled with liquid) which is placed inside your uterus to record the length and strength of the contractions.

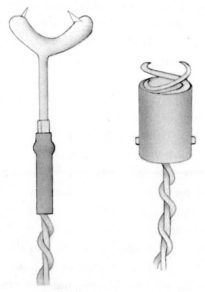

FETAL MONITOR PROBES

The external monitor is safer because it is less invasive and it can be used when the membranes are still intact. But it is also less accurate, and it is impossible to move around once you are connected. Even shifting to get more comfortable on the bed interferes with the printout, so you may be told to lie very still. This causes aches and pains—and probably would even if you were not having a baby. Sometimes the printout is only clear when you are lying on your back. But this position is dangerous in labor because the uterus may press on the large blood vessels in the lower part of your body and slow down the return of blood to your heart. This will make you feel sick, dizzy, or faint, and will reduce the blood flow to the baby. For this reason, EFM can cause the very conditions it is designed to reveal.

The internal monitor, which involves placing a clip on the baby's scalp, may also immobilize you, though without the tight bands around your abdomen it is easier to move around, and since the electrode is fixed to the baby's head, it cannot shift away from it.

But the clip cannot be put in place until the membranes have ruptured, and this is sometimes given as a reason for artificially rupturing them. This procedure, known as amniotomy, also allows the doctor to see whether or not the amniotic fluid is clear. The presence of meconium (the baby's first bowel movements) in the amniotic fluid may be a sign that the baby is under excessive stress. Once the membranes have ruptured, however, the protective cushioning of fluid in front of the baby's head, around the cord through which the blood flows to the baby, and over the fetal surface of the placenta, is reduced. In most labors in which there is no intervention the membranes do not rupture spontaneously till toward the end of the first stage, when the cervix has dilated to about nine centimeters. When they are ruptured early, the baby's head is exposed to the effects of uneven pressure during contractions and the parietal bones—the skull bones, which are like a cap divided in the middle by a suture and with the fontanelle (soft spot) at the front—may become misaligned and a swelling, called a caput, can develop under the scalp.[8] This is usually harmless, but it is occasionally a sign that there has been bruising deeper down—and the brain lies directly beneath.

There is a third kind of continuous monitoring—telemetry. With this method, radio waves record the fetal heart rate and you do not need to be immobilized. The machinery can be put in your pocket as you walk about, and the recording picked up in another room some distance away. Telemetry is not in general use, however, and when it is available the woman is still often kept in bed. This is not necessary: a similar system is in fact used by zoologists to monitor the heart rates of wild birds and animals.

There is no evidence that routine monitoring saves babies' lives.[9] It can certainly make birth more difficult for the mother, however, since there is a greater chance of cesarean section, which brings its own risks.[10] Whether or not a woman has a cesarean section, she is more likely to acquire an infection if on the internal type—and this risk increases the longer monitoring continues.[11] Many babies delivered by forceps or cesarean section because EFM indicated fetal distress are actually in vigorous condition at birth and need not have had such a delivery.[12] Signs of apparent distress may have been picked up because their heads were squeezed or because they were drowsy from pain-killing drugs received through the mother's blood-stream.[13]

Electronic monitoring is sometimes used together with scalp blood analysis. If there seem to be heart-rate abnormalities, the baby's head is pricked, and some blood drawn off and analyzed. This offers a guide as to whether or not the baby ought to be delivered immediately by forceps or cesarean section. When these two methods of assessing fetal well-being are used together, convulsions can be prevented in several babies in every thousand.[14] It is not known whether convulsions have any long-term effects on babies, though it would seem better to avoid them if possible. But there is a price to pay. That price is being strapped up or having a wire stuck in the baby's head (with the slight risk of a scalp abscess), being more or less immobilized, having many other kinds of intervention when the monitor does not work properly or the printout is wrongly interpreted, and an increased risk of forceps delivery or cesarean section.

♦ ♦ ♦ Record your thoughts about electronic fetal monitoring and anything you wish to find out more about from your doctor or midwife. ♦ ♦ ♦

AMNIOTOMY

Many obstetricians practice routine artificial rupture of the membranes as soon as the woman is admitted to the hospital and seems to be in labor, or at three or four centimeters dilation of the cervix, whether or not they wish to put an electrode on the baby's head.

The advantages are that if the baby has passed meconium into the amniotic fluid, showing that it *may* be in trouble, this can be seen. It also allows access to the baby's scalp for blood analysis, and electronic monitoring of the fetal heart rate, and may make labor shorter if the cervix is already ripe.

But there are disadvantages. In many hospitals it is the rule that once the waters have broken delivery must take place within twelve hours (or twenty-four, depending on your obstetrician). If you don't deliver by then, it will be a cesarean birth, and if it looks as if you are not going to deliver within these time limits, labor may be artificially speeded up. Amniotic fluid lubricates the baby, the cord, and the membranes. So it protects the baby's head, prevents the cord from being squashed, and helps blood flow freely between the placenta and the baby. There may be a lot of pressure against the cord, the placenta, and the baby's head during strong contractions after the membranes have ruptured, and the heart rate may slow down. If the membranes are ruptured when the presenting part is high, the cord, or an arm, may drop down.[15]

You may decide that amniotomy should not be done unless your doctor or midwife can convince you that it will be helpful in your particular labor—either because there is reason to be concerned about the condition of the baby and they want to insert a scalp electrode, or because labor is taking a very long time, you are already half dilated, and amniotomy may trigger the extra spurt of uterine activity you need.

THE INTRAVENOUS DRIP

Having an intravenous drip set up so that drugs and fluids can be introduced straight into your bloodstream is another procedure that forms part of the obstetric management of labor. Some obstetricians believe that a vein should always be opened and fluids dripped in so that the woman does not get dehydrated and drugs can be introduced straight into her bloodstream in an emergency. They consider it better for the woman to receive intravenous glucose than to be allowed to eat or drink, in case she has to have general anesthesia for a cesarean section, when she might inhale her stomach contents.

But in ensuring against one risk, this kind of obstetric management exposes you and the baby to two others. The first is water intoxication, when an excess of fluids in the body upsets its chemical balance. If severe, that could lead to brain damage. Water intoxication is more likely to occur if you are also having Demerol, Pitocin, or continuous epidural anesthesia, since they decrease the flow of urine. The other risk involves the intravenous fluid used, which is usually dextrose, a glucose solution. In the United States, high concentrations are given—20 to 30 percent—while in Britain a much lower concentration of 10 percent is the norm. There may be problems for the baby with high concentrations of sugar. Dextrose crosses the placenta, and if the baby is born with a high level of sugar in its bloodstream, but this is not kept up after birth, it can become hypoglycemic—that is, the blood sugar can drop to an abnormal level. This is one cause of convulsions. (A British anesthetist, Professor Selwyn Crawford, has stated that intravenous sugar solution is a "poison." [16])

Even if a dextrose intravenous drip is not used routinely on every woman, it is common practice to order one if a woman's blood sugar drops while she is in labor. During pregnancy you store more sugar than usual in your bloodstream to meet your baby's needs. If you don't have any food while in labor, but are using a lot of energy—especially if labor is long—you use this up and start to burn fat. If you don't drink, you are also likely to get dehydrated. Starvation plus dehydration produces ketosis. Acids called ketones build up in your bloodstream and you get a headache, become drowsy, and tend to hyperventilate. Ketosis is much more common than an emergency cesarean section requiring general anesthesia, so it would seem that avoiding starvation and dehydration by eating and drinking when you wish is a sensible course to follow.

If you develop ketosis, you could have either an intravenous dextrose drip or glucose drinks. In one hospital that has stopped using intravenous drips for ketosis, it has been discovered that ketones disappear from the mother's urine after a while if she has plenty of sweet drinks. So it is important to eat and drink when you want. Most women do not want to eat once labor is well established, and if they do, or if their stomach is already overloaded, they vomit. On the other hand, in the early phases, before your cervix is half-dilated you may enjoy foods that are easily digested: soup, smooth vegetable and fruit purées, and honey (not milk or high-fiber vegetables). Your natural thirst is a good guide to when and how much to drink. Ice water, sweetened juices or lemon tea can be very pleasant. In strong labor the stomach shuts down, but you can still absorb glucose in liquid form. Most women also enjoy sucking ice cubes.

♦ ♦ ♦   This is another subject to discuss with your doctor or midwife. Make a note of the questions you want to ask, concerning both general practice and specifically what happens if ketones appear in the urine.   ♦ ♦ ♦

EPISIOTOMY

When the crown of the baby's head pushes against the tissues of the perineum and can be seen like a wrinkled walnut just inside the vagina, surgical intervention is usually made—an episiotomy. This is an incision in the perineum to enlarge the vaginal outlet. It was introduced by obstetricians when they took over from midwives, and has now become one of the routine procedures of childbirth, performed on the majority of women having first babies—and many

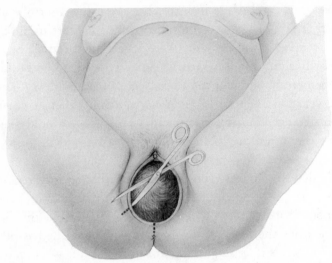

EPISIOTOMY: MEDIOLATERAL (LEFT) AND MIDLINE

having second and subsequent babies, too. In 1920 Joseph DeLee first recommended the practice of routine episiotomy and forceps delivery, claiming that this would prevent the fetal head from becoming a "battering ram" and suffering prolonged pounding and congestion leading to brain damage.[17] No proof for this statement has ever been produced. In a randomized controlled study done at the Rotunda Hospital in Dublin, babies were found to be in equally good condition at birth whether their mothers had an episiotomy, a tear, or an intact perineum.[18]

There is also the woman to consider. Women's feelings about episiotomy have hardly been investigated at all. Instead, there are numerous studies on different ways of performing an episiotomy and methods of suturing afterward. In the few research projects in which women have been asked what they think, inquiry has usually been restricted to how they feel during the six weeks after childbirth, and often only in the first week. Most doctors do not realize that women can have problems with an episiotomy and the suturing of the perineum for months, and sometimes even years, afterward.

My own research indicates that women are often shocked by the pain they experience.[19] Many have stitches that are supposed to dissolve but do not, and eventually either have to be removed or become embedded in scar tissue. Some women are sutured so tightly that there is no space for the swelling of tissue that always follows injury. They often say they cannot sit comfortably when holding the baby, and it is especially difficult when breast-feeding. Some are left with painful lumps of scar tissue months after the birth, and sexual intercourse is extremely painful—or even impossible. Only 22 percent of the episiotomy mothers said that intercourse was comfortable within the first month, compared with 39 percent of those with tears and 64 percent of those who had no injury to the perineum. Women with episiotomies tended to have pain lasting longer than three months. Another recent study in England also demonstrates that episiotomy is often performed unnecessarily, causes pain both at delivery and in the weeks after, and makes intercourse uncomfortable.[20] An episiotomy might be worth it if it had long-term benefits, but there is no evidence that it does anything to improve the condition of a woman's perineum or her pelvic muscles, and it certainly sometimes causes sexual problems.

Though there are situations in which a baby has to be born quickly, and an episiotomy is then done for a practical reason, from an anthropological point of view most episiotomies serve a ritual function and mark with a dramatic flourish the significance of the act of delivery by genital mutilation of the mother.

There is now a growing awareness among obstetricians and midwives that far too many episiotomies are done, and women having babies are asking searching questions about this surgical intervention.[21]

♦ ♦ ♦ If you decide you want to avoid an episiotomy, discuss the subject with your doctor or midwife well before labor starts. You can say that you do not want an episiotomy unless you are forewarned, are given an explanation of why you need one, and have agreed to it. You may want this written in your notes. Practice pelvic floor exercises, especially the elevator exercise (see chapter 5). Concentrate on feeling your perineum bulge down like a heavy bag of soft fruit. Also practice light, rather quick breathing with your mouth open while you feel soft and loose below. This helps during contractions as the baby is sliding out. Regularly massage the skin in and around your vagina with warm oil and concentrate on visualizing yourself open while you do this. Ask whoever is supporting you in labor to use the word "open" rather than "push." Push only when you most want to, and only as hard as you want to. Remind the person attending you that you would like to deliver without an episiotomy. When you feel the baby's head pressing through your vagina and beginning to stretch you wide open, rest your fingers lightly on the head and get into a position where you can look down and see the birth of your baby. That way you will realize when it is sensible to stop pushing and start *breathing* the baby out instead. ♦ ♦ ♦

CESAREAN SECTION

With a cesarean section the obstetrician achieves ultimate control over birth—he cuts another, artificial orifice and lifts the baby out. Through the act of surgery, he has acquired the female power of giving birth. It is his expertise, his surgical skill that produces the baby.

In the 1970s the cesarean rate in the United States increased threefold and now almost one woman in five has a cesarean birth. Though rates are lower in Europe, there is virtually an epidemic of cesarean sections throughout the Western world. An analysis of the U.S. increase gives a good indication of why most cesareans are done.[22] The most frequent reason is that *labor is slow*—dystocia. Thirty percent of the rise in cesarean sections has been attributed to dystocia. So if you would prefer to avoid a cesarean section, think ahead about the things that will help you cope with a long, tiring labor—for example, the freedom to walk about and get in the shower or bath to relax, being given a lot of encouragement and, above all, *not being hurried.*

Repeat cesareans comprise another 25 to 30 percent of the increase. A repeat cesarean section is often done because there is concern that the scar from the previous operation may rupture. So if you want to have a vaginal birth after a previous cesarean section (VBAC), tell your doctor or midwife that you do not wish your labor to be augmented with Pitocin, as this increases the risk of that happening.

Breech births are responsible for 10 to 15 percent of the increase. When a baby is born bottom first, there is a chance that the delivery of the head will be delayed, resulting in a lack of oxygen. A cesarean section for a breech birth should not be necessary if

♦ you have a normal pelvis.

♦ the baby is expected to weigh less than eight pounds.

♦ the baby is curled up into a ball with its head forward on its chest —*a frank breech.*

Fetal distress accounts for another 10 to 15 percent of the increase. This diagnosis is made more often when electronic monitoring is used. As a result, cesarean section rates tend to go up threefold when monitoring is first used in a hospital, but fall later when there is more experience with the interpretation of the printout. There are steps you can take to ensure that your baby gets enough oxygen: be well nourished, in good health, and rested when labor starts; decline induction and oxytocin stimulation; avoid drugs in labor; move about, and when you want to lie down, do so on your side rather than on your back; breathe rhythmically, stay relaxed, rest between contractions; have emotional support so that you stay confident and calm; in the second stage choose upright positions and avoid prolonged breathholding and frantic straining.

The disadvantages of a cesarean section are that it

♦ increases the risk of birth for the mother. The mortality rate is almost four times as high as for a vaginal birth, largely due to the effects of general anesthesia.

◆ is more likely than a vaginal birth to result in infection (sometimes a risk as high as 65 percent). Infection may occur in the lining of the uterus, the urinary tract, or in the wound itself.

◆ can lead to the birth of a premature baby if it is mistimed, with all the associated risks of prematurity.

◆ is more likely to result in the delivery of a baby who has breathing difficulties after birth, whether or not the baby is premature. This may be because uterine contractions and the passage through the birth canal, by squeezing out excess fluid from the lungs and massaging the baby, provide an important respiratory stimulus.

◆ introduces the additional risk of rupture (separation in the muscle wall) of the uterus in future births. With a lower-segment transverse incision rather than a vertical incision, however, this risk is slight.

Though we may think of cesarean sections as being done to save babies' lives, they are often performed for less pressing reasons, and a great many may not be necessary.

If you are a candidate for a cesarean section but would like to deliver vaginally, you will need to bring this out into the open with your doctor, discuss it fully, and have a birth plan reflecting the outcome of this discussion. You will be asking for a "trial of labor." This takes place when it is not known whether or not a woman can deliver vaginally, and is conducted in the hospital with everything ready for a cesarean section if necessary. It is a trial of the uterus and not of the woman having the baby! Obstetricians are increasingly reluctant to allow a trial of labor and advise, or insist on, an elective (planned-in-advance) cesarean section because they believe it is safer.

This is happening particularly often when there is a breech presentation. Sometimes a woman is told that if she insists on trying for a vaginal birth she will end up with a brain-damaged baby. This is just a threat and is not supported by the facts. A Canadian study of breech babies that followed the children until they were eight years old concluded: "There appears to be no difference in the subsequent health and development of breech infants whether delivered vaginally or by Caesarean section."[23]

Bear in mind, however, that if you have an oddly shaped or very small pelvis, or if the breech baby is likely to be very big, or has its legs extended, a cesarean birth may be safer in the end. Suppose that after detailed discussion you decide that a cesarean section would be wiser—what then? You need not simply hand yourself over to your obstetrician. Discuss the different ways in which the operation can be done and the different kinds of anesthesia. Let your doctor know the things that are most important to you about the birth and the time afterward. One vital aspect of good care in birth, as noted earlier, is being able to have someone with you who is on the same wavelength and gives strong and loving emotional support. This is true whether or not you have a vaginal birth, and in many ways a woman who is having a cesarean section needs that support even more urgently than when labor is proceeding normally. Contact one of the cesarean birth organizations listed under Useful Addresses for further information, and work out a birth plan that meets your needs (see chapter 19).

17

◆ CEREMONIAL BIRTH ◆ PROCEDURES

Ever since the mid-eighteenth century, when maternity hospitals were first established in England for the indigent poor so that doctors could practice on them, ceremonial procedures have accumulated which regulate everything that happens inside a hospital. These rules often erect a rigid barrier between the woman in childbirth and those attending her, and make her the passive object of care.

In those first charity hospitals, the patients were poor, powerless —and female. The doctors were powerful, well off—and male. As professional men, they were separated by the gulf of social class not only from their impoverished patients but also from the nurses, who came from the working class, and they treated them accordingly. Midwives were not employed in these hospitals, since it was probable that they would have known a great deal more about childbirth than the doctors. Instead, nurses were engaged who would be sure to defer to the doctors and take their orders from them.

Specialist doctors, the majority of them male, are still at the top of the hospital hierarchy, controlling both the patients at the bottom and the female nurses who carry out their orders. Rules and regulations provide what is intended to be a standard setting for birth, often prevent the exercise of individual initiative by any member of the staff, and attempt to ensure that every patient is treated in exactly the same way.

Most routine procedures performed on women in childbirth are of only marginal benefit to them. Some make labor more uncomfortable and difficult. But they are part of the immutable ceremonial order of the hospital. And if these ceremonies are ignored or neglected, many staff members are anxious that chaos and confusion will result. Sometimes these ritual procedures, even when of no practical value, make patients feel secure, too.

In addition to their social function of regulating behavior in the hospital, these ceremonies are also part of the armor with which some doctors, nurses, and midwives protect themselves from the anxiety experienced when dealing with the dangerous passages and major life crises of birth, sickness, and death. The initiation every medical student goes through—learning to dissect a corpse, and not see it as a dead person but as a collection of anatomical parts—is the first step in a training process that tends to screen out the doctor's awareness of the patient as an individual. As an intern, the doctor learns to perform ceremonies in obstetrics that depersonalize the woman and because they make initiative and decision making unnecessary, reduce the anxiety provoked by uncertainty.[1] Task-oriented rather than woman-oriented care encourages caregivers to deny their own feelings and to detach themselves from any personal contact with patients which might prove threatening.[2] Perhaps this is why even when research shows a procedure is unnecessary, causes discomfort or distress to the mother, or can actually be dangerous, it continues to be performed. This chapter looks at some of these unnecessary ceremonies and customs.

ADMISSION CEREMONIES AND ENVIRONMENT

Shaving

On admission to the hospital it has been the general practice to prepare the patient by shaving her perineal hair. This was first done in the nineteenth century to poor women who were having their babies in charity hospitals, to get rid of lice. It preceded the introduction of antiseptic procedures by Lister.

Studies showing that it was useless were first done in the 1960s.[3] Doctors were very nervous about undertaking any research on this subject. In one California study women who were not going to be shaved were made to wash between their legs with pHisoHex for a whole month before delivery.[4]

It was not until 1980 that a midwife researcher, Mona Romney, showed that not only did shaving have no effect on infection, but it produced great discomfort for women after the birth, with itching and burning as the hair started to grow again. She concluded: "Most patients disliked shaving and we can present no evidence to support its continued use. . . . We believe that perineal shaving is an unjustified assault and should be abandoned."[5]

Subsequent investigations with scanning electron microscopes revealed that shaving, even by skilled hands, always produces nicks in the skin which may be invisible to the naked eye but can be entry points for microorganisms and are therefore a focus for infection, even if there is no episiotomy or tearing. An editorial in the *Lancet* advised that since "preoperative shaving increases the rate of postoperative wound infection, this traditional surgical practice should be dropped."[6]

Purging

Another routine admission procedure is the giving of an enema (or suppositories) to empty the lower bowel. The idea behind this is to avoid contamination of the perineum by feces. Most women dislike it intensely and some have said that the pain produced by a large, strong enema was worse than any pain they had from contractions. Research has shown that "the enema should be reserved for women who have not had their bowels opened in the past twenty-four hours and have an obviously loaded rectum."[7] The author of this study commented: "Contamination after an enema was especially difficult to control, since it was more likely to be fluid." This research was of particular interest as the staff in the hospital where it was done were very unhappy about the project when it started and thought there would be mess everywhere. But they soon realized this was not so, and that labor was much more pleasant for women when they did not have their bowels emptied artificially. As a result, they surreptitiously omitted the enema or readily agreed with the woman when she demurred, so that the study had to be ended prematurely. Simply asking questions about procedures can start a process of change.

Immobilization

In many hospitals women in labor are put to bed. Most women are more comfortable moving about during contractions and getting into positions in which they can lean forward. They spontaneously crouch, kneel, or squat as labor advances and the birth approaches. The most uncomfortable position of all is lying down flat on your back, and there is evidence that it makes the first stage of labor longer and unnecessarily painful.[8] If a woman is lying on her back, either with her legs drawn up or suspended in the air in the lithotomy position, she is not only uncomfortable, but has to work much harder to push the baby out.

If you have anesthesia, or anything but the smallest dose of pain-relieving drugs, there may be no alternative *but* to be in bed. One study of mobility in labor seemed to demonstrate conclusively that women do not want to leave their beds. This is hardly surprising, as in that hospital most women had already received large doses of Demerol and it would have been difficult for them to stand up, let alone walk around.[9]

If you decide that you don't want to be in bed all the time, you can prepare yourself for active birth, and some guidelines for this are in chapter 5.

Loss of privacy

In many hospitals the delivery room is a public arena and some labor wards are like a busy airport or railroad waiting room. Even when each woman has her own labor room, there is often no privacy. People barge in and out without knocking, or if they do knock, do not wait for an answer. Doctors and nurses chat to each other about irrelevant topics or discuss the management of the woman's labor as if she were a log of wood. Sometimes the attendants talk about a delivery that went wrong, or another particularly interesting case, in her presence, and seem unaware that this can be terribly frightening.

If you would prefer an intimate atmosphere for your labor, it may be a good idea to say in your birth plan that you would like as much peace and privacy as possible and to have continuity of care from just one or two nurses or midwives. You may find that dimming lights and playing music also helps.

Isolation

One element of transitional rituals in traditional societies—puberty rites, for example—is separation of the novitiate from family and friends, from all the ordinary, everyday human relationships which have significance, and removal to a special place of isolation. In the twentieth century, until the mid 1970s, a woman having a baby in our Western culture was often similarly isolated from those closest to her. When she entered the hospital her husband was forced to leave her in professional hands, taking away with him a suitcase of her clothes and personal belongings. She became merely another maternity case.

The introduction of husbands into the labor room changed all that, but this has still not come about in many countries, notably the Soviet Union, where the father of the baby may not be allowed to step over the threshold of the hospital. After the birth he must stand in the street watching to see if by a sign through a window his wife can tell him whether they have had a girl or a boy.

The change came in the West partly because of the insistence of couples that they wanted to be together for this supremely important event in their lives. (One father, for example, given permission to be with his wife during labor, but not for delivery, handcuffed himself to the side of the delivery table.) It also happened because doctors began to see that when a woman had a companion with her she was calmer, needed fewer drugs for pain relief, and was a more cooperative patient. So the medical profession's acceptance of the father's presence during childbirth was double-edged. Some obstetricians quickly learned that they could collude with a man to keep the woman obedient, talk science together over her head, and persuade her to submit to interventions she did not really want. Threatening that her partner would be sent away if they did not both conform to the rules was a method of further ensuring patient compliance.

In the early days, the man might be told to sit in a corner and not speak or move. Gradually, however, it was discovered that he could be of real assistance in giving both physical and emotional support and in helping out with nursing chores. The danger now is that the special intimacy between a couple can be exploited by professionals for whom management of the father has become as much a skill as management of the woman in labor. He may be directed, for example, to watch the electronic fetal monitor, to tell her when contractions are coming. For any man who is unsure of his role and lacks confidence in his ability to give the right emotional support, this can lead to his concentrating on the machinery instead of keeping in touch with his partner's emotional experience. He has become part of the team and is no longer on her side, representing her wishes and helping her with his special understanding of her needs.

Though fathers are allowed in the labor and delivery room now, and are here to stay, it is sometimes very much on the hospital's terms and with a carefully scripted part to play. Other members of the family and friends, on the other hand, are often still denied entrance. The mother may not be allowed another woman with her in labor, for example, and if she has the baby's father with her, may be denied the right to have another support person as well.

Transfer to the delivery room

In many hospitals a woman is still moved to another room for delivery. This often entails tremendous emotional upheaval and disorientation. She is under the stress of almost continuous contractions and suddenly her whole environment changes. Unless there are reasons why she needs to be in a specially equipped theater for an operative delivery, this should not happen. It is now being realized that there is less risk of cross-infection and far less physical disturbance and emotional stress as she starts the second stage if each woman has her own private birth room in which she can labor and deliver.

MANAGEMENT OF THE SECOND STAGE

Drapes and masks

These were originally introduced in the nineteenth century in an attempt to create a sterile environment for birth. In fact, bacteria are transferred by doctors and nurses on their hands and clothing, not by ordinary breathing and talking, and there is less infection when staff members do not wear masks.[10] The wearing of masks, said the

Lancet, is "no more than an expensive ritual."[11] One tremendous advantage when those who are caring for you do *not* wear masks is that you can see their faces and relate to them as individuals.

Cheerleading and pushing to order

Cheerleading in the second stage also has a ceremonial quality. It may make everyone feel good, because there is a sense of all being in it together and at last getting somewhere. It can seem that if only the mother would push harder and longer the baby's head would appear, so everyone present exhorts her to greater effort. They may tell her to hold her breath for ten, fifteen, or even twenty seconds—and count them out for her. She may be cajoled, bullied, and threatened with a forceps delivery if she does not try harder. When she holds her breath for a really long time, goes red in the face and gasps with effort, she is likely to be praised and told that she is doing it right now. Dripping with sweat, eyes bulging, little blood vessels bursting in her cheeks and eyes, and falling back exhausted once each contraction is over, she struggles to obey the commands of her cheerleaders and tackles the second stage of labor as if she were in a prize fight.

Telling a woman when and how to push, and encouraging her to work as hard as she can, is no new obstetric invention. It has been hallowed by time, and tends to be taken for granted as the only way of giving help in the second stage. Yet it has many disadvantages. It is not only that the woman feels desperate, as if the baby will never be born, or that she is left afterward with aching muscles and a sore throat, as if she had a bad dose of flu. When she holds her breath for a long time—more than about six seconds—and simultaneously exerts effort, there are changes in her heart rate and blood pressure, and the oxygen content of the blood going through to the baby is reduced. As she deliberately holds her breath and pushes hard, her blood pressure drops until she comes up for air and gasps, when it shoots up again. She may get dizzy and faint in much the same way as some people suffering from constipation do as they struggle to empty their bowels (the reason why heart attacks often occur in the bathroom). It is not surprising that if a woman strains like this for a long time—an hour or more—abnormalities in the baby's heart rate may be discovered. This practice has led to the conclusion that the second stage of labor is always dangerous for the baby, so that strict time limits are set on it by obstetricians. It is not, however, the length of time itself, but the prolonged straining and breath holding that put the baby at risk.

So this is another subject you may want to discuss in advance with your caregiver. Is any time limit set on the second stage? If so, what is it? Will you be told to push or can you take the second stage at your own pace? In the process of discussing this, you will realize that another question is raised: When is the second stage believed to start? It is one thing for a doctor to say, "I don't like the baby's head to be too long on the perineum," and quite another to say that you only have an hour from full dilation of the cervix before you must be at the point of delivery. The second stage is sometimes considered to be the whole process following full dilation until delivery of the baby. It is much more in line with physiology to consider it as the time during which you are pushing spontaneously. Since a woman does not get an overwhelming urge to push until the baby's head is on the perineum, this means that there is often a lull following full dilation during which she is not doing anything deliberate to push the baby out and responds to the contractions very much as if they were first stage ones—that is, breathing and relaxing with them. However, another ceremony which has become an integral part of childbirth is to urge the woman to push at this point—because, she is often told, "the baby is just sitting there waiting to be born." If she says she does not want to yet, she may be coaxed into trying and persuaded to hold her breath. She often feels bewildered by this and also worried that her body is not working correctly. She may feel rather like a little girl sitting on her potty unable to produce.

When a woman starts pushing before her body is ready for it, she may tire herself out by the time she can really work with her uterus to press the baby through the birth canal. Moreover, her pushing is ineffective because she feels no physical urge telling her exactly when and for how long each push should last and how strong it should be. She may feel guilty and disheartened by this.

In the process of being born, the baby's head comes down through different levels of the pelvis called "stations." These are identified by numbers from minus four—where the top of the baby's head is four

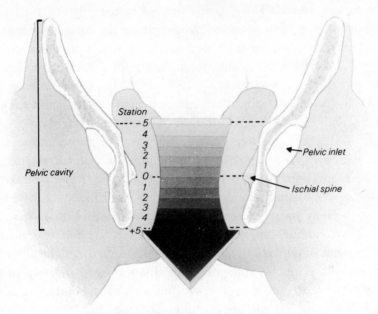

THE STATIONS OF BIRTH, FRONT VIEW

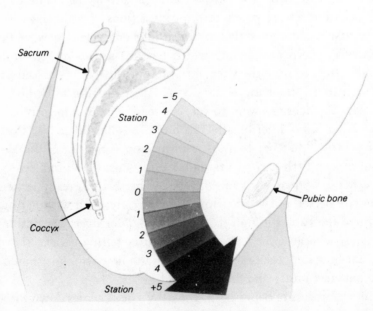

THE STATIONS OF BIRTH, SIDE VIEW

centimeters above the ischial spines (the small parts of the pelvis projecting into the sides of the pelvic cavity)—through zero—where the head is level with the ischial spines—down through plus one to plus five, the position at birth.

If by the time the cervix is completely dilated the head is already low, the pushing urge comes at or around full dilation. When the baby's head is high, there is no spontaneous desire to push. In fact, contractions often get weak and far apart, or may cease entirely for about twenty minutes—sometimes longer. This is a marvelous opportunity to have a rest and get refreshed in preparation for the active second stage. Having your hair brushed or a luxurious back massage, taking a shower, strolling around and breathing some fresh air, are all good things to do during this interval. This lull has been called "the latent phase of the second stage," and it corresponds to the gentle introduction to labor many women have at the beginning of the first stage.[12] It is only when the head comes down through the cervix onto the perineal tissues that the contractions will build up again, when what is known as Fergusson's reflex is established. (It is a fair bet that Fergusson, who was a man, never felt it, but as with many other female physiological functions, a man's name is attached to it.)

Getting a baby born is not only a matter of achieving full dilation. Tissues in and around the birth canal and the perineum need to open up before the baby can be pressed through the vagina without injury to the mother. Full dilation of the cervix precedes this further dilation. Forcing the baby down through a rigid passage is difficult for the mother and can be hard on the baby, too. A British professor of obstetrics has stated categorically: "It is a serious fault to force delivery merely because a set time has elapsed on the clock. Women must not be urged to commence bearing down merely because the cervix is fully dilated."[13]

When she pushes because she is being told she must, or because she feels she ought to, the mother's blood pressure sometimes goes up and there are late decelerations of the fetal heart. This means that the heart rate gets slower at the end of a contraction and remains slow after it has finished. A forceps delivery is then done because of fetal and/or maternal distress.

All this can be avoided if you are allowed to take your own time.

Labor should not be a competition to see how quickly it can be over. It is not only a question of being able to find your own rhythm once you are in the second stage, but also of being able to enjoy the rest period which often comes after full dilation, and of waiting to push until *you* want to, until it is impossible to ask whether you should or should not because that is the only thing you *can* do!

Some women want to push *before* they are fully dilated. The custom then is to instruct them not to push, and if they cannot obey anesthesia may be given at this point, in case forceful pushing produces trauma to the cervix. A premature urge to push often occurs if the baby is occipito-posterior (facing forward). Ordering a woman not to push when she finds it unavoidable causes anxiety, especially if there is nothing that she can do instead. A change of position, leaning forward or being on all fours, is a more effective way of helping. But, in fact, research has failed to show that there is any harm in gentle pushing before the cervix is fully dilated. Pushing like this is quite different from the kind of pushing that starts when a woman is in a state of panic because she has been told not to.

Commands to push or not to push are another way ritual intrudes on a woman's trust in her own body, often causing anxiety and distress.

MANAGEMENT OF
THE THIRD STAGE

The time from delivery of the baby until the delivery of the placenta and membranes constitutes the third stage of labor. As soon as the baby is born, the placenta starts to separate naturally from the inner lining of the uterus. This happens because the uterus continues to contract, and since the placenta cannot contract, it is automatically peeled off. The placenta is attached to the wall of the uterus like a postage stamp stuck on stretched elastic. If you let the elastic spring back, the stamp automatically peels away.

But this process can be delayed by things done at the time of birth and immediately afterward. The first intervention that can cause problems is the simple act of clamping the cord while blood is still pulsating through it.[14] Until the seventeenth century the cord was simply cut, not clamped. But when doctors began to take over from midwives, and as women began to give birth in bed rather than on birth stools, the practice of cord clamping was introduced in order to avoid soiling the bed linen. When blood cannot drain through the cord, the placenta becomes solid and compact like a firmly packed cushion, a blood clot forms behind it where the blood cannot flow, and it sometimes gets stuck. So doctors began to pull on the cord in order to get the placenta out before the cervix closed up, and taught midwives to do this, too. If this is done before the placenta has fully separated, blood oozes from partially torn blood vessels. As a result, there is greater blood loss than if everything was left to happen naturally, and sometimes the placenta is retained while at the same time the woman is hemorrhaging.

In the 1930s ergonovine, an alkaloid of a fungus that grows on rye, was developed and used to make the uterus contract harder. This meant getting the placenta out more quickly still, lest it become trapped inside the firmly contracted uterus. Since then, synthetic oxytocic drugs have also been developed for this purpose, and their use, with ergonovine or alone, is now standard practice in obstetrics. An injection is given in the mother's thigh to force the uterus to contract as soon as the baby's anterior shoulder is delivered, or immediately following the birth. Then the cord is clamped to avoid large amounts of excess blood being forced into the baby's circulation by these abnormally strong contractions. This is followed by "controlled cord traction," delivery of the placenta by pulling on the cord before the cervix closes up. All this is done to avoid postpartum hemorrhage (PPH). The idea is that if the placenta is expelled quickly and the uterus can clamp down on itself, the pools of blood formed when the fingerlike projections all over the maternal side of the placenta are sheered away will close rapidly so that there is minimal blood loss. The drugs employed are useful, and can be life-saving if there is heavy bleeding, but there are disadvantages to their routine use, as there are also with early cord clamping and pulling on the cord.

♦ When the cord is clamped while still pulsating, the baby is cut off from its oxygen supply and thrown onto its own resources. There must be no delay in the start of breathing.

♦ Early cord clamping also deprives the baby of blood that is rightly its own. It is especially important for a premature baby to receive this blood.

♦ The third stage tends to last longer when the cord is clamped while blood is still pulsating through it. The placenta usually separates easily if it is allowed to bleed.[15]

♦ Ergonovine causes a rise in the mother's blood pressure and can result in headaches, dizziness, ringing in the ears, palpitations, and cramps in the legs and back. It makes any nausea and vomiting much worse.

♦ Once ergonovine has been given, if the clamping of the cord is left for as long as three minutes the baby gets overtransfused as the contractions of the uterus force blood into its body. One result of this is that many babies develop jaundice because they have more red cells than they can cope with.

♦ When the cord is pulled, it sometimes breaks accidentally. Occasionally, too, when part of the placenta is still attached, some gets left behind. If part or all of the placenta gets trapped in the contracted uterus, there must be manual removal under general anesthesia. If it has not separated, the uterus is occasionally even pulled inside out.

♦ For a woman who is Rh negative with a Rh positive baby there is a special disadvantage to these procedures. As the placenta is peeling off, some fetal blood cells can escape into her circulation. This is more likely to happen when the cord is clamped early, because a good deal of the baby's blood is in the placenta at this stage, and as pressure rises in the placenta some blood vessels may burst. This results in isoimmunization (the build-up of antibodies in her bloodstream), which can jeopardize the next pregnancy.[16]

If you want to have a natural third stage you can ask

♦ to be in an upright position (squatting or kneeling) for delivery of the placenta, so that gravity helps its expulsion;

♦ not to be given ergonovine or any form of oxytocin unless you start to bleed heavily;

♦ not to have the cord clamped until it has stopped pulsating;

♦ to deliver the placenta yourself by pushing.

Remember, though, that if an injection to make the uterus contract *is* given, the cord *should* be clamped to prevent the baby from receiving too much blood.

HOW THE BABY IS TREATED

Handling at delivery

How would you react if told that there was a species of animal that hung its young upside down at birth and hit it! That used to be the practice when a baby was born, and there are doubtless some doctors who still do it. The standard TV scene of delivery shows a doctor suspending a screaming baby from its heels as he announces through his mask, "It's a boy!" This practice is unnecessary and may be harmful. Frederick Leboyer claims that sudden extension of the spine after being curled up in the uterus could be painful and shocking for the baby, and may cause physical harm: "The spinal column has been strained, bent, pushed, and twisted to the limits of its endurance— and now it is robbed of all support. And the head, so supremely involved in the passage outward—now it also is dangling, twisting. And this at the very moment when, in order to calm this vast terror, this panic, what is essential is a coming together with the mother, a *reuniting.*" [17]

At birth the baby encounters cold air and noise of a very different kind from that experienced in the uterus, is placed in unfamiliar contact with cloth, metal, and plastic, and is put under bright lights for the first time. It is a dramatic transition from the warmth, comfort, glowing light, and velvety softness of the uterus. Hands touch the baby, sometimes roughly as if the child were a lump of meat, sometimes tenderly, expressing reverence for the new life.

You may want to think about the environment your baby is born into and the way your child is welcomed to life. You can ask, for example, that the birth take place in a dimly lit room, that the voices of the attendants be lowered and that there are no extraneous sounds, that the baby be delivered straight onto your abdomen, and that you are in skin-to-skin contact for as long as you choose. When the birth is straightforward, it is often possible for you to lift the baby from your body yourself, especially if you have help and encouragement to do so. This is an incredible experience!

EYEDROPS

In some countries the baby must receive eyedrops as prophylaxis against gonococcal blindness. Silver nitrate treatment was introduced in Germany by Dr. Crede in the nineteenth century and is still often used, though today there are better alternatives—tetracycline and erythromycine—which do not irritate the eyes and may be even more effective.[18] In some countries, for example the United Kingdom, eye treatment for newborn babies has been discarded unless it is shown to be needed. This may be another issue to consider, perhaps discuss with a pediatrician, and include in your birth plans.

BONDING TIME

A new rite has been added to the care of the newborn in the hospital —"bonding time." In theory it is a marvelous idea, and acknowledges a new concern about the relationship between mother and baby and the need for nurses and doctors to understand the emotional aspects of the postpartum experience. In practice, it becomes another ceremonial procedure.

Feeling you have to bond in ten minutes flat (or knowing that people are watching you to see if you are bonding correctly) is unlikely to help you fall in love with your baby. It can be even more difficult if the baby is then taken to the nursery. Even having the baby close to your bed but being told not to disturb it interferes with spontaneous behavior and emotions.

Many women do not fall in love with their babies immediately. You need time to be close to your baby and to get to know each other. As you think ahead to the hours and days after birth, consider what is likely to help you most to relax and enjoy your baby. In many new mothers' experience, it is best to be free to cuddle the baby whenever you want, have lengthy sucking sessions in which you ignore time and just enjoy being together, and have the baby in bed whenever and for as long as you choose. On the other hand, you may also want to know that someone will keep an eye on the baby if you wish to sleep and find it difficult to drop off if the baby is in your bed, as some women do; or you may feel that you simply must have a night of more or less undisturbed sleep and need to know there is someone there to care for the baby if you decide to do this.

You will get more ideas about how you would like those days after birth to be if you talk to other new mothers and find out how it was for them. Breast-feeding is undoubtedly the best start to life for any baby; to help you decide whether you want to nurse your baby, you may find it helpful to read my book *The Experience of Breastfeeding*.

Incorporate your wishes for after the birth in your birth plan. Remember to be flexible and think about what you might want if you are very tired, or uncomfortable with stitches in your perineum. Whatever happens, you will then have prepared for your baby's first days of life outside your body with forethought and understanding.

◆ AUTONOMOUS BIRTH ◆

18

◆ THE CONCEPT OF ◆
AUTONOMY

AUTONOMY: freedom, liberty, scope, self-determination,
  noninterference, emancipation
AUTONOMOUS: independent, unconstrained, unconfined,
  unhindered, unshackled

Roget's Thesaurus

There are two distinctly different styles of birth, *obstetrically managed* birth and *autonomous* birth. Before you start to draw up your birth plan you need to consider which of these overall styles of childbirth you prefer. By "autonomous" I mean that you make your own informed decisions after considering the alternatives and give birth in an environment where you have the self-confidence to act spontaneously. You may need a great deal of help from other people to do this. Or you may have everything within yourself to give birth using your own power and energy.

The term "natural childbirth" often implies a labor and delivery without intervention of any kind. Sometimes, however, intervention is helpful and is safer for the baby or results in a more positive birth experience for the mother. An autonomous birth is one in which the woman is free to do exactly what she feels like doing—moving about or lying down, if that is what she wants at the time—and in which she decides what help she needs. It is not only a matter of active birth and being able to move about—though this is important—but of being an active birthgiver rather than a passive patient. It is basically a question of who accepts the main responsibility, and ultimately of where the power lies—with the obstetrician or with you. Whether labor turns out to be natural or assisted, straightforward or complicated, short or long, with or without pain-relieving drugs, when it is an event for which a woman accepts personal responsibility, considers the advantages and disadvantages of different alternatives, comes to her own decisions, and has the freedom to follow them through, it is an autonomous experience.

Autonomous birth is not just a matter of writing down how you would like your birth to be, or of not having people do things to you against your will. It is something much more positive than that. Autonomous birth entails

♦ choosing an environment for birth in which you are free to be yourself. You can forget your public, polite, performing self and surrender to intensity of feeling. You prepare yourself as fully as you can to meet the stresses and challenges of childbirth and to ride the waves of a powerful and fathomless experience.

♦ being able to rely on continuing companionship in labor from someone of your choice who in no way represents or reinforces the power of the hospital, but is there to support *you* and can be your anchor in a stormy sea.

♦ having a midwife or doctor who understands what you are trying to do and who knows how to give positive support. Some professionals do not realize that if you hope to manage without drugs or any other intervention in labor it is not enough simply to leave you alone to get on with it. You need positive support for what you are doing. If labor is long or tiring, or you hit a storm in the late first stage, or if there is a delay at any phase, you will need other kinds of help: warm encouragement, emotional support, suggestions about ways in which you can deal with the challenges yourself (such as breathing and relaxation, walking about, taking a hot shower or relaxing in the bath, being massaged where you have pain or there are signs of tension, kissing and cuddling and nipple stimulation from someone you love to stimulate your uterus).

♦ seeking the information you need in order to weigh up the pros and cons of different courses of action and learning how to use obstetricians and other professionals as valuable resource people.

This is far from straightforward, since access to information is controlled by those in power, and the very act of seeking knowledge is seen by some doctors as threatening. Yet one thing is clear: "If you don't know your options, you don't have any." [1]

♦ speaking and acting with assurance so that your wishes are clearly understood and you define the limits of what other people do to you. As we have seen already in chapter 10, it is not easy to be assertive in childbirth unless you have developed the habit of calm, confident assertion in the rest of your life. For many women labor is an overwhelming experience in which they feel swept along by forces beyond their control. This is why, however much knowledge you have about alternatives, and however sure of yourself you feel during pregnancy, assertiveness should not be left to chance and you need to practice and cultivate it during pregnancy.

♦ having the strength that comes from flexibility and awareness of the alternatives in any situation you are likely to encounter, and avoiding the weakness inherent in rigidity.

♦ ♦ ♦ Consider the different elements of autonomous birth as I have outlined them in this list, and if this is the kind of birth you want, use it to assess your own strengths in preparing for such an experience. Make a note of each of your strong points. Then look over the list again to see where you need to do more work and perhaps seek help to prepare yourself for an autonomous birth. Note any decisions you want to make as a result of this. ♦ ♦ ♦

Autonomous birth is not necessarily easy, straightforward, or brief. Jan's labor, for instance, was at times stormy and frustrating. But she was clear in her mind about what she wanted and approached the whole experience with verve, had loving care from her partner and women friends, and with enlightened support from her midwives, succeeded in having an autonomous birth.

In the early phases she was so excited that she overreacted to the initial signs of labor and expected the baby to be born almost any minute. She phoned me and asked if I thought she should go into the hospital yet. I urged her to stay at home, see friends, go for walks, eat when she was hungry, and keep moving. However, this latent phase of labor, during which her contractions became increasingly painful, lasted close to eight hours. She remained keyed up and too alert to rest properly. Her husband called me and said, "She is exhausting herself with her own determination." Here is Jan's own description of what happened:

The atmosphere in the house truly felt festive—like we were getting ready for a special event. P. and I walked down to the supermarket—good, brisk walk with contractions coming every five minutes. Then we had dinner of rich chicken broth, whole wheat bread—contractions still maintaining the same intensity, lasting forty to forty-five seconds every five to six minutes. From 9 P.M. to 11:30 or 12 could manage the contractions by holding on to the mantlepiece and rocking. Also walked around the house frequently. Around 12 started to hang from Bill's shoulders—bend at the knees and sway from foot to foot. That as it turns out was going to be my most enduring and comfortable position.

I *nicely* insisted that I wear my own blue cotton shirt, not regulation gown. We went to the big Active Birth Room—good atmosphere. When given an internal I was only three to four centimeters dilated. The midwife who admitted me put a fetal heart monitor on—seemed alarmed by a sudden fall in heartbeat—put an oxygen mask on me. Bill annoyed, as it was the machine's fault and should not have been a cause of worry for us.

I managed to doze off during contractions. Bill sat in front of me while Cathy rubbed my lower back—felt very good. To my great happiness the lovely midwife who shared the parentcraft class—Heather—was our midwife. Couldn't have been better. Started suggesting alternative positions for dealing with contractions—on all fours—raising the height of the bed so that I could lean on pillows—birthing stool. I was still finding that hanging from Bill's shoulders was the best way to deal with the contractions. Starting to say "Oh God!" a lot of the time.

At 10:30 Heather suggested a shower. Cathy talked me though the next half-hour in the shower. During a contraction

I held on to a vertical bar and literally belly danced, trying to relax my rectum and allow the head to drop, dilating the cervix. Between contractions I sat on a bench, dropped my head, attempted to let everything go limp while Cathy sprayed me with water. I was so relaxed on occasions that I would fall asleep, only waking because another contraction was coming.

Bill was lying on the bed, the midwife was sitting chatting to him and a young student nurse, all very jolly. The contractions were tough. I remember saying to Cathy, toward the end of the shower, "I physically can't take much more, I am just so tired."

But when I returned to the room the urge to push came. The energy was unbelievable. Heather did another internal and confirmed that I was about nine centimeters and yes, I could start pushing. Hallelujah! What a turnabout in my energies! I became euphoric—remember loading film in the camera between contractions, tried several different positions—on all fours, but didn't find this to be as successful as sitting in a very vertical position or squatting on the bed with arms around the shoulders of midwife and student nurse.

The pushing sensation is a most extraordinary one—the whole universe being pushed into the rectum. The sun was shining brightly into the room. I felt a cocoon of support around me. The pushes were strong. Never needless chatter. Episiotomy was discussed, with the unanimous decision to avoid it if possible—meant twice panting like a frenzied dog in spite of the fact that the uterus continued to push.

When Heather said to feel the head, the emotion building up in me was like a volcano about to erupt. Once the head and shoulders had emerged I pulled him up onto me. I remember very well the tears of joy and relief and disbelief as he lay on my chest—me fumbling with a breast which he was not at all interested in. He cried immediately but soon stopped.

I had a small lateral vaginal tear. An experienced doctor handled it beautifully while I cuddled William. Then he and I just lay together for a while, and Heather brought me in toast and tea.

The euphoric feeling was with both Bill and me and we only had to look at each other or the baby and we'd start to cry.

Plans often need adapting in the light of experience. But this need not deprive you of autonomy. Tricia, for example, very much wanted to have her second baby at home. Because she had had a cesarean delivery with her first child, however, her doctor was unhappy with the suggestion, but he agreed that she should have a natural birth if possible. "After a great deal of thought and discussion and soul-searching," Tricia explained to me, "we decided to have the baby in the hospital. We felt happy with this decision because we were very fortunate to find an excellent obstetrician who feels as we do, that birth is a normal, natural process, which should not be interfered with unless there are very strong indications for doing so. She thought our requests—no electronic monitoring; no artificial rupture of membranes, no episiotomy, and no injection to help expel the placenta—were perfectly understandable." This is how Tricia's labor went:

After two false labors, I went into labor proper at 5 A.M. My husband stayed off work and we had a lovely morning playing with our daughter, walking the dog, and shopping. At 12 noon the contractions began to demand my relaxation and attention. By 2 P.M. I felt the need to breathe through them. By 4:30 P.M. I had to do upper-chest breathing and occasionally had to disappear into the bedroom with my husband to regain control over the contractions by relaxation and breathing. Fortunately, my mother was here to play with my daughter, so my husband was able to give me his full attention, without which I could not have coped.

By 8:30 P.M. I was only four centimeters dilated and the contractions had been coming at intervals of two minutes—lasting for one minute—for some time. I was beginning to feel that I might not be able to manage if I had many hours to go. At 9:30 P.M. I asked my husband to phone the hospital and inform them that we were going in. As he put the phone down, I began to shake and feel sick. I knew that these were signs of transition, but didn't dare hope that I was so far on.

The half-hour car journey was very trying, but once in the

delivery room I vomited, which gave me enormous relief. They asked Michael what we did and didn't want, and put a mattress on the floor for us. I suddenly heard myself grunting and felt frightened that they would tell me I couldn't push yet. I felt then that I would lose control. Much to my relief, they told me to push, and they ruptured the membranes.

We had wanted some pictures of the delivery, but I was unable to let my husband go to take them, so the pediatrician kindly took over this role. After a couple of contractions when I felt quite confused, I got into the rhythm of pushing. The midwife went out of her way to avoid doing an episiotomy. I had a quick second stage of twenty minutes and Sophie was delivered at 11:06 P.M.

I enjoyed my labor and delivery enormously. In fact it was the best day of my life. It was the most fulfilling thing I have ever done.

I feel that I have held the universe in my hands.

19

◆ DRAWING UP YOUR ◆
BIRTH PLAN

One way of helping yourself toward autonomy in childbirth is to construct a birth plan based on all the notes you have already made as you have gone through this book. It will give those caring for you a clear idea of what you want and provide a good basis for discussion. Here are some general guidelines for writing your plan: At the beginning there should be a brief outline of principles relating to *behavior,* not attitudes. You can't change people's attitudes, but you can monitor what they do. You might want to say, for example, "Except in an emergency, if intervention of any kind is proposed, I want to be told what it is, its effects and side effects, and why it is considered necessary, and have time to discuss this with my partner in private." Or you could say, "For me, effective pain relief by whatever means available is of primary importance," or "I want to be certain that the person who cares for me in labor is someone with whom I have already established a relationship."

The birth plan should go on to list particular requests. Emphasize the positive rather than simply saying that you don't want something. For instance, "No episiotomy!" sounds like part of a manifesto. It may make the doctor or midwife anxious about what to do if there is stress on your perineum and you are about to tear. It is better to say: "I would prefer a tear to an episiotomy, and hope to be able to deliver slowly to avoid any perineal wound."

If you are having your baby in the hospital, make sure that your plan covers everything that happens from the time you are admitted.

There are problems with birth plans in some hospitals because they have a system of "standing orders." This means that when a woman is admitted labor is conducted according to a protocol that is applied to all patients of that doctor or nurse-midwife, or sometimes to all patients in the hospital. This may be quite different from the things you have negotiated. You can ask in advance whether standard care is provided until your own doctor arrives, and make an arrangement with him or her and with the head nurse to ensure your wishes are respected from the moment you go into the hospital.

Your plan should not be vague. "I want an active birth" may leave someone unfamiliar with the term unable to understand what you mean. Be clear and specific: "I wish to be free to be out of bed and move around throughout labor."

Show that you are aware that in labor you may want something different from what you envisaged in pregnancy: "I want to be able to eat during labor, if I feel like it at the time."

Your plan should take into account the care you would like to have if there are deviations from the normal: "I am happy to have electronic fetal monitoring if labor is prolonged, the baby is in an unusual position, or there are deviations from the normal which are fully explained to me. Otherwise I should like to have intermittent monitoring."

Think of building your birth plan in several stages. To begin with, write down the things that are most important to you, together with any interventions you particularly want to avoid. This should be followed by a discussion with your doctor or midwife. You may then want to find out more about particular aspects of care or procedures about which you have not already made up your mind, so you will need to talk to other women who have had babies, do some reading, and so on. By thirty-six weeks you should have a clear idea of what you want and of your priorities. Talk it over freely with the person who is going to be your birth companion. Then draw up a new, modified birth plan and discuss this at one of your prenatal visits. You can ask your caregiver to confirm your discussions by indicating on the final version that you have talked together about these subjects and that you are in agreement. One copy should go with your notes, and you should have another with you in labor. Then there can be no confusion.

Bear in mind that doctors and midwives are very anxious about birth plans. You may find you need to reassure them about why you want a birth plan. Explain that you are flexible and will accept intervention if you consider it necessary, and that you are glad to have advice (even though sometimes in the end your conclusion may be different from theirs).

Here are some examples of birth plans drawn up by real women— not models on which to base your own. First a short simple one:

BIRTH PLAN

To the midwife who attends me in labor

If my labor proceeds in a spontaneous and natural manner with no complications, then the following points are of main concern to me. It will help me to relax more if I feel they can be taken into consideration.

1. If possible, I would like my baby to be born in a room where the lights can be dimmed after delivery.
2. Unless it is absolutely necessary, I would prefer not to be continually monitored by machinery that prohibits my movement.
3. Because I worry about their effect on the baby, I would prefer that drugs not be administered unless I request them.
4. If I am not too exhausted after delivery and the baby is fine, I would like the baby to be placed on me. Also, I would prefer that the cord not be clamped until it has stopped pulsating unless there is a specific reason for doing so.
5. After delivery and provided all is well, I would like to keep my baby with me in order to breast-feed on demand and I would be grateful for any help or advice from the staff.

The following birth plan is in the form of suggestions for a woman to consider. It is used at McMaster University Hospital, Hamilton, Ontario.

BIRTH PLAN

It is always helpful to give some thought in advance to your baby's birth, and to your stay in hospital. Putting your plans in writing will help you to clarify them in your own mind and will allow us to discuss them with you.

Pregnancy

Are you taking (or have you taken) any childbirth education classes?

The hospital maternity tour? If not, do you plan to take any?

Labor and Birth

1. *If all goes normally.* (Please make note of anything that may be important to you, such as who you might wish to have with you, your plans in regard to medication, epidural, place, or position for birth, etc.)
2. *Contingency plans.* (Please note your thoughts about what you might want done if things don't go the way you planned; if, for example, you have a long or difficult labor, require more pain relief than you had anticipated, need forceps, episiotomy, or a cesarean; if the baby is premature or ill. It is often valuable to think about things like this in advance.)
3. *Personal plans.* (Do you wish to take photos, bring in a tape recorder for music, or do you have any special requests to bring to our attention?)

Postpartum

(Any special plans about baby feeding, or baby care?)

For our information

Who will be the doctor for the baby in the hospital?

If you have a boy, do you wish him to be circumcised?

Do you plan on early discharge from hospital?

Thank you. This sheet will be kept with your chart, and will serve as a guide to those who will be caring for you in hospital.

A problem with hospital-designed birth plans, however, is that they define your parameters of choice; they are like set menus. They are very useful in getting women, some of whom might not have thought beforehand about what they wanted or did not know that there were any alternatives, to make decisions about the kind of care they prefer. But they may have the effect of actually preventing some alternatives from ever being considered. So if hospitals do devise their own birth plans, it is important that they discuss and develop them with women having babies, preferably through some kind of study group in which there can be a free exchange of ideas with the staff.

The next birth plan is a sample one devised by the organization Choice, a member agency of Women's Way in Philadelphia.

BIRTH PLAN

We have written this birth plan in partnership with our midwife so that we can be involved in the birth of our baby. This is an ideal plan, based on our hope that labor and birth will be normal and that Joanna and the baby will not have problems. We know that there may be problems or emergencies, and that we may need to use a medication or procedure we would rather avoid. If this happens, we would like to have the problem explained and our questions answered, so that we can give our informed consent.

As long as there are no problems with Joanna's or the baby's health:

1. Paul, the baby's father, would like to be present during labor and birth.
2. Joanna would rather not be shaved or have an enema.
3. She would rather not have an IV inserted unless labor is very long, or medication is needed.
4. Joanna and Paul have learned breathing and relaxation exercises. If it is needed, she would prefer to use a mild medication to ease the pain before using anesthesia. We would like to avoid general anesthesia.
5. As long as she is comfortable, she would like to walk or sit during labor.

6. If labor contractions are not strong enough, we would like to strengthen them by doing these things if possible: walking, taking a warm shower; then, if necessary, amniotomy, and uterine stimulation only if essential.

7. We would like to have our baby's heart monitored by the midwife using a fetoscope, and contractions monitored by the midwife listening to Joanna's description of them and feeling her abdomen to tell their strength and length. If it is needed, we would rather use external than internal electronic monitoring.

8. Joanna would like to give birth in the same room she labors in, in a position that is comfortable for her.

9. If possible she would like to avoid an episiotomy.

10. After the baby is born, we would like to have one to two hours with her to hold her, nurse her, and get to know each other. If there is a problem with the baby's health and she must go to the nursery right away, Paul would like to go with her, and Joanna would like to join them when she can.

11. If a cesarean birth is needed, we would rather use regional anesthesia, and Paul would like to be in the delivery room. If possible, we would like to spend time together before the baby is sent to the nursery.

12. While Joanna and the baby are in the hospital, we would like the baby to room in so that she can feed her whenever she is hungry.

We look forward to working with you during labor and the birth of our baby.

Joanna Adamson
Paul Adamson

I agree to honor the wishes of Joanna and Paul as long as labor is normal and the mother and baby's health allows it. If a problem comes up, I will discuss it with them before taking the necessary medical steps.

Susan Brown, C.N.M.

As you can see, the advantage of this one is that it is signed by the caregiver, in this case the nurse-midwife. Like other birth plans, it is not a legal contract, but when plans are signed in this way it gives them a certain formal status which suggests that they are morally binding.

It is sometimes asserted that birth plans do not work, and never can, because it is the doctor who is ultimately in control. It is true that in the last resort a woman may be coerced into compliance with caregivers who do not respect her right to make decisions. But birth plans can be a valuable way of opening negotiation with caregivers, building communication, and, indeed, of educating them about what women want. It is through such ventures, through pressure put on the medical system primarily from outside, rather than from changes doctors and nurses themselves introduce, that childbirth can be improved for *all* women, not only those who are vocal and know what they are seeking.

You may be surprised by your caregivers' readiness to cooperate with your birth plans, even in a hospital which a few years earlier was not open to suggestions from patients. Kathy, for example, told me that she was very unsure about how her birth plan would be received in a hospital in the Midwest which was not known for being progressive. She was pleased when she was invited to go on a tour of the labor and postnatal wards and encouraged to ask as many questions as she wanted: "A senior nurse said that they might be introducing a proforma birth plan to be issued at the first prenatal visit —not to impose anything on the mother but to give her something to think about, if she wanted to." When Kathy met the head nurse she produced her birth plan, but the head nurse seemed "rather put out that I had felt it necessary to put my wishes in writing, since most of what I had asked for was standard practice." Here is Kathy's birth plan.

BIRTH PLAN

I would like the birth of our baby to be as natural as possible, as long as the life and well-being of me and the baby are not endangered.

Enema: No.

Shaving: No.

Artificial breaking of waters: Only if necessary. Please discuss first.

Induction: Only if necessary. Please discuss and check dilation first.

Electronic fetal monitoring: Internal—preferably only in the event of an epidural. External—not continuously. Monitoring for a few minutes at a time every half-hour (say) would be perfectly acceptable.

Position: As I feel the need at the time. I am likely to want to move around, at least in the early stages.

Pain relief: None if I can manage without. If Demerol is used, please start with 50 mg, and check dilation first. Epidural only after discussion.

Episiotomy: I would rather matters went slowly enough for this not to be necessary. I would prefer to tear rather than be cut. Please discuss first.

Delivery of baby: Onto my stomach immediately. I would like the baby to be able to suckle if it wants.

Cutting the cord: Not until it has stopped pulsating (at the earliest).

Syntometrine injection: If this can be avoided, so much the better, otherwise not until the cord is cut.

Aspiration of mucus: If the baby is breathing satisfactorily, then no aspiration please.

Environment: At delivery or before, lights dimmed; no unnecessary noises please.

Section: If time, then epidural; I realize that a general anesthetic may be necessary. I would like a trial of labor first, please. To the best of my knowledge I am not allergic to penicillin.

Feeding: Breast-feeding only, on demand both day and night.

My husband Dave knows and is thoroughly familiar with the contents of this birth plan; he will be able to discuss any aspects as required if I am not in a fit state to do so!

As it turned out, Kathy didn't get all the things she asked for in her birth plan, but the relationship with her caregivers was so good and discussion so open that from her point of view the birth went exactly as she wished. This is how she described labor:

At 5 A.M. I woke to find myself leaking. At 6:30 A.M. contractions started and seemed to me to be very close—closer than I had expected so early on—about three to four minutes—deep breathing and concentrating on the rest of me helped—especially shoulders and legs. I went into the hospital and was examined—two centimeters.

I was put on an external monitor for half an hour. The midwife brought me some toast, tea, and marmalade. I managed half a slice and half a cup, but no more. Somewhere around this time my body demonstrated its lack of need for an enema by emptying itself from both ends, so I made no further attempt to eat any breakfast.

I sipped water using a straw—a godsend. I couldn't hold a cup—Dave had to for me. I vaguely remember hearing music —Haydn, Vivaldi. I rocked back and forth through these contractions—I really felt I could not move about but this small movement helped. I asked for Demerol at 9:45. When they examined me, they said that as I was eight centimeters dilated and perhaps I could manage without it. This news bucked me up tremendously. Sometimes I forgot to breathe in-between contractions. Dave realized and reminded me. I remember trying to work out my rate of dilation per hour given that I'd gone from two to eight centimeters in three hours, to give me some idea of how long it would take to get to ten centimeters. But I gave up.

When I said I was getting a different feeling, like pushing, people seemed to turn up rather suddenly. The midwife examined me and said I was 9½ centimeters and that there was a lip which was swelling. She suggested that I should turn over and stick my bottom in the air to drop the baby back and allow full dilation, but it seemed too much of an effort, so she said she'd try something first, and on the next contraction she flipped the lip over the head and we were straight into the second stage at around 11 A.M. Dave helped me to get up and squat. I leaned forward on to my hands. I tried hanging on to Dave around his neck, but it didn't work so well, so I reverted to all fours. I began breathing too hard between contractions, and when the midwife asked me whether I was still having a contraction, I calmed down. The pain of the contractions had gone. Instead, there was the pain of stretching skin. At one point I said, "It hurts," and Dave said, "It's got to," and so I carried on.

The midwife, when she could feel the head coming, asked me to sit back so she would have more control. Dave was on my right, helping me to push from that side, and I held a lever on the left. At first they wanted little pushes, which Dave translated into terms I could cope with in a rhythm—push, relax, push, relax. Then panting, then back to push, relax. Then, "You can feel the head if you like. Do you want a mirror?" "No, thank you." What an extraordinary feeling, to touch the head! In between contractions I could relax totally, and the sitting-back position, knees up, helped. It took several contractions to deliver the head. What a relief then! The stretching eased dramatically. Then some more for the shoulders, and suddenly I let go and the baby was on my stomach. Time: 11:25 A.M.

The cord stopped pulsating very soon and then they clamped it. For the delivery of the placenta I should have got up again and squatted, and not been in such a hurry perhaps; but I didn't want to leave it too long so we agreed that I should have a Syntometrine injection and the placenta came away soon after. I had first degree tears to the labia and inside; the midwife thought I might get away with no stitches, but called the doctor anyway who decided to stitch, to guarantee a clean mend.

Afterward the midwife commented on how relaxed I'd been and this had undoubtedly helped the birth and minimized the tearing. The baby's head was apparently rather big.

At 1 P.M. we returned to my room. How strange! The last time I was in that elevator I was carrying Blob. Now I was carrying Michael.

Look back at Kathy's birth plan. Nearly everything was just as she wanted. Though she asked for Demerol once she was having strong contractions, the midwife, realizing that she wanted as natural a birth as possible, encouraged her to cope without it by letting her know how fast she was dilating. Kathy had asked for a few minutes of electronic monitoring every half-hour or so. In fact, her midwife thought it was better to do continuous monitoring for half an hour early in labor to make sure that all was well, and then to monitor the baby's heart using a fetal stethoscope which did not involve any electronics at all. To avoid an episiotomy the midwife worked closely and carefully with her so that birth could be slow and gentle. She had a uterine stimulant after the cord was cut because she was impatient to deliver the placenta, but this was only done after discussion and with her agreement. Kathy feels that her birth plan worked well.

One of the great criticisms of birth plans is that a woman may set her sights on an ideal and be very shocked if labor is difficult or there are complications. This is why it is important also to make contingency plans to cope with the unexpected. Julie and Philip had decided on a home birth and Julie's sister, Penny, who is a midwife, was looking forward to caring for her in labor. In the event, the baby was breech, and after talking it over they decided that it would be safer to have the baby in a hospital where there was an intensive-care neonatal unit. So she rewrote her birth plan in this way:

BIRTH PLAN

We are obviously disappointed at not being able to have the home birth that we had planned, but we recognize that the hospital is the safest place to have a breech birth. The following points reflect what we would consider to be the ideal experience for us and while we are aware that it may not be possible to fulfill some of these wishes, we would like to maintain a flexible approach all around with full consultation at all stages in order to have a positive experience.

Vaginal breech delivery—first stage of labor

1. I would like to start labor spontaneously and not be induced unless it is decided that the baby might be at risk.

2. I would like an active first stage of labor, at home with my midwife (my sister) monitoring the fetal heart regularly with her pocket sonic-aid. Unless there are reasons to transfer early, I would like to stay at home until labor is well established, the cervix being well dilated (but obviously not leaving it too late).

3. Once in the hospital I would like my labor support to be continued by Philip (my husband), Penny (my sister and independent midwife), and Sue (an independent midwife who has been sharing my antenatal care with Penny).

4. I would prefer intermittent to continual fetal monitoring without a fetal scalp electrode (unless there is suspected fetal distress), and I would prefer telemetry in order to enable me to move around to encourage normal physiological processes, help with pain, etc.

5. No acceleration with synthetic oxytocin unless necessary.

6. Epidural? I would prefer not to have one if I'm coping well but recognize that if I'm not relaxed for delivery it would be a useful aid.

Second stage and delivery

1. Any chance of not being in the lithotomy position? I really would prefer to be upright on the birthing bed in a suitable position.

2. Episiotomy? I'd prefer *not* and if it is considered completely necessary would rather have a midline cut.

3. Forceps? Any chance of delivering the head without forceps —Mauriceau Smellie-Veit method?

Third stage

1. No Syntometrine unless necessary.

2. Unless the baby needs resuscitation, I would prefer the cord not to be cut until the placenta is delivered by me, in an upright position, baby at the breast.

3. I don't mind the baby having Vitamin K orally.

Cesarean delivery

1. Under epidural if possible.
2. Philip and Penny present in supporting role.
3. Baby to breast immediately if well.
4. If general anesthetic, could Penny be there as an observer in order to fill me in on the experience afterward?
5. If an elective cesarean section, would it be possible for me to start labor normally and then have the section in early labor?

Postnatally

1. I would like to go home as soon as possible since my sister (midwife) will be staying with me full time to follow through my postnatal care.
2. I would like the baby next to me, or in bed with me, all the time.
3. I want to fully breast-feed on demand—please no water or dextrose. Thank you.

Julie says that when thinking ahead to the birth she was "very scared . . . it was like a bad dream." But she was relieved when a scan at thirty-eight weeks revealed that her pelvis was large enough for her to deliver the baby vaginally. She felt grateful that she was at a hospital where breech babies were not delivered by cesarean as a matter of course.

This is what happened when she went into labor:

Labor—first stage

Saturday/Sunday—Minor contractions, heavy shows. Feeling relieved now that Penny has arrived from London and is with me.

Sunday 7 P.M.—Contractions increasing. Labor really starts. Eat a large pasta meal and make sure everything is packed for the hospital. Need Philip near me now at all times.

9 P.M.—Waters break. Telephone hospital; want us to come in immediately.

10 P.M.—Penny drives Philip and me to the hospital where we meet midwife, Jackie. From the first moment I meet her, she makes me feel very positive about being in the hospital. I give Jackie the birth plan. She is wonderful and makes me feel anything is possible, encouragingly shows us the birthing bed, rocking chair. Contractions are now very strong and painful, needing my full concentration. With each contraction I need to hold on to Philip.

10:15 P.M.—Joanna, a midwife who is also a homeopath, whose childbirth classes we attended, arrives.

10:30 P.M.—Meet Dr. Livingstone, the registrar. Together we go through the birth plan. His reaction is very positive— what a relief! At this point he cannot commit himself, but is happy about delivering the baby on the end of the bed, trying without drugs for pain relief, and avoiding forceps. He basically says, "Let's see how it goes." His approach and attitude make all the difference in the world. Dr. Livingstone goes to bed leaving Jackie, Joanna, Philip, Penny, and me to finish first stage.

Monday 11 P.M. to 6 A.M.—To the background of music (mostly Mozart), supported by Philip, Penny, and Joanna, I go through the first stage, changing position from the rocking chair to sitting on the bed. The fetal heart and contraction monitors are taken off, except for occasional reading between 1 and 5 A.M. When it is in use, Jackie's hand holds it—really good of her, as I find the straps uncomfortable. In between contractions I suck ice cold water from a sponge and have the occasional glucose tablet. Joanna gives me homeopathic remedies. I try not to look at the clock as I find this stage endless.

At the height of every contraction my friends give help by close eye contact. I remember vividly Penny and Joanna's strong and compassionate eyes saying, "You can do it," "You're doing brilliantly," and thinking, "I'm not, and want pain relief."

I ask in desperation, "How much longer, how many more hours?" Their reply is honest, but not comforting, yet I am glad of their honesty as I continue to trust them. At peaks of contractions Penny holds my head and I feel anchored and able to cope.

I feel complete dependancy on Philip, Penny, and Joanna— need all their strength, think if Philip breaks down now that will be it—he doesn't. His strength is solid. I want to cry but know I have to keep strong.

As I am having no drugs for pain relief, my body's own pain defenses come into action—I hallucinate and feel completely out of my head. I watch a cupboard on the wall in front of me become larger and smaller over and over again.

6 A.M.—Transition comes. It feels like the end of the world —I've had enough—no break from the intense pain. At this point Jackie comes in, does an internal and says I am fully dilated. Penny and Joanna jump up and down with delight. I hold on to Philip who continues to give me unfailing strength.

Labor—second stage

Monday 6:00 to 7:20 A.M.—I now want to stand up. When I feel a contraction, I link my hands around Philip's neck and, still standing, push as this overriding urge comes.

6:30 A.M.—Dr. Livingstone arrives and to everyone's surprise decides to take on the delivery as he finds us—standing. The lights are still dimmed, as they have been throughout. He lies down on the floor, between my legs.

This is the stage I have most dreaded and always imagined I would not be able to cope with. To my surprise it is not painful, but an indescribable, overpowering, opening sensation that makes me want to shout each time I push.

I continue with my hands around Philip's neck and let him take all my weight as I push down.

Penny kneels on the floor next to Dr. Livingstone and tells me what is happening in an encouraging and reassuring way: "Baby's leg is just coming out now." Although Dr. Livingstone offers to tell us the baby's sex, and for me to hold the baby's legs as they are coming out, I refuse, as I just want to concentrate on pushing and getting our baby born. Still I cannot believe or take for granted that our baby will be all right.

It is amazing to see my baby's legs hanging from inside me. I remember thinking, "I've been pregnant for the last nine months and now I can see there really *is* a baby inside me!" Dr. Livingstone, with his hands, gently delivers our baby—NO FORCEPS, NO EPISIOTOMY.

7:20 A.M.—Our baby girl is born, followed by the placenta landing on Dr. Livingston's head! (He is still lying on the floor.) The baby is rushed away by the surprised and slightly anxious pediatrician, but everything is fine. I have a beautiful healthy daughter. Dr. Livingstone seems as delighted as we were.

I walk over to see her as she lies on the pediatrician's table, eyes wide open, calmly and alertly taking everything in. She is so beautiful!

I have feelings of such love for Philip, Penny, Joanna, Jackie, and Dr. Livingstone—and overwhelming love for Amy, who is so precious as not to be real. In fact, at first I do not want to hold her—I am shaky, so am glad for Philip to cuddle her. I feel proud that I have not taken any drugs for pain relief. It is wonderful to have her sucking right away from my breast. I feel so grateful to everyone! As the moments go by I realize more and more just what Dr. Livingstone's bold and skillful actions have enabled me and my baby to experience. I shall always be grateful to him.

Because I had no drugs for pain relief and a positive and straightforward birth I can leave the hospital after only five hours and go home where Penny will continue my postnatal care for ten days.

However straightforward your pregnancy, and even if you very much want an autonomous birth, it is wise to consider the possibility of a cesarean section and what a cesarean birth plan would be like. After all, nearly one woman in every four ends up with cesarean birth in the United States. Some women do not want to consider the possibility because they believe that it they do so it will act as a kind of softening up process and make them more ready to think that a section is really necessary. On the other hand, a woman who has not thought ahead to what she would want if a cesarean seemed the safest manner of delivery tends to be thrown off course and is unable to act assertively and make any decisions herself. Here is one woman's cesarean birth plan. Your own may be very different, but the issues dealt with are all ones which you may want to consider.

CESAREAN BIRTH-PLAN REQUESTS

I should like to

♦ wait for labor to start before the cesarean section is performed;

♦ discuss all procedures in advance;

♦ have my partner with me during prepping, administration of anesthesia, and the birth;

♦ be shaved only as necessary;

♦ be given medication only after receiving information about it;

♦ have epidural anesthesia for the operation;

♦ if I should need general anesthesia, have my partner stay with me so that he can hold the baby immediately after delivery;

♦ have no curtain obstructing my view;

♦ have a mirror so that I can watch the birth if I wish;

♦ hold the baby immediately after delivery and breast-feed on the delivery table; have baby stay with me all the time unless he/she needs to be taken to the nursery;

♦ be consulted about it first if I am awake and the baby needs to be taken to the nursery;

♦ have my partner and the baby go with me to the recovery room;

♦ have rooming-in as soon as possible;

♦ know that no artificial milk will be given to the baby;

♦ breast-feed on demand;

♦ not be separated from the baby unless I wish it;

♦ have a visit from my three-year-old, and a chance for her to meet the baby, as soon as possible.

If a baby needs to go to the special-care nursery, you can also make contingency plans. You may, for example, sketch out something like this:

- ◆ If our baby has to be in the nursery we would welcome the opportunity of unrestricted visiting.

- ◆ We should like to be able to touch, and if possible, hold, our baby.

- ◆ It would help a great deal if all procedures and any medication given to the baby could be explained to us.

- ◆ Since I plan to breast-feed my baby if possible, I want to use a breast pump and should like to know that my baby will not, unless absolutely necessary, have any artificial feedings.

- ◆ We should like to be kept fully informed about our baby's condition at all times.

- ◆ If our baby is severely ill and there is no hope, we wish to have all tubes and other apparatus removed so that the baby can die in our arms.

- ◆ If our baby has a severe handicap, we should like a full discussion with the pediatrician before any drug treatment is started or surgery embarked on, to consider whether it would be better for the child to have nurturing only, and explore all options.

You may feel that it demands too much of you to contemplate the death of a baby. Some women believe that if they let themselves acknowledge that there is even the faintest possibility of such a thing happening this can somehow make it more likely to occur in reality. It is understandable that we don't want to dwell on such thoughts. Yet many of us secretly fear that we may lose the baby, and the dread is made still worse by feeling isolated and alone with it. It may seem in bad taste to voice such fears, largely because it tends to disturb other people's equanimity and make them anxious—especially caregivers. The result is that when things go terribly wrong and a baby dies—and even when there is the best care it must be remembered that 4 out of every 1,000 babies die at or around the time of birth—a woman may be completely unprepared emotionally, and actions may be undertaken on her behalf that are very different from those she would have wanted herself.

Even if you do not think in terms of a plan, this is a subject you should discuss with your partner or someone else close to you so that, to a certain extent at least, you can sort out in your own mind how you would wish things to be and the degree to which you would want to be involved in making decisions about what happens. Here are one woman's thoughts about this. She did not hand this to her doctor, but had it in her suitcase packed for the hospital, in case it was needed.

If my baby dies at birth I should wish

♦ to see and hold the baby;

♦ to have undisturbed time alone with the baby;

♦ not to be on a ward or corridor with mothers of newborns;

♦ to have a private room, with a bed for my partner too;

♦ not to have tranquilizers or drugs which blunt or delay grieving;

♦ to arrange a funeral ourselves.

Thinking about such choices, making painful decisions, looking at the whole birth experience with openness and honesty—all this helps to forge self-confidence and prepare you to be an active birthgiver instead of a passive patient, and—more than that—to be in touch with the heart of life and to grow in new awareness and understanding of yourself and others.

♦ AFTERWORD ♦

Throughout this book I have been exploring choices and decision making. As you will have realized, this is not simply a matter of stating preferences, as if you were selecting dishes from a menu. If your caregivers are so accommodating that this is what it seems like, it is worth thinking about who composed the menu in the first place, since it may be that you are being offered a very limited range of choices. Some hospitals, for example, are now instituting their own birth plans. There is the danger that this both formalizes and restricts a woman's choice so that consideration of matters that do not appear on the birth plan can be quietly and politely discouraged. In the face of such an apparently liberal attitude on the part of the hospital, it may seem demanding to explore and discuss other issues.

Knowledge brings power. But the profession of medicine restricts access to knowledge for all those who are not within its membership. Whereas at first it seems that choosing how you want to have your baby is a matter of learning about pregnancy and birth and making decisions based on that information, it soon becomes obvious that the information we need is closely guarded. This is especially clear when we inquire about what goes on inside hospitals. We are fed crumbs of information which those controlling the institution allow us to receive, and even that is often inaccurate.

Getting information entails acquiring power. It is a political act. It means joining together with others who have similar concerns to work for social change.

Through striving to achieve autonomy in childbirth—the biological act that epitomizes a woman's role as mother, nurturer, and homemaker—conformists become nonconformists, assimilators become dissidents, charming, polite, compliant women become political activists.

Birth is not only a matter of producing a top-quality baby, a first-class product, as many obstetricians believe. Nor is it only a matter of the mother's physical well-being or even her emotional fulfillment. The way we experience pregnancy and birth today raises political issues that have a profound significance for our own lives, for those of our children, and for all those who come after us.

♦ REFERENCES ♦

1. CURTAIN UP ON PREGNANCY

1. Barbara Katz Rothman, *The Tentative Pregnancy: Prenatal Diagnosis and the Future of Motherhood* (New York: Viking, 1986).

2. THE EARLY WEEKS

1. Barbara Pickard, "Vitamin B_6 During Pregnancy," *Nutrition and Health* 1 (1982), pp. 78–84.
2. K. Niswander and M. Gordon, *The Collaborative Perinatal Study: The Women and Their Pregnancies* (Philadelphia: W. B. Saunders, 1972).
3. "Vaginal Bleeding in Early Pregnancy," editorial, *British Medical Journal* 6 (1980), p. 470.

3. DRUGS AND HEALTH

1. U.S. Department of Health, Education and Welfare, *The Health Consequences of Smoking for Women: A Report of the Surgeon General* (Washington, D.C., 1980).
2. K. Praeger et al., "Smoking and Drinking Behavior before and during Pregnancy of Married Mothers of Live-Born Infants and Stillborn Infants," *Public Health Reports* 99 (1984), pp. 117–23.
3. N. R. Butler and E. D. Alberman, eds., *Perinatal Problems: The Second Report of the 1958 British Perinatal Mortality Survey* (Edinburgh: Churchill Livingstone, 1969).

4. M. Stjernfeldt et al., "Maternal Smoking during Pregnancy and Risk of Childhood Cancer," *Lancet* 1 (1986) pp. 1350–52.

5. N. R. Butler and H. Goldstein, "Smoking in Pregnancy and Subsequent Child Development," *British Medical Journal* 4 (1973), pp. 573–75.

6. Peter C. Buchan, "Cigarette Smoking in Pregnancy and Fetal Hyperviscosity," *British Medical Journal* 286 (1983), pp. 13–15.

7. M. B. Meyer and J. A. Tunascia, "Maternal Smoking, Pregnancy Complications and Perinatal Mortality," *American Journal of Obstetrics and Gynecology* 128 (1977), p. 494.

8. D. O. Ho Yen et al., "Why Smoke Fewer Cigarettes?" *British Medical Journal* 284 (1982), pp. 1905–7.

9. R. Olegard, K. G. Sabel, and M. Aronss, "Effects on the Child of Alcohol Abuse during Pregnancy," *Acta Paediatrica Scandinavica* Suppl. 275, (1979), pp. 112–21.

10. J. W. Hanson, A. P. Streisguth, and D. W. Smith, "Effects of Moderate Alcohol Consumption during Pregnancy on Fetal Growth and Morphogenesis," *Journal of Paediatrics* 92, no. 3 (1978), pp. 457–60.

11. R. J. Sokol, S. I. Miller, and G. Reed, "Alcohol Abuse during Pregnancy: An Epidemiologic Study," *Alcoholism: Clinical and Experimental Research* 4, no. 2 (1980), pp. 135–45.

12. J. Kline, Z. Stein, and P. Shrout, "Drinking during Pregnancy and Spontaneous Abortion," *Lancet* 2 (1980), pp. 176–80.

13. S. Harlap and P. H. Shiono, "Alcohol, Smoking and Incidence of Spontaneous Abortion in the First and Second Trimesters," *Lancet* 2 (1980), pp. 173–76.

14. H. O. Rosett et al., "Patterns of Alcohol Consumption and Fetal Development," *Obstetrics and Gynecology* 61 (1983), pp. 539–46.

15. P. L. Doering and R. B. Stewart, "The Extent and Character of Drug Consumption during Pregnancy," *Journal of the American Medical Association* 239 (1978), pp. 843–46.

16. Yvonne Brackbill, Karen McManus, and Lynn Woodward, *Medication in Maternity* (Ann Arbor: University of Michigan Press for the International Academy for Research in Learning Disabilities, 1985).

17. Ibid.

18. Bruce H. Wooley, "Herbal Pharmacology and Toxicology," *Journal of Collegium Aesculatium,* (December 1983), pp. 1–11.

19. R. K. Siegel, "Ginseng Abuse Syndrome—Problems with the Panacea," *Journal of the American Medical Association* 241 (1979), pp. 1614–15.

4. CHOOSING THE RIGHT FOOD

1. Madeleine H. Shearer, "Malnutrition in Middle-Class Pregnant Women," *Birth and the Family Journal,* 7, no. 1 (Spring 1980), pp. 27–35.
2. A. Stewart Truswell, "Nutrition for Pregnancy," *British Medical Journal* 291 (1985), pp. 263–66.
3. John Dobbing, ed., *Prevention of Spina Bifida and Other Neural Tube Defects,* (London: Academic Press, 1983).
4. K. Laurence et al., "Increased Risk of Recurrence of Pregnancies Complicated by Fatal Neural Tube Defects in Mothers Receiving Poor Diets and Possible Benefit of Dietary Counselling," *British Medical Journal* 281 (1980), pp. 1592–94.
5. R. C. Goodlin et al., "Clinical Signs of Normal Plasma Volume Expansion during Pregnancy," *American Journal of Obstetrics and Gynecology* 145 (1983), pp. 1001–9.
6. Thomas H. Brewer, *Metabolic Toxemia of Late Pregnancy* (New Canaan, Conn.: Keats Publishing Inc., 1982).
7. R. Collins, S. Yusef, and R. Peto, "Overview of Randomised Trials of Diuretics in Pregnancy," *British Medical Journal* 290 (1985), pp. 17–23.
8. A. Lechtig et al., "Effect of Food Supplementation during Pregnancy on Birthweight," *Pediatrics* 56 (1975), pp. 508–19; D. Rush, S. Stein, and M. Susser, "A Randomized Controlled Trial of Pre-natal Nutritional Supplementation in New York," *Pediatrics* 65 (1980), pp. 685–97.
9. O. A. C. Viegas et al., "Dietary Protein Energy Supplementation of Pregnant Asian Mothers at Sorrento, Birmingham I: Unselective during Second and Third Trimesters," *British Medical Journal* 285 (1982), pp. 589–91.
10. O. A. C. Viegas et al., "Dietary Protein Energy Supplementation of Pregnant Asian Mothers at Sorrento, Birmingham II: Selective during Third Trimester Only," *British Medical Journal* 285 (1982), pp. 592–95.

5. EXERCISE

1. Susan L. Woodward, "How Does Strenuous Maternal Exercise Affect the Fetus? A Review," *Birth* 8, no. 1 (1981), pp. 17–23.
2. J. F. Newhall, "Scuba Diving in Pregnancy," *American Journal of Obstetrics and Gynecology* 140 (1981), pp. 893–94.

3. G. Turner and I. Unsworth, "Intrauterine Bends?" *Lancet* 1 (1982), p. 905.
4. M. E. Bolton, "Scuba Diving and Fetal Well-Being," *Undersea Biomedical Research* 7 (1980), pp. 183–89.
5. Frederick Leboyer, *Inner Beauty, Inner Light: Yoga for Pregnant Women* (New York: Alfred A. Knopf, 1978).
6. C. A. Collins et al., "Maternal and Fetal Responses to a Maternal Aerobic Exercise Program," *American Journal and Obstetrics and Gynecology* 145 (1983), p. 702.
7. Janet Balaskas, *Active Birth* (New York: McGraw-Hill, 1983); and *The Active Birth Partners' Handbook* (London: Sidgwick and Jackson, 1984).
8. Sheila Kitzinger, *Women as Mothers* (New York: Vintage Books, 1980); R. J. Atwood, "Parturitional Posture and Related Birth Behavior," *Acta Obstetrica et Ginecologica Scandinavica* Suppl. 57 (1976), pp. 1–25; R. W. Wertz and D. C. Wertz, *Lying In: A History of Childbirth in America* (New York: Free Press, 1977); G. Engelmann, *Labor Among Primitive People* (St. Louis, 1882).
9. P. Dunn, "Obstetrics Delivery Today, for Better or Worse?" *Lancet* 1 (1976), pp. 790–93; W. I. Hampton, "Practical Considerations for the Routine Application of Left Lateral Sims' Position for Vaginal Delivery," *American Journal of Obstetrics and Gynecology* 131 (1978), pp. 129–33; M. A. Hugo, "A Look at Maternal Positions during Labour," *Nurse Midwifery* 22 (1977), pp. 26–7; Y. C. Lieu, "Effects of an Upright Position during Labor," *American Journal of Nursing* 74 (1974), pp. 2203–5; C. Mendez-Bauer et al., "Effects of Standing Position on Spontaneous Uterine Contracility and Other Aspects of Labor," *Journal of Perinatal Medicine* 3 (1975), pp. 89–100; I. N. Mitre, "The Influence of Maternal Position on Duration of the Active Phase of Labor," *International Journal of Gynaecology and Obstetrics* 12 (1974), pp. 181–83.
10. A. M. Flynn and J. Kelly, "Continuous Fetal Monitoring in the Ambulant Patient in Labour," *British Medical Journal* 2 (1976), pp. 842–43.

6. THE ENVIRONMENT IN PREGNANCY

1. W. R. Lee, "Working with Visual Display Units," *British Medical Journal* 291 (1985), pp. 989–91.
2. A. Kurpa et al., "Birth Defects and Video Display Terminals," *Lancet* 2 (1984), p. 1339.

3. V. J. Bayne, "A Trade Union Response to the Allegations of Reproductive Hazards from VDUs, in *Allegations of Reproductive Hazards from VDUs,* ed. B. G. Pearce, (Loughborough, Eng.: Humane Technology, 1984), pp. 161–75.

4. L. D. Longo, "Environmental Pollution and Pregnancy: Risks and Uncertainties for the Fetus and the Infant," *American Journal of Obstetrics and Gynecology* 137 (1980), pp. 162–73.

5. L. D. Longo, "The Biological Effects of Carbon Monoxide on the Pregnant Woman, Fetus and Newborn Infant," *American Journal of Obstetrics and Gynecology* 129 (1977), p. 69.

6. K. Hemminki et al., "Spontaneous Abortions in Hospital Staff Engaged in Sterilising Instruments with Chemical Agents," *British Medical Journal* 285 (1982), pp. 1461–63.

7. Sheila McKechnie, "Reproductive Hazards in Employment: Protect the Fetus, Yes, but not at the Expense of the Adult Woman," *Medical World,* June 4, 1981, p. 5.

7. EMOTIONAL CHANGES

1. R. Kumar and K. Robson, "Previous Induced Abortion and Antenatal Depression in Primipara," *Psychology and Medicine* 8 (1978), pp. 711–15.

2. Richard L. Naeye and Ellen C. Peters, "Causes and Consequences of Premature Rupture of Fetal Membranes," *Lancet* (1980), pp. 192–94.

8. WHAT KIND OF PRENATAL CARE?

1. Jean Donnison, *Midwives and Medical Men* (London: Heinemann Educational Books Ltd., 1977); Margot Edwards and Mary Waldorf, "The Midwife Question," in their *Reclaiming Birth* (New York: Crossing Press, 1984); Margarita Artschwager Kay, ed., *Anthropology of Human Birth* (Philadelphia: F. A. Davis Co., 1982); Shelly Romalis, ed. *Childbirth: Alternatives to Medical Control* (Austin: University of Texas Press, 1981). Richard W. Wertz and Dorothy C. Wertz, *Lying-In: A History of Childbirth in America* (New York : The Free Press, 1977).

2. Shirley Ardener, ed. *Defining Females* (London: Croom Helm, 1978); Sheila Kitzinger, *Women as Mothers* (New York: Vintage Books, 1980);

Carol P. MacCormack, ed., *Ethnography of Fertility and Birth* (London: Academic Press, 1982).

3. Kitzinger, *Women as Mothers;* and "The Social Context of Birth: Some Comparisons between Childbirth in Jamaica and Britain," in *Ethnography of Fertility and Birth.*

4. Wendy D. Savage, "Antenatal Care in Britain," *Nursing* 21 (1980), pp. 909–11.

5. See Alison Macfarlane and Miranda Mugford, *Birth Counts, Statistics of pregnancy and childbirth.* (London: H.M.S.O., 1984).

6. *Infant and Perinatal Mortality 1980* (London: Office of Population Censuses and Surveys, 1982).

7. As reported in *The Guardian,* September 13, 1984.

8. Ann Oakley, *The Captured Womb* (Oxford: Blackwell, 1984).

9. Ibid.

10. Marion H. Hall, P. K. Ching, and I. McGillivray, "Is Routine Antenatal Care Worth While?" *Lancet* 2 (1980).

11. Ibid.

12. Mary J. Houston and Lesley Page, *Midwifery: Practice and Research* (Edinburgh: Churchill Livingstone, forthcoming).

13. Gordon Bourne, *Pregnancy* (London: Pan Books, 1975).

14. Ann Oakley, *Women Confined* (Oxford: Martin Robertson, 1980); Hilary Graham, "Problems in Antenatal Care," Department of Health and Social Security, Child Poverty Action Group Conference, 1978; Sally Macintyre, "Consumer Reaction to Present-Day Antenatal Services," in *Pregnancy Care for the 1980's,* ed. Luke Zander and Geoffrey Chamberlain (London: Royal Society of Medicine and Macmillan, 1984); Sheila Kitzinger, "What Do Women Want?" in *The Management of Labour,* ed. John Studd (Oxford: Blackwell Scientific Publications, 1985).

15. Sarah Robinson, "Responsibilities of Midwives and Medical Staff: Findings from the National Survey," *Midwives Chronicle,* March 1985.

16. G. Chamberlain et al., *British Births* (London: Heinemann, 1970).

17. Ibid.

18. H. D. Kleinert et al., "What Is the Value of Home Blood Pressure Measurement in Patients with Mild Hypertension?" *Hypertension* 6 (1984), pp. 574–78.

19. E. Brien, D. Fitzgerald, and K. O'Malley, "Blood Pressure Measurement: Current Practice and Future Trends," *British Medical Journal* 290 (1985), pp. 729–34.

20. R. M. Carey et al., "The Charlottesville Blood Pressure Survey: Value

of Repeated Blood Pressure Measurements," *Journal of the American Medical Association* 236 (1976), pp. 847–51.

21. Rory Collins, Salim Yusef, and Richard Peto, "Overview of Randomised Trials of Diuretics in Pregnancy," *British Medical Journal* 290 (1985), pp. 17–23.

22. J. Fidler et al., "Randomised Controlled Comparative Study of Methyldopa and Oxprenolol in Treatment of Hypertension in Pregnancy," *British Medical Journal* 286 (1983), pp. 1927–30.

23. M. Ounstead and C. W. G. Redman, letter to the *British Medical Journal* 290 (1985), p. 1080.

24. Collins, "Overview of Trials of Diuretics."

9. DECIDING ABOUT SPECIAL TESTS

1. J. Murphy et al., "Conservative Management of Pregnancy in Diabetic Women," *British Medical Journal* 288 (1984), pp. 1203–5.

2. "Second Report of UK Collaborative Study on AFP in Relation to Neural Tube Defects," *Lancet* 2 (1979), pp. 651–62.

3. J. B. Holton, "Assessment of Fetal Immaturity and Prediction of Respiratory Distress Syndrome," in *Prevention of Handicap through Antenatal Care,* eds. A. C. Turnbull and F. P. Woodward (Amsterdam: Elsevier, 1976).

4. B. N. Hibbard et al., "Can We Afford Screening for Neural Tube Defects? The South Wales Experience," *British Medical Journal* 290 (1985), pp. 293–95.

5. Professor John Edwards, personal communication.

6. Barbara Katz Rothman, *The Tentative Pregnancy: Prenatal Diagnosis and the Future of Motherhood* (New York: Viking, 1986).

7. Medical Research Council Working Party on Amniocentesis, "An Assessment of the Hazards of Amniocentesis," *British Journal of Obstetrics and Gynaecology* 85, suppl. 2 (1978).

8. L. N. Reece, "The Estimation of Fetal Maturity by a New Method of X-ray Cephalometry: Its bearing on Clinical Midwifery," *Proceedings of the Royal Society of Medicine* (January 18, 1935, pp. 489–504), quoted in Ann Oakley, *The Captured Womb: A History of the Medical Care of Pregnant Women,* (Oxford: Blackwell's, 1984).

9. R. W. A. Salmond, "The Uses and Value of Radiology in Obstetrics," in *Antenatal and Postnatal Care,* ed. F. J. Browne, (London: Churchill, 1935).

10. Oakley, *The Captured Womb.*

11. A. Stewart et al., "Malignant Disease in Childhood and Diagnostic Irradiation in Utero," *Lancet* 2 (1956), p. 447.

12. Doris Haire, "Fetal Effects of Ultrasound: A Growing Controversy," *Journal of Nurse Midwifery* 29, no. 4 (1984).

13. H. F. Stewart and M. E. Stratmeyer, *An Overview of Ultrasound: Theory, Measurement, Medical Applications and Biological Effects* (Washington, D.C.: Department of Health and Human Services, Food and Drug Administration, Publication 82–8190, Bureau of Radiological Health, 1982).

14. American College of Obstetricians and Gynecologists, *Diagnostic Ultrasound in Obstetrics and Gynecology,* ACOG Technical Bulletin no. 63 (1981). Office of Technology Assessment, "Policy Implications of the Computed Tomography (CT) Scanner: an Update," Appendix B, in *Research and Development of CT and Other Diagnostic Imaging Technologies* (Washington D.C., 1981).

15. M. Edwards and P. Simkin, *Obstetric Tests and Technology: A Consumer's Guide* (Seattle, Wash.: The Pennypress, 1980).

16. American College of Gynecologists, *Diagnostic Ultrasound.*

17. J. P. Neilson, S. P. Munjanja, and C. R. Whitfield, "Screening for Small-for-dates Fetuses: A Controlled Trial," *British Medical Journal* 289 (1984), pp. 1170–82.

18. B. Bolsen, "Question of Risk Still Hovers over Routine Prenatal Use of Ultrasound," *Journal of the American Medical Association* 247 (1982), pp. 2195–97; Stewart and Stratmeyer, *Overview of Ultrasound.*

19. D. Liebeskind et al., "Diagnostic Ultrasound: Effects on DNA and Growth Patterns of Animal Cells," *Radiology* 131, no. 1 (1979), pp. 177–84.

20. American College of Gynecologists, *Diagnostic Ultrasound.*

21. Penny Simkin, Janet Whalley, and Ann Keppler, *Pregnancy, Childbirth and the Newborn* (Deephaven, Minn.: Meadowbrook Press, 1984); International Childbirth Education Association, "Diagnostic Ultrasound in Obstetrics," 1983 position paper.

22. U.S. Department of Health, Education and Welfare, *Antenatal Diagnosis,* National Institutes of Health Publication No. 79 (1973).

23. R. E. Myers, "Maternal Anxiety and Fetal Death," in *Psychoendocrinology in Reproduction,* ed. L. Zichella and P. Pancheri (Amsterdam: Elsevier, 1979).

24. A. Grant and P. Mohide, "Screening and Diagnostic Tests in Antenatal Care," in *Effectiveness and Satisfaction in Antenatal Care,* ed. M. Enkin and I. Chalmers (London: Spastics International, 1982).

25. Richard Hamilton, *The Herpes Book* (Boston: Houghton Mifflin Co., 1980).

26. Zane A. Brown, "Herpes Update" (Paper presented at Utah Perinatal Conference, Salt Lake City, October 1985).
27. J. F. Pearson and J. B. Weaver, "Fetal Activity and Fetal Well-being: An Evaluation," *British Medical Journal* 1 (1976), pp. 1305–7.
28. R. Homburg et al., "Management of Patients with a Live Fetus and Cessation of Fetal Movement," *British Journal of Obstetrics and Gynaecology* 87 (1980), pp. 804–7.

10. SAYING WHAT YOU WANT

1. Helen Roberts, *Patient Patients* (London: Pandora Press, 1985).
2. Ann Oakley, *Women Confined: Towards a Sociology of Childbirth* (Oxford: Martin Robertson, 1980).

11. BIRTH PLANS

1. Harold Francis, "Obstetrics: A Consumer-Oriented Service? The Case Against," *Maternal and Child Health* 10, no. 3 (1985), pp. 69–72.
2. R. P. Lederman et al. "The Relationship of Maternal Anxiety, Plasma Catecholamines and Plasma Cortisol to Progress in Labor," *American Journal of Obstetrics and Gynecology* 132 (1973), p. 495.
3. Michael Klein, "Contracting for Trust in Family Practice Obstetrics," *Canadian Family Physician* 29 (1983), pp. 2225–27.
4. R. Sosa et al., "The Effect of Support on Perinatal Problems," *New England Journal of Medicine* 303 (1980), pp. 597–600.
5. Sheila Kitzinger, *Women as Mothers* (New York: Vintage Books, 1980).
6. S. V. D. Anderson, "Siblings at Birth," *Birth* 6 (1979), pp. 80–87.
7. R. Campbell, I. M. Davies, and A. J. Macfarlane, "Perinatal Mortality and Place of Delivery," *Population Trends* 20 (1982), pp. 9–12.
8. R. Campbell, lecture in symposium, *Statistics and Policy Making in the Maternity Services,* Royal Society of Medicine, December 1984.
9. Marjorie Tew, "The Case Against Hospital Deliveries: The Statistical Evidence," in *The Place of Birth,* ed. Sheila Kitzinger and John A. Davies (London: Oxford University Press, 1978); Marjorie Tew, "Is Home a Safer Place?" *Health and Social Service Journal,* September 12, 1980, pp. 702–5.
10. Iain Chalmers, National Perinatal Epidemiology Unit, Oxford, personal communication.

11. J. F. Murphy et al., "Planned and Unplanned Deliveries at Home: Implications of a Changing Ratio," *British Medical Journal* (1984), pp. 1429–32.

12. S. M. I. Damstra-Wijmenga, "Home Confinement: The Positive Results in Holland," *Journal of the Royal College of Practitioners* 34 (1984), pp. 425–30.

13. G. W. Taylor et al., "How Safe Is General Practitioner Obstetrics?" *Lancet* 2 (1980), pp. 1287–89.

14. Michael Klein et al., "A Comparison of Low Risk Women Booked for Delivery in Two Different Systems of Care," *British Journal of Obstetrics and Gynaecology* 90 (1983), pp. 118–22, and 123–28; Michael Klein, Diana Elbourne, and Ivor Lloyd, "Booking for Maternity Care: A Comparison of Two Systems," *Royal College of General Practitioners,* Occasional Paper 31 (1985).

15. R. C. Goodlin and I. B. Frederick, "Postpartum Vulvar Edema Associated with the Birthing Chair," *American Journal of Obstetrics,* 146, no. 3 (1984), p. 334.

12. GETTING IN TOUCH WITH YOUR BABY

1. D. Purpura, "Consciousness," *Behavior Today,* June 2, 1975, p. 494.

2. C. M. Nistretta and R. M. Bradley, "Taste in Utero: Theoretical Considerations" in *Taste and Development: The Genesis of Sweet Preference* ed. J. M. Weiffenbach (Washington, D.C.: Government Printing Office, 1977), pp. 51–69.

3. K. C. Pratt, A. K. Nelson, and K. H. Sun, *The Behavior of the Newborn Infant* (Columbus, Ohio: Ohio State University Press, 1930).

4. K. R. Kobre and L. R. Lipsitt, "A Negative Contrast Effect in Newborns," *Journal of Experimental Child Psychology* 14 (1972), pp. 81–91.

5. C. K. Crook, "Taste Perception in the Newborn Infant," *Infant Behavior and Development* 1 (1978), pp. 52–69.

6. R. Artal, M. Rosen, and R. Sokol, "Fetal Response to Sound," *Contemporary Ob./Gyn.* 5 (1975).

7. M. Clements, "Observations on Certain Aspects of Neonatal Behaviour in Response to Auditory Stimuli" (Paper presented at the 5th International Congress of Psychosomatic Obstetrics and Gynaecology, Rome, 1977).

8. R. G. Eisenberg, "Auditory Behaviors in the Human Neonate," *Journal of Auditory Research* 5 (1965), pp. 159–77.

9. David B. Chamberlain, *Consciousness at Birth: A Review of the Empirical*

Evidence (San Diego, Calif.: Chamberlain Communications, 1983), pp. 26–49.

10. W. S. Condon and L. W. Sander, "Neonate Movement Is Synchronized with Adult Speech: Interaction or Participation and Language Acquisition," *Science* 183 (1974), pp. 99–101.

11. N. Hack and M. Klaus, *The Amazing Newborn* (Film distributed by Ross Laboratories, Columbus, Ohio, 1976).

12. A. DeCasper and W. Fifer, "Of Human Bonding: Newborns Prefer Their Mothers' Voices," *Science* 208 (1980), pp. 1174–76.

13. H. Truby and J. Lind, "Cry Sounds of the Newborn Infant," *Newborn Infant Cry*, J. Lind, ed., *Acta Paediatrica Scandinavica* Suppl. 63 (1965), pp. 7–59.

14. M. Wertheimer, "Psychomotor Coordination of Auditory and Visual Space at Birth," *Science* 134 (1961), p. 1692.

15. L. Salk, "The Role of the Heart Beat in the Relations between Mother and Infant," *Scientific American,* May 1973, pp. 24–29.

16. H. P. Roffwarg, J. N. Muzio, and W. C. Dement, "Ontogenetic Development of the Human Sleep-Dream Cycle," *Science* 152 (1966), pp. 604–619.

17. A. B. Roberts et al., "Fetal Activity in 100 Normal Third Trimester Pregnancies," *British Journal of Obstetrics and Gynaecology* 87 (1980), pp. 480–84.

18. Chamberlain, *Consciousness at Birth.*

19. J. F. Pearson and J. B. Weaver, "Fetal Activity and Fetal Wellbeing: An Evaluation," *British Medical Journal* 1 (1976), pp. 1305–1307.

20. This outline is based on information given in Chamberlain, *Consciousness at Birth,* and in three papers delivered at the European Congress of Perinatal Medicine, Dublin, 1984: E. E. van Woerden Petal, "Distribution of Movements within Behavioral States of the Human Fetus"; J. I. P. de Vries, "Incidence of Specific Movement Patterns during the First Half of Gestation"; and K. Maeda et al., "New Ultrasonic Doppler Fetal Actogram and the Analysis of FHR Changes Related to Fetal Movement."

13. ON THE THRESHOLD OF THE UNKNOWN

1. Clare M. Andrews, "Changing Fetal Position," *Journal of Nurse Midwifery* 25, no. 1, (1980), pp. 7–12.

2. G. R. Evaldson, A. Malmborg, and C. E. Nord, "Premature Rupture

of the Membranes and Ascending Infection," *British Journal of Obstetrics and Gynaecology* 89 (1982), p. 793.

3. P. Duff, R. D. Huff, and R. S. Gibbs, "Management of Premature Rupture of Membranes on Unfavourable Cervix in Term Pregnancy, *Obstetrics and Gynecology* 63 (1984), p. 69.

4. M. F. Schutte et al., "Management of Premature Rupture of Membranes: The Risk of Vaginal Examination to the Infant," *American Journal of Obstetrics and Gynecology* 146 (1983), p. 395.

15. DEALING WITH PAIN

1. John J. Bonica, "Labour Pain," in *Textbook of Pain,* ed. Patrick D. Wall and Ronald Melzack (New York: Churchill Livingstone, 1984).

2. Reported in *Irish Medical Times,* March 30, 1984.

3. Grantly Dick-Read, *Childbirth without Fear,* 9th ed., (London: Heinemann, 1942).

4. Bonica, "Labour Pain."

5. Ibid.

6. B. M. Morgan, S. Rehor, and P. J. Lewis, "Epidural Analgesia for Uneventful Labour," *Anaesthesia* 35 (1980), pp. 57–60.

7. E. Tronick et al., "Regional Obstetric Anesthesia and Newborn Behavior: Effect over the First Ten Days of Life," *Pediatrics* 58 (1976), pp. 94–100.

8. J. F. Pearson and P. Davies, "The Effect of Continuous Lumbar Analgesia on the Acid-base Status of Maternal Arterial Blood during the First Stage of Labour," *Journal of Obstetrics and Gynaecology of the British Commonwealth* 80 (1973), pp. 218–24; J. F. Pearson and P. Davies, "The Effect of Continuous Lumbar Analgesia upon Fetal Acid-base Status during the First Stage of Labour," *Journal of Obstetrics and Gynaecology of the British Commonwealth* 81 (1974), pp. 971–74.

9. J. W. W. Studd et al., "The Effect of Lumbar Epidural Analgesia on the Rate of Cervical Dilatation and the Outcome of Labour of Spontaneous Onset," *British Journal of Obstetrics and Gynaecology* 87 (1980), pp. 1015–21; J. S. Crawford, "The Second Thousand Epidural Blocks in an Obstetric Hospital Practice," *British Journal of Anaesthetics* 44 (1972), pp. 1277–96.

10. I. J. Hoult, A. H. MacLennan, and L. E. S. Carrie, "Lumbar Epidural Analgesia in Labour: Relation to Fetal Malposition and Instrumental Delivery," *British Medical Journal* 1 (1977), pp. 14–16.

11. Crawford, "The Second Thousand Epidural Blocks."

12. Tronick, "Regional Obstetric Anesthesia."

13. J. W. Scanlon et al., "Neurobehavioral Responses of Newborn Infants after Maternal Epidural Anesthesia," *Anesthesiology* 40 (1974), pp. 121–28; Tronick, "Regional Obstetric Anesthesia"; B. A. Liebermann et al., "The Effect of Maternally Administered Pethidine or Bupivicaine on Fetus and Newborn," *British Journal of Obstetrics and Gynaecology* 86 (1979), pp. 598–806; B. A. Leibermann et al., "The Influence of Maternal Analgesia on Neo-natal Behavior: II epidural bupivicaine," *British Journal of Obstetrics and Gynaecology* 88 (1981), pp. 407–13.

14. Murray W. Enkin, commentary on "Epidural Analgesia," *ICEA Review* 5 (1981), p. 2.

15. Dr. Wendy Savage in evidence to the tribunal investigating her management of five childbirth cases, London, February 1986.

16. John J. Bonica, *Obstetric Analgesia and Anaesthesia,* 2d ed. (Amsterdam: World Federation of Societies of Anesthesiologists, 1980).

17. Michel Odent, *Birth Reborn* (New York: Pantheon Books, 1984).

18. Gayle Peterson, *Birthing Normally: A Personal Growth Approach to Childbirth* (Berkeley, Calif.: Mind/Body Press, 1981); Claudia Panuthos, *Transformation Through Birth* (South Hadley, Mass.: Bergin and Garvey, 1984); Rahima Baldwin and Terra Palmarini, *Pregnant Feelings* (Berkeley, Calif.: Celestial Arts, 1986).

19. Odent, *Birth Reborn.*

20. Sheila Kitzinger, *Women's Experience of Sex* (New York: Putnam, 1983); Ina May Gaskin, *Spiritual Midwifery* (Summertown, Tenn.: Book Publishing Co., 1978); Odent, *Birth Reborn.*

21. Ronald Melzack, "Acupuncture and Related Forms of Folk Medicine," in *Textbook of Pain,* ed. Patrick D. Wall and Ronald Melzack (New York: Churchill Livingstone, 1984).

22. L. Auginstinsson et al., "Pain Relief during Delivery by Transcutaneous Electrical Stimulation," *Pain* 4 (1977), pp. 59–65.

23. W. S. Kroger, *Clinical and Experimental Hypnosis,* 2d ed. (Philadelphia: J. B. Lippincott, 1977); P. Stone and G. D. Burrows, "Hypnosis and Obstetrics," in *Handbook of Hypnosis and Psychosomatic Medicine,* ed. G. D. Burrows and L. Dennerstein (Amsterdam: Elsevier, 1980), p. 37.

24. Jeannine O' Brien Medvin, *Prenatal Yoga and Natural Birth* (Monroe, Utah: Freestone Publishing Co., 1974); Ma Anand Ganda, *Yoga et Maternité,* Paris: EPI, 1979).

25. Barbara A. K. Porter, "Water and Birth, the Pros and Cons," editorial in *ICEA News* 23 (1984), p. 3.

26. Odent, *Birth Reborn.*

16. OBSTETRICALLY DIRECTED BIRTH

1. Harold Francis, "Obstetrics: A Consumer-Oriented Service? The Case Against," *Maternal and Child Health* 10, no. 3 (1985), p. 69.
2. Kieran O'Driscoll and Declan Meagher, *Active Management of Labour* (Philadelphia: W. B. Saunders, 1980).
3. Ibid.
4. Ibid.
5. Editorial, *British Journal of Obstetrics and Gynaecology* 93 (1986), pp. 105–8.
6. James Owen Drife, "Pre-term Rupture of the Membrane," *British Medical Journal* 285 (1982), p. 583.
7. Sheila Kitzinger, *The Complete Book of Pregnancy and Childbirth* (New York: Alfred A. Knopf, 1980).
8. Roberto Caldeyro-Barcia, "Some Consequences of Obstetrical Interference," *Birth and the Family Journal* 2, no. 2 (1975), pp. 34–37.
9. H. David Banta and Steven B. Thacker, "Assessing the Costs and Benefits of Electronic Fetal Monitoring," *Obstetrical and Gynecological Survey*, 38, 8 (supplement) (1979), pp. 627–42.
10. G. Tutera and R. O. Newman, "Fetal Monitoring: Its Effect on the Perinatal Mortality and Cesarean Section Rates and Its Complications," *American Journal of Obstetrics and Gynecology* 122 (1975), pp. 750–54.
11. D. M. Okada, A. W. Chow, and V. T. Bruce, "Neonatal Scalp Abscess and Fetal Monitoring, Factors Associated with Infection," *American Journal of Obstetrics and Gynecology* 129 (1977), pp. 185–89.
12. G. S. Sykes et al., "Fetal Distress and the Condition of Newborn Infants," *British Medical Journal* 287 (1983), pp. 943–48.
13. P. Curzen et al., "Reliability of Cardiotocography in Predicting Baby's Condition at Birth," *British Medical Journal* 289 (1984), pp. 1345–47.
14. Dermot Macdonald et al., "The Dublin Randomised Controlled Trial of Intrapartum Electronic Fetal Heartrate Monitoring," (Paper presented at the Twenty-third British Congress of Obstetrics and Gynaecology, Birmingham, England, July 1983).
15. R. Schwartz et al., "Fetal Heart Rate in Labors with Intact and with Ruptured Membranes," *Journal of Perinatal Medicine* 1 (1973), pp. 153–65; S. G. Gabbe et al., "Umbilical Cord Compression Associated with Amniotomy," *American Journal of Obstetrics and Gynecology* 126 (1976), pp. 353–55; M. Martel et al., "Blood Acid-Base at Birth in

Neonates from Labors with Early and Late Rupture of Membranes," *Journal of Pediatrics* 89 (1976), pp. 963–67.

16. Lecture in refresher course for midwives, Birmingham, England, 1984.

17. Joseph DeLee, "The Prophylactic Forceps Operation," *American Journal of Obstetrics and Gynecology* 1 (1920), pp. 34–44.

18. R. F. Harrison and M. Brennan, "Fetal Outcome after Episiotomy or Perineal Tear," (Paper given at European Congress of Perinatal Medicine, Dublin, Ireland, 1984).

19. Sheila Kitzinger with Rhiannon Walters, *Some Women's Experience of Episiotomy* (London: National Childbirth Trust, 1981).

20. Jennifer Sleep et al., "West Berkshire Perineal Management Trial," *British Medical Journal* 289 (1984), pp. 507–90.

21. Sheila Kitzinger and Penny Simkin, eds. *Episiotomy and the Second Stage of Labor,* 2d ed. (East Seattle, Wash.: Pennypress, 1986).

22. "Cesarean Childbirth," Report of Task Force, Office of Research Reporting (National Institutes of Health Consensus Development, Bethesda, Maryland, 1980).

23. Shirley Huchcroft et al., "Late Results of Cesarean and Vaginal Deliveries in Cases of Breech Presentation," *Canadian Medical Association Journal* 125 (1981), pp. 726–30.

17. CEREMONIAL BIRTH PROCEDURES

1. I. E. P. Menzies, "The Functioning of Social Systems as a Defence against Anxiety," pamphlet 3 (London: Tavistock Institute, 1981).

2. Joan Raphael Leff, "Fears and Fantasies of Childbirth," *Pre- and Perinatal Psychology Association of North America Journal,* (Spring 1985), pp. 14–18.

3. H. Kanton et al., "The Value of Shaving the Pudendal Perineal Area in Delivery Preparation," *Obstetrics and Gynecology* 25 (1965), p. 509.

4. Albert E. Long, "The Unshaved Perineum at Parturition," *American Journal of Obstetrics and Gynecology* 99 (1967), pp. 333–36.

5. Mona L. Romney, "Pre-delivery Shaving: An Unjustified Assault?" *Journal of Obstetrics and Gynaecology* 1 (1980), pp. 33–35.

6. Editorial, "Preoperative Depilation," *Lancet* 1 (1983), p. 1311.

7. M. L. Romney and H. Gordon, "Is Your Enema Really Necessary?" *British Medical Journal* 282 (1981), pp. 1269–71.

8. R. Caldeyro-Barcia, *Physiological and Psychological Bases for the Modern and Humanised Management of Normal Labor,* Scientific Publication 858

(Montevideo, Uruguay: Latin American Center of Perinatology and Human Development, 1980).

9. T. J. McManus and A. A. Calder, "Upright Posture and the Efficiency of Labour," *Lancet* 1 (1978), pp. 72–74.

10. Morag A. Hunter and Delores Williams, "Mask Wearing in the Labour War," *Midwives Chronicle,* January 1985, pp. 12–14.

11. Editorial, "Behind the Mask," *Lancet* 1 (1983), pp. 197–98.

12. Penny Simkin et al., *Pregnancy, Childbirth and the Newborn* (Deephaven, Minn.: Meadowbrook Press, 1984).

13. G. M. Stirrat, *Obstetrics* (London: Grant McIntyre, 1981).

14. Sally Inch, "Management of the Third Stage of Labour—Another Cascade of Intervention?" *Midwifery* (1985), pp. 114–22.

15. "Should the Cord be Clamped?" *World Medicine,* January 28, 1969.

16. Inch, "Management."

17. Frederick Leboyer, *Birth without Violence* (New York: Alfred A. Knopf, 1976).

18. R. Rothenberg, "Opthalmia Neonatorum Due to Neisseria Gonorrhoeae," *Sexually Transmitted Diseases* 6 (1979), pp. 187–91.

18. THE CONCEPT OF AUTONOMY

1. See Diana Korte and Roberta Scaer, *A Good Birth, a Safe Birth* (New York: Bantam Books, 1984).

♦ FURTHER READING ♦

Note: ICEA (International Childbirth Education Association) is listed under Useful Addresses, below.

Anderson, Ann-Marie. *The American Way of Birth*. Philadelphia: Temple University Press, 1987.

Anderson, Sandra Van Dam, and Penny Simkin. *Birth—Through Children's Eyes*. Seattle: Pennypress, 1981.

Ashford, Janet Isaacs, ed. *Birth Stories*. Trumansburg, N.Y.: Crossing Press, 1984.

———. *The Whole Birth Catalogue*. Trumansburg, N.Y.: Crossing Press, 1983.

Balaskas, Janet. *Active Birth*. New York: McGraw-Hill, 1985.

Baldwin, Rahima, and Terra Palmarini. *Pregnant Feelings*. Berkeley: Celestial Arts, 1986.

Baldwin, Rahima. *Special Delivery: The Complete Guide to Informed Birth*. Berkeley: Celestial Arts, 1979.

Barrington, Eleanor. *Midwifery Is Catching*. Toronto: NC Press, 1985.

Bean, Constance. *Methods of Childbirth*. Garden City: Doubleday, 1982.

Bing, Elizabeth, and Libby Colman. *Making Love During Pregnancy*. New York: Bantam, 1977.

Chesler, Phyllis. *With Child*. New York: Berkley, 1981.

Cohen, Nancy Wainer, and Lois J. Estner. *Silent Knife: Caesarean Prevention and Vaginal Birth after Caesarean*. South Hadley, Mass.: Bergin and Garvey, 1983.

Davis, Elizabeth. *Heart and Hands*. Berkeley: Celestial Arts, 1987.

Edwards, Margot, and Mary Waldorf. *Reclaiming Birth*. Trumansburg, N.Y.: Crossing Press, 1984.

Gaskin, Ina May. *Spiritual Midwifery.* Summertown, Tenn.: Book Pub., 1978.

Grad, Rae, et al. *The Father Book: Pregnancy and Beyond.* Washington, D.C.: Acropolis, 1981.

Greenspan, Stanley I., and Nancy Thorndike Greenspan. *First Feelings.* New York: Viking, 1985.

Huggins, Kathleen. *The Nursing Mother's Companion.* Cambridge: Harvard Common Press, 1986.

Inch, Sally. *Birth Rights.* New York: Pantheon, 1985.

Korte, Diana, and Roberta Scaer. *A Good Birth: A Safe Birth.* New York: Bantam, 1984.

Leboyer, Frederick. *Birth Without Violence.* New York: Knopf, 1976.

La Leche League International. *The Womanly Art of Breastfeeding.* Franklin Park, Ill: La Leche, 1981.

McKay, Susan. *The Assertive Approach to Childbirth* (pamphlet). ICEA.

————. *Assertive Childbirth.* New York: Prentice-Hall, 1983.

McKee, Lorna, and Margaret O'Brien. *The Father Figure.* London: Tavistock, 1982.

Noble, Elizabeth, *Childbirth with Insight.* Boston: Houghton Mifflin, 1983.

————. *Essential Exercises for the Childbearing Year.* Boston: Houghton Mifflin, 1982.

————. *Having Twins.* Boston: Houghton Mifflin, 1980.

Oakley, Ann. *The Captured Womb: A History of the Medical Care of Pregnant Women.* Oxford: Blackwell, 1984.

Odent, Michel. *Birth Reborn.* New York: Pantheon, 1984.

Panuthos, Claudia. *Transformation Through Birth: A Woman's Guide.* South Hadley, Mass.: Bergin and Garvey, 1984.

Peterson, Gayle. *Birthing Normally: A Personal Growth Approach to Childbirth.* Berkeley: Mind/Body Press, 1981.

Presser, Janice, Gail Sforza Brewer, and Julianna FreeHand. *Breastfeeding.* New York: Knopf, 1983.

Rose, Jeanne. *Yes, I'm Having a VBAC* (pamphlet). ICEA.

Rothman, Barbara Katz. *The Tentative Pregnancy.* New York: Viking, 1986.

Savage, Beverly, and Diana Simkin. *Preparation for Birth: The Complete Guide to the Lamaze Method.* New York: Ballantine, 1987.

Schwartz, Leni. *The World of the Unborn: Nurturing Your Child Before Birth.* New York: Marek, 1981.

Simkin, Penny, Janet Whalley, and Ann Keppler. *Pregnancy, Childbirth, and the Newborn.* Deephaven, Minn.: Meadowbrook, 1984.

Sousa, Marion. *Childbirth at Home.* New York: Bantam, 1977.

Young, Diony. *Changing Childbirth: Family Birth in the Hospital.* Rochester, N.Y.: Childbirth Graphics, 1982.

Young, Diony, and Charles Mahon. *Unnecessary Caesareans—Ways to Avoid Them* (pamphlet). ICEA.

♦ USEFUL ADDRESSES ♦

BREASTFEEDING

La Leche League International
P.O. Box 1209
Franklin Park, Ill. 60131-8209

CESAREANS

Cesarean Prevention Movement
P.O. Box 152, University Station
Syracuse, N.Y. 13210

Information on preventing unnecessary cesareans.

C/Sec
22 Forest Road
Framingham, Mass. 01701

Support for those who have had a cesarean section.

CHILDBIRTH

American Academy of Husband-Coached Childbirth (Bradley Method)
P.O. Box 5224
Sherman Oaks, Calif. 91413
Tel: (213) 788-6662

American Society for Psychoprophylaxis in Obstetrics (ASPO)
1411 K Street, NW
Suite 200
Washington, D.C. 20005
Tel: (202) 783-7050

Lamaze classes.

International Childbirth Education Association (ICEA)
P.O. Box 20048
Minneapolis, Minn. 554320-0048
Tel: (612) 854-8660

A wide range of childbirth classes.

National Association of Parents and Professionals for Safe Alternatives in Childbirth (NAPSAC)
Route 1, Box 646
Marble Hill, Mo. 63764

Umbrella organization of alternative birth movement, pro-home birth, anti-abortion.

HOME BIRTH

Association for Childbirth at Home International
P.O. Box 39498
Los Angeles, Calif. 90039

Provides information on home birth for parents and teachers.

Informed Homebirth/Informed Birth and Parenting
P.O. Box 3675
Ann Arbor, Mich. 48106

Information on training in birth alternatives for parents and teachers; news-letter; childbirth educator certification and midwifery skills workshops.

MIDWIVES

American College of Nurse-Midwives
1522 K Street, NW
Suite 1120
Washington, D.C. 20005
Tel: (202) 347-5445

Midwives Alliance of North America
c/o Concord Midwifery Service
30 South Main Street
Concord, N.H. 03301

LESBIAN PARENTING

Groups for Lesbians Considering Parenthood
P.O. Box 3173
Oakland, Calif. 94609

WOMEN'S HEALTH

Boston Women's Health Book Collective
47 Nicholls Avenue
Watertown, Mass. 02172
Tel: (617) 924-2681

Information on women's health issues and list of women's health centers all over USA.

Coalition for the Medical Rights of Women
1638-B Haight Street
San Francisco, Calif. 94117

Resource center.

National Women's Health Network
224 Seventh Street, SE
Washington, D.C. 20003
Tel: (202) 543-9222

Consumer advocacy and information clearing house on all women's health issues.

SMOKING

American Cancer Society
4 West 35th Street
New York, N.Y. 10001
Tel.: (212) 736-3030

Smokenders, Inc.
50 Washington Street
Norwalk, Conn'. 06854
Tel.: (800) 243-5614

✦ INDEX ✦

Note: italicized page numbers indicate tables.

Sheila Kitzinger is one of the world's foremost childbirth educators, and is also a social anthropologist. She studied at Oxford University and has conducted research on birth, breast-feeding, and motherhood in cultures around the world. She lectures widely on the social and psychological dimensions of birth and parenthood, is a member of Britain's Advisory Board of the National Childbirth Trust, and is a Consultant to the International Childbirth Education Association. Her many best selling books include *Birth Over Thirty, The Complete Book of Pregnancy and Childbirth, The Experience of Childbirth,* and *Women's Experience of Sex.* Sheila Kitzinger is married to Uwe Kitzinger, President of Templeton College, Oxford. They have five daughters and live near Oxford, England.